MEXICO'S RUINS

SUNY series in Latin American and Iberian Thought and Culture

Jorge J. E. Gracia and Rosemary Geisdorfer Feal, editors

MEXICO'S RUINS

Juan García Ponce and the Writing of Modernity

Raúl Rodríguez-Hernández

State University of New York Press

Cover photo: Claudia Schaefer

Published by
State University of New York Press, Albany

Printed in the United States of America

For information, address State University of New York Press,
194 Washington Avenue, Suite 305, Albany, NY 12210-2384

Production by Judith Block
Marketing by Michael Campochiaro

Library of Congress Cataloguing-in-Publication Data

Rodríguez-Hernández, Raúl.
Mexico's ruins : Juan García Ponce and the writing of modernity / Raúl Rodríguez-Hernández.
p. cm. — (Suny series in Latin American and Iberian thought and culture)
Includes bibliographical references and index.
ISBN-13: 978-0-7914-6943-9 (hardcover : alk. paper)
ISBN-10: 0-7914-6943-3 (hardcover : alk. paper)
ISBN-13: 978-0-7914-6944-6 (pbk. : alk. paper)
1. García Ponce, Juan—Criticism and interpretation. 2. Literature and society—Mexico. 3. Politics and society—Mexico. I. Title. II. Series.

PQ7298.17.A7Z86 2007
868'.6409—dc22

2006002190

10 9 8 7 6 5 4 3 2 1

Contents

Preface

In the following text, I shall examine a trilogy of García Ponce's novels, several collections of essays on art and literature, and a number of short stories, in the context of a modernizing Mexican State and questions of citizenry. I shall focus on cultural issues related to modernity, relations between the Americas and Europe, aesthetics and narrative structures, the role of the storyteller, and inter-artistic influences and their often ambiguous results. I begin with a chapter on theory, addressing in particular concepts of philosophers Walter Benjamin, Jürgen Habermas, Theodor Adorno, as well as the notions of the ruin developed by anthropologist Quetzil Castañeda. I will explore here as well some of the central tropes of modernity, including the modern itself as a trope and the allegory of the ruin whose material existence is tinged and tangled with those bits that have fallen or disappeared on the road to modernity, much like the statue of salt subsumed under official monuments which constantly call the attention of García Ponce and his narrators. I shall follow these theoretical issues and initiatives with a more focused and textual consideration of the telling of these stories and how (or if) they are to be told. Who gets to tell what, and in what form, will constitute chapters 2 through 7, ending with a return visit to the theories deployed throughout. García Ponce suggestively revisits the literary text as others return to pay homage to the Ángel de la Independencia or to other equally 'ruinous' monuments. He wonders aloud whether literature is a means to an end or an end in itself. The conclusion leads readers to the vision of continuity and rupture we will find in both his own writings and in the theoretical propositions of Jameson, Habermas, and Benjamin regarding the ongoing project of modernity. In "Los medios del fin" [the means to an end], from *Desconsideraciones*, he writes that

> las obras nos dicen, en el mejor de los casos; pero su acción no termina en el momento de decir ni su realidad se cierra con este acto. Como los monumentos públicos, a los que la costumbre ha hecho invisibles

> una vez pasada la sorpresa que nos produjo encontrar donde antes no solíamos ver más que un espacio vacío a un militar montado a caballo y con la espada desenvainada, a un pensativo político de cráneo abultado y con las manos en la espalda o a una atractiva mujer desnuda transformada en alegoría de la virtud, los libros, las obras, siguen diciendo en silencio. [Works speak to us, in the best of cases, but their action does not end in the moment of speech nor does their reality end with this act. Like the public monuments, which the daily custom of seeing has made invisible to us once we have recovered from the initial surprise of finding, where only empty space was before, a military figure on horseback with sword in hand; a pensive politician with a large head and hands clasped behind his back; or an attractive nude woman representing the quality of virtue, books, written works, keep on speaking to us in silence.] "Los medios del fin" (2001 73–74)

How the production of new texts represents allegories of these monumental structures—of literature or the arts in general—is the subject of our discussion. What might García Ponce do, in the space of the Jamesonian period and the rupture, with all of those texts that continue to "speak to us in silence"?

My text explores the layers of meaning as sediments or traces of cultural concerns in *Crónica de la intervención* [Chronicle of an Intervention], *De ánima* [On the Spirit, the Soul], and *Inmaculada o los placeres de la inocencia* [Inmaculada or the Pleasures of Innocence] with an eye toward other narrations and other representations from the works of Octavio Paz, Carlos Fuentes, Robert Musil, José Luis Cuevas, Manuel Felgúerez, the painter Balthus, Pierre Klossowski, Georges Bataille, Heimito von Doderer, Margo Glantz and a cacophony of other voices amid the din of Mexican modernity. After taking into consideration the constitutive elements of García Ponce's tripartite set of storytelling panels and the triptych formed by the three novels, I expand the discussion to include both his last published novel entitled *Pasado presente* [Present Past] (1993) as the capstone of his narrative construction and *Personas, lugares y anexas* [People, Places, and Surroundings or the Spaces In Between] (1996) as his last text which continues to speak to readers even from the depths of silence.

R.R.-H.

Rochester, New York
April 2006

Acknowledgments

I am very grateful to a number of individuals and institutions who have contributed to the writing of this book. I would especially like to thank Debra Castillo, Walter Cohen, Jonathan Culler, Peter Hohendahl, and Geoffrey Waite, all from Cornell University, for their encouragement, support, and patience from the outset. They were the first readers of the very first drafts of this project, and patience was certainly the order of the day to get through it all. Their suggestions have proved invaluable, and I shall always recall my Cornell days with fondness and intellectual delight.

I am also indebted to The College of the University of Rochester, whose junior leave policy gave me the chance to finally complete what I had been working on for a while, and whose financial support allowed me to acquire some of the scholarly material not available outside of Mexico. In addition, the generous travel funds provided by Thomas DiPiero, then Chair of the Department of Modern Languages and Cultures, helped me open doors in Mexico to access archives and interview writers, all of which has enhanced any reading I could have otherwise done of García Ponce's texts. I am appreciative of Tom's continued support and of his open-door office policy for junior faculty. This access to departmental support on a daily basis has meant more than he might realize.

The constructive comments of the two anonymous readers at the State University of New York Press were most helpful to me as I reread the manuscript to prepare it for final submission. I greatly appreciate the time and care they gave to reviewing my work, and their suggestions for making it better. I also thank the editors of this series for their generous support of this project and for adding my book to such an excellent group of volumes. Special thanks to Claudia Schaefer for being there and for the technical expertise on computers she doesn't think she has.

To my parents in Mexico, Luis Rodríguez-Murueta and María Hernández de Rodríguez, I send my gratitude for helping me keep my priorities straight, "al mantener mis pies pegados a la tierra." Finally, I am appreciative of the friendship and support of my in-laws in the United States: thanks to Helen and Cal Schaefer. Sadly, Cal did not live long enough to see this project come to fruition, but he shall always remain in my heart as "my good friend."

Finally, I am grateful to John Benicewicz of the Permissions Department of Art Resource in New York and to Eliana Glicklich of the Artists Rights Society of New York for all their help with obtaining permissions to reproduce the two Balthus paintings included in Chapter 6. They have been wonderful resources for my sometimes naive inquiries, and have been a big help in moving this process along. I also thank the Museum of Modern Art in New York and Art Resource for granting me these permissions.

CHAPTER ONE

Traces of Theory, Tropes of Modernity

Perhaps it goes without saying that in order for ruins to exist, something whole must have preceded them. Nations and communities are built; they neither appear out of thin air nor disappear without a trace. They rest on principles as much as they do on the columns of their architectural creations; they are constructed on and through foundational documents; they are framed in legal and moral terms; they arise bit by bit as their founding generations erect the walls and portals that enclose or keep out. Even vestiges of those communities wiped out by natural disasters survive as traces amid the ash and sediment of volcanic rubble, buried under the silt of ocean deposits, or in the piles of debris remaining after great winds have blown through. Throughout the course of history these aspects of the social and the cultural lives of nations and their citizens leave behind remnants of all sorts.

Anthropologist Quetzil E. Castañeda proposes that cultural identities, in his case specifically referring to the Maya culture of Mexico's Yucatán peninsula, are invented and reinvented continually "through certain textual guises, forms, and tropes" (*Museum* 1). So we might conclude that besides the physical rubble, or perhaps even as a reading of its multiple strata, narratives themselves remain that rise as monuments or cultural markers to societies and their projects. While Castañeda posits his argument on the commercial guidebook as a prime mediating force in the production of utopian landscapes of "truth" (*Museum* 3) for tourists, I am concerned with the genealogy of the connections between the ruin as trope and its previous existence as the remnants of a purportedly resplendent past in which (one is told) all contemporaries have a stake. Such a connection, if not a "historical continuity"(Casanova 241) in the sense that some such as Octavio Paz and Carlos Fuentes have proposed, just might assist in articulating the problematic that most defines post-revolutionary Mexico: modernity. In particular, I call upon the models put forward by Walter

Benjamin for the development of an urban social critique to illuminate my discussion of the writings of Juan García Ponce and their context as components of what David Harvey calls the "creative destruction" (1) of European modernity and what Sibylle Fischer recasts as the "brutal modernity" (23) of transatlantic societies. The threefold Benjaminian models consist of the archaeological, the memorial, and the dialectical (Gilloch, *Myth* 13). The first involves the recovery and preservation of the traces from the past. The second privileges the forces of memory over the tug of amnesia. The third, and the most useful for us here, concerns "the momentary mutual recognition and illumination of past and present" (Gilloch, *Myth* 13) through an encounter with evocatory images.[1]

While I do not propose to graft these categories in situ onto Mexican culture, they nevertheless provide a pathway into the oppositional challenges to what are constituted as the myths of the modern. Eschewing the lure of some general notion of modernity as either radical break on the one hand or new inscription of the past on the other, I instead suggest, with Fredric Jameson, that what we will examine is "a dialectic of the break and the period" (23). The trope of construction and ruin, therefore, signals this dialectic in as much as new constructions are undertaken all the time, many of which fall under the rubric of modernity's supposed innovations, the shadows and vestiges of previous, simultaneous, or even nightmarish otherness still haunt those configurations. Anthony Giddens refers to this internal set of contradictions as "the darker side of modernity," which is frequently seen as outweighed by its "opportunity side" (7). Without an absolute historical (and historiographic) beginning and lacking a moment of definitive rupture, under this schema Mexico's modernity becomes a significantly more difficult concept to quantify as it emerges as a more challenging notion to narrate. If, as Jameson submits, "tropes are themselves the signs and symptoms of a hidden or buried narrative" (40), then modernity needs to be considered less a singular conceptual category than changing narratives grounded in specific spaces and moments.

Illuminating the impressive task of uniting Brazil as a modern entity, Todd A. Diacon uses the trope of the telegraph wire as "stringing together a nation" (3). In addition to the power of the centralized federal government, the extension of health care to even the most remote territory, and the early twentieth-century universal conscription law, only the lines of the telegraph wires could establish contact and connectedness across Brazil's vast geographies. Thus it is that Brazil is invented and reinvented, as Castañeda proposes, through the electrified lines laid out under the authority of engineer Cândido Mariano da Silva Rondon. This trope reveals the loneliness of the frontier life for those engineers and telegraph workers who settle an unknown geography which then becomes interconnected in the lightning flash of the telegraph spark. The intersection of open spaces and closed communication fires up encounters across the board, from politics to public works, from family structures to religious communities. The "Modern Brazil" of his title does not appear at some absolute date or time, springing out of the vast expanses of *os sertões* as wires are stretched across previously open spaces, but as an alternation of events and encounters among political structures, medical initiatives, civic rituals, military interventions, international expeditions, industrial investments, and advances in communications. Singing telegraph wires are the tropic manifestation (or the Jamesonian symptom) of a narrative of "creative destruction" that ends with the linkage of Brazilian states unified by certain ideologies of modernization.

If for the case of Brazil the hope of the "wired nation" (Diacon 16) trope serves best to address the modernizing forces at work, for Mexico the ruin solidifies and transforms sometimes ambiguous social experience into a tangible material form.[2] The language of construction resounds throughout the historical and literary texts issuing forth from Benedict Anderson's imagined communities as cultures rise and fall, as they erect monuments to their greatest ideals and seek to prevail over rivals. References to the fashioning of buildings themselves and to the elucidation of cultural goals through them abound among the records taken from the stone bases of the pyramids and the stelae of Bonampak, from the ball courts of Chichén Itzá and the zócalos of Spanish settlements; they continue to appear in modern times among the architects of the political and cultural revolution that began in Mexico in 1910. In a larger sense there is little difference, really, between the organizing precepts of the builders of Teotihuacán or the designers of the modern nation. Each sets out a blueprint to serve as the ideal model for conduct and for belonging to a collectivity. Each envisions what society's members must aspire to and makes it visible—in word or image—to all, to either live up to or fail to attain. Whether among the monumental tombs and mausoleums Anderson refers to (9), in the *crónicas* of the conquest that detail the mythical founding of Tenochtitlán,[3] in the blocks of stone that enclose the sacred spaces of Teotihuacán, or in the philosophical treatises on nationhood penned by Samuel Ramos we find the accumulated acts of construction of the nation followed by their remnants.

Taking as a point of departure the double strands of national narrative the historian Arthur Schmidt attributes to the last six decades of the twentieth century, Mexico may be said to have had two conflicting outlooks—"revolution to evolution" and "revolution to demolition" (25). The first would unify the nation under the myth of an ongoing revolution into whose vessel all historical events would fit. The second is, of course, the narrative of rupture we have mentioned which mobilizes citizens on the road of modernity from the Reforma onward. Most engaging is the notion of "demolition," both as the implied razing of the past and as that "creative destruction" through which we might cast modernity. Demolition produces ruins of the cultural as well as of the cement kind. If we turn to Octavio Paz at this juncture, he seems to agree on a very material level of cultural constructs. In "América Latina y la democracia" [Latin America and Democracy], he writes that "[l]a arquitectura es el espejo de las sociedades. Pero es un espejo que nos presenta imágenes enigmáticas que debemos descifrar" [Architecture is the mirror of societies. But it is a mirror that presents us with enigmatic images which we have to decipher] (165). Leaving aside the similarity between Paz's mirror image and Carlos Fuentes's use of the "buried mirror" of the Conquest, visible supports of modernist ideologies appear to converge on the facades of the emergent nations as they choose dwellings, offices, stadiums, and arenas to stand in for their power behind the scenes.

When Ramos addresses the "abandono de la cultura en México" [abandonment of culture in Mexico] (83) in 1934, after the implementation of the educational reforms suggested under Minister of Education José Vasconcelos, he cites a lack of interest in advanced studies and a corresponding loss of respect for intellectual activity as results of this popularizing process in which quantity substituted for quality. The verb he employs to mark this cultural turn—to him, for the worse—is that interest in higher education and the life of the mind "ha decaído" [has declined] (83). Such a crumbling and, in the end, fall indicate that a collective cultural edifice had been erected to the ideals of the Revolution but that, over time, those same utopian endeavors had fallen short. The inevitable outcome is "decaimiento" or a collapse into decay, ruin, and loss. The radical impulse to counteract reforms that seem to have run their course comes through in the language of this philosophical essay on the state of Mexican culture as Ramos studies the need to construct a new subject confident of the social and cultural edifice in which he or she lives. The question lies in just how this might come about and what to do with the material of the demolished structures. Evolutionary theory requires its preservation; demolition theory constructs the garbage dumps of cities and ideas.

These philosophical constructions are at once "marvelous and horrible," in the words of Octavio Paz when he writes of the forces contained in pre-Columbian sculptural images that apply to theoretical systems as well. He clarifies that "[h]orror . . . is fear and repulsion, but it is also respect and veneration for the unknown or the sublime. Horror is not terror; it is fascination, bewitchment" ("Will for Form" 5). A fascination with the evocatory powers of the artifact (a previous construct in ruin) establishes a link to Benjamin's third category of the dialectical model of critique, proceeding beyond forgetting and mere nostalgia into the realm of analysis. "Bewitchment" with the monuments to a society's glories is the first model of experience; when only the traces of those luminous times remain, another sort of fascinating circumstance occurs, equal in power but different in form. This is the encounter with the ruin in Benjaminian terms, what Castañeda calls "a dialogical process of reflective intercalation" (*Museum* 17) effected by the questioning subject. Holding together contradictory elements, what Jameson sums up as "belonging and innovation" (57), the ruin would then place questioning individuals on double ground, tangibly forcing an encounter with a force field of associations which had previously been relegated to the more facile continuity/rupture, evolution/demolition opposites. Both "marvelous and horrible," modernity brings entire systems into contention. As Jameson invites readers to think of this flash point, he reiterates that "the trope of 'modernity' is always in one way or another a rewriting, a powerful displacement of previous narrative paradigms . . . the affirmation of the 'modernity' of this or that generally involves a rewriting of the narratives of modernity itself which are already in place and have become conventional wisdom" (35–36). So Castañeda's "dialogical process of reflective intercalation" is nothing more than the restatement of the idea that there is no singular modernity (as Jameson's title echoes), let us say a European version versus an American one, but a constant, reiterated, and challenged confrontation of ideologies. Harvie Ferguson elaborates, "Modernity calls into existence, as well as a new social world, new forms of knowledge and self-understanding" (189). As Jürgen Habermas famously states, modernity is a project never completed (3).

Among the "splendors" (according to Paz) of the unfinished edifice of what has emerged as modern Mexico, we find temples as well as promises (the imminent return of the god Quetzalcoatl, for instance, or the capitalist dream of Carlos Salinas de Gortari), ethnic *mestizaje* as well as social revolution, invasion as well as innovation, creation as well as destruction. As Carlos Fuentes concludes, the "unfinished business" of contemporary Mexican culture rests on the "concrete problem" embodied in a very material structure, which can be used as a metaphor for the "bewitching" encounter described above. He writes, "There is a very tall hotel in Mexico City that has never been finished. Year after year builders add to its height, but one can always look right through its hive of gaping stones. When, if ever, will it receive its hypothetical guests?" (*Buried Mirror* 316). The empty shell of the hotel-in-progress (even if later completed) is a visible sign of two simultaneous processes linked to two temporal moments. The first is the utopian urge of progress and modernization, symbolized by the upward surge of construction (reflected in official government discourse as much as it is for Fuentes in sweeping architectural design). Curiously, Paz mirrors this same notion of "upward thrust" and "vertical movement" ["Will for Form" 15–16] in construction in his evaluation of the condensation of time-space symbolism in the architecture of the pyramid. A similar verticality is at the core of Fuentes's gaze upon the changing skylines of the metropolis of Mexico City as it expands and contracts with post-revolutionary design. Calling it "the Cinderella city" during the 1960s ("New Wave" 126), Fuentes anchors the development of the Mexican nation of modern times in the surge of economic and architectural development after the Revolution. The falling away of the previous "mythical facade" ("New Wave" 128), however, gives way to the ambiguous constructions meant for incipient tourism and international display. The second process involves the paradoxical concept of construction-as-ruin since the wearing down of the girders and scaffolding witnesses the element of time passing, the constant threat of entropy overtaking the forces of construction. The "hive of gaping stones" simultaneously suggests a drive toward completion and an accompanying deterioration, for the structure of the hive is both presence and absence, both stones and spaces. The "hypothetical guests" can only be intuited, of course, in the interstices, but they form as central an aspect of this project in their imagined arrival as do the floors and rooms of the building they will (some day) occupy.

I suggest that the project of modernity might be considered through this double visual image: a thrust toward the future but a wrenching toward decay, a "creative destruction" not devoid of brutality in the form of political institutions which "operat[e] like a modernizing, rationalizing machine that k[eeps] turning in disregard of human needs" (Fischer 23). The PRI (Partido Revolucionario Institucional) [Institutional Revolutionary Party] created an efficient metro system, luxurious embassies, government offices on a scale that is able to deal with daily concerns, and even the tourist mecca teasingly called the Zona Rosa, but what of the killing of students and workers in 1968, what of the buildings devastated by the 1985 earthquake that never were rebuilt, what of the murder of presidential candidate Luis Donaldo Colosio or the lack of housing or potable water for citizens, to say nothing of the indigenous uprising in Chiapas? The brutality factor could be analyzed as that which is deemed necessary to keep the machine of modernity in motion without the intrusion of technological glitches or dissident opinion. The ruin is not an either/or proposition; it is both construction and destruction. Castañeda finds this very same promising dilemma in the etymology of the word ruin: "derived from Latin *ruina*, a falling down, from *ruere*, to rush, and *origo*, to rise—[ruins] entail movements in opposing directions: a 'falling down' and a 'rising up'" ("Aura" 452). We cannot lose sight of the paradox of a city in the throes of 'progress' and modernization evincing not only an image of rising vertically but of static verticality in its standing in place. The ruins of the modern are not stone but steel; they rust and do not crumble. Yet the same impulses that apply to the reading of the ruin of antiquity are found in the paralyzed structure of the real and metaphorical hotel. Will the building progress or *decaer* [decline, fall] as Mexican culture did in the eyes of Ramos? The two tendencies do not cancel one another, but like the "dialectic of the break and the period," coexist within an ambiguity worthy of critical examination.

Ruins are the result of wear, time's passage, dilapidation, conquest, replacement, erosion, abandonment, transformation, or a combination of these factors. If we speak of ruins in literal terms, we might conjure up fallen statues, crumbling buildings, remnants of walls or pillars, columns in decay, arches precariously suspended overhead, rusty bridges long condemned to traffic, dusty highways leading to nowhere, or overgrown archaeological sites in the middle of the jungle. In a more symbolic form, however, we could evoke complex images of aged human beings whose life stories are written on their very skin, fragments of cultural detritus collected on library shelves or in museum cases, worn out discourses, or the ghostly shadows of previous glories embodied in aesthetic or linguistic turns of phrase. I propose to examine both material vestiges of construction and deconstruction, and imagined ruinations. In these two strands—the imagined and the 'real'—the reader might find narratives of the rise of modern Mexico and see how they intertwine and collide to produce counternarratives, where one might imagine a revelation among the ruins. The writings of Juan García Ponce are the cornerstone of my project, for among his lengthy and monolithic texts many of these contrary impulses are brought to light. Let us now frame his literary works in a general cultural edifice of both mortar and image.

From the longer historical perspective, Mexico was invaded in the sixteenth century by Spanish conquerors who arrived at a period of 'ruin' in the Aztec empire, since by that time it had declined in both royal lineage and imperial splendor into a killing machine demanding economic and blood sacrifice to perpetuate its hegemony. Ceremonial buildings and complexes were at their peak, but the underlying narratives of social cohesion revealed weakened structures of community. As the writer Elena Garro portrays in her short story "La culpa es de los tlaxcaltecas" [Blame it on the Tlaxcalans], the Tlaxcalans were just one of the conquered peoples who assisted the incoming European soldiers in the hopes of escaping the yoke of Aztec domination. The process of disintegration of the grand empire and its grand narratives left the geography and culture(s) in ruins, ripe for

European imperialism and its own narrations of mastery. Yet even this process produces new forms of narration and constant readjustment. The remains of this early period lie buried under layers of silt and debris that attest to past history, weather patterns, volcanic eruptions, broken dreams, and collective sympathies. But they also lie beneath newer constructions: what better way to offer evidence of entropy and decline, vanquishment and death, than to build atop the old? One system replaces the other, but the facade gives evidence of (false) continuity. The ruins of the old are also part of the glorious 'new,' for the same stones used in worship of native deities become the foundations for the syncretic institutions of an idealized *mestizaje*. Like the descent into the Templo Mayor in the very center of the modern Mexican capital or the secret side doors to the Great Pyramid of Cholula, which sits buried under the church of Nuestro Santuario de los Remedios, entrances and exits to the discourses of the past can be 'discovered' and 'rediscovered' through the archaeology of cultural debris. It would be difficult to avoid seeing the enormous mound of earth on which the sanctuary sits, or the handrail to the stairway leading down into the internal excavation, but the path to its heart lies hidden to the eye at first glance. The physical remains of two cultures lie one atop the other as a "palimpsest that operates like a 'text,' in the sense that Derrida has defined it: a text is a giant machine for reading and writing other texts" (Castañeda, *Museum* 98). It is hardly an unproblematic construction, yet it "bewitches" the observer in its very problematizing of cultural discourses and counter-discourses and in its potential as a site for self-fashioning amid contradiction. One is left to wonder whether this giant interpretative machine functions along the lines of the brutal "modernizing, rationalizing machine" or if the capacity to rewrite and innovate can win.

Octavio Paz projects a reading of the ruin as text in his collection of essays entitled *Vislumbres de la India: un diálogo con la condición humana* [Glimpses of India: A Dialogue with the Human Condition]. The title itself gives the reader a hint that for this particular observer walls, palaces, towers, and frescoes all provide a glimpse of something more than mortar and stone. As official ambassador and then as private traveler, Paz experienced an obvious fascination with traces of the subcontinent's past, which he then paralleled with Mexico's own. The ornamental arches, nooks, niches, corridors, terraces, and gardens he saw upon disembarking from his ocean liner "son los corredores de un sueño fastuoso, siniestro e inacabable" [are the corridors of a magnificent dream, sinister and endless] (*Vislumbres* 13). Both glorious dream and endless demonic nightmare, the colonial architecture of India astonished Paz into a "repentina fascinación" [sudden fascination] (*Vislumbres* 16) with the myriad of historical times and feelings it seems to evoke. The light shining through the crevices reveals hidden forces at work and secret ideas underlying the construction. In the mausoleums of vast cemeteries, he contemplated what Anderson proposes as imagined communities in their own right: "el universo reducido a sus elementos geométricos esenciales. . . . Abolición del tiempo convertido en espacio y el espacio en un conjunto de formas simultáneamente sólidas y ligeras, creadoras de otro espacio hecho, por decirlo así, de aire. Edificios que han durado siglos y que parecen un parpadeo de fantasía" (the universe reduced to its essential geometric elements. . . . The abolishing of time converted into space, and space in a conjunction of forms at once solid and light, the creators of another space made, as it were, of air. Buildings that have lasted centuries and that seem only a single fantastic blink {of an eye}] (*Vislumbres* 23). Air and stone combine to conjure up collective dreams of past, present, and future, dreams that seem solid but melt into nothingness. Even as communities go the way of the ruin, they can be reimagined as solidly and inclusively utopian collectivities or, alternately, as vast social projects gone awry. The language of the stones, also reflected in Paz's poetry collection *Piedra de sol* [Sun Stone], provides the ruins with voices which he then deciphered for us. These voices seem to call him back to India time and again after his service as a diplomat ended in 1968, and he rewrote himself time and again onto the exterior faces of the stones.

If the arrival of European culture and its hegemonic imposition over former empires did not encounter material ruins per se but ebullient cities, although the decline of the imperial monarch was evidence of other decay related to the social and religious structures, this event produced a scenario for the ruin to become a tourist splendor of modern times. While few Spaniards would gaze upon indigenous edifices as remnants of better times, nineteenth and twentieth century archaeologists would find in them what Laura U. Marks terms "[f]etishes and fossils . . . as two kinds of objects that condense cryptic histories within themselves. Both gather their peculiar power by virtue of a prior contact with some originary object . . . Fetishes and fossils translate experience through space and time in a material medium" (224). Like a fossil compressed into layers of earth, the "fascinating" ruins and traces of original Mesoamerican cultures survive compressed into the "cryptic" monoliths and temples of their modern cities. The fossil's remains are pertinent as relics of meaning, for they have to be unearthed or cleaved from rocks in a secret, primordial landscape. The "cryptic" nature of the language of the stones (à la Paz in his privileged role as translator) is doubled by the similarly enigmatic message of the fossil. In each instance we require an interpreter, but in each we may write our own version as well. All of these form palimpsestic layers of discursive debris.

The identification of Mexico as a site of ruinous fascination has been and continues to be a commonplace of guidebooks and travelers alike. From the popular Frommer to Fodor, from Lonely Planet to the more erudite Knopf Guides, we find a celebration of the ruin as a carved-in-stone identifying symbol of the nation owing to its mysterious, powerful, and "originary" link to the past. As a palimpsest, in Castañeda's terms once again, we see traces of prior cultures inscribed on the surfaces of these stones, but we also contribute to their meanings by writing ourselves onto them and by producing new communities of readers around them. This discursive practice produces a sense of the subject as it recalls—in Benjamin's spark of memory recovery—others who then are either wiped away to produce a clean slate or phantasmatically written into contemporary narratives of individual and nation. In his meditation on ruins as mainstays of modern culture, museum director Christopher Woodward argues that "[w]hen we contemplate ruins, we contemplate our own future. To statesmen, ruins predict the fall of Empires, and to philosophers the futility of mortal man's aspirations. To a poet, the decay of a monument represents the dissolution of the individual ego in the flow of Time; to a painter or architect, the fragments of a stupendous antiquity call into question the purpose of their art. . . . Each spectator is forced to supply the missing pieces from his or her own imagination and a ruin therefore appears different to everyone" (2–3, 15). Such a conquering of the forces of amnesia, as Benjamin refers to them, calls on the imaginary to furnish meaning—or not—for what is present before our eyes. At this moment, then, either a tabula rasa comes into being (in the schema of the modernist rupture), or a promising constellation of meanings is evoked. Rather than a true emptiness, nevertheless, even the blank slate remains as a material surface on which shadowy traces might eventually be deciphered. Then, conjecture on the violence exerted to prevent readers from this text can also be brought into view.

Nineteenth-century travelers and adventurers rediscovered the world of Mesoamerican ruins and continued to inscribe on their words, drawings, and watercolors the "missing pieces" of cultural narrative of which Woodward writes. Classical nudes appear in Jean-Frédéric Waldeck's paintings of Maya sites, idealizing human and architectural forms into a harmonious whole. Europe and America are clearly integrated into some 'natural' scheme. In his artistic works the romantic myth of the noble savage acquires visible form and imbues indigenous feminine form with the whiteness and roundness of Rubenesque figures. Explorers appear in top hats and cutaway jackets, indicating with their walking canes the crumbling lintels and doorways of Mexican and Guatemalan archaeological sites. No beads of sweat evident anywhere, these metropolitan travelers stroll the ruins amid jungle foliage and hard-working natives. Daily life is indeed represented on the canvases and watercolor papers, but archaeological ruins are the mere backdrops for such activity. Ruins frame work, but they do not belong to its world; they are solid evidence of the vestiges of something else. In 1841, John Lloyd Stephens (United States ambassador to Central America and budding journal writer) and Frederick Catherwood (the illustrator) produced two volumes entitled *Incidents of Travel in Yucatán* that pursue a similar enchantment with ruins as auratic signs. Both wonderment and loss, they indicate for two modern Europeans something genuine and legible missing in their own culture. Stephens writes that his contemplation of such scenes "inspired in me a state of excitement more acute than any I had experienced among the ruins of the Old World" (qtd. in *Route of the Mayas* 131). Their celebration of this moment in detailed words and images captures the spark of revelation for both men. Stephens writes that his journey is one of fascination akin to Paz's: "In a few years, even these [ruins of Labná] will be gone; and as it has been denied that such things ever were, doubts may again arise whether they have indeed existed" (30–31). The old stones of the New World are the key to these explorers' enchantment with the hidden ruins which they offer to preserve in journal and sketchbook lest they disappear into the jungles or be relegated to the domain of the mirage. While the Spanish feel no urge to do the same with the buildings they find upon arrival in a wondrous new world already imagined as utopia, for these represent beliefs and systems contrary to Christianity, romantic era wanderers read other stories into these edifices. But neither roots out contradiction between the imaginary and the real; a singular thread of discourse winds its way across stones and rubble to join all together.

After the pathways of the romantics began to recede and become overgrown as elaborate and aesthetic ruins in progress, another era of romantic-like fervor accompanied the early twentieth century as Mexico prepared to fight one of the bloodiest revolutions in history. Fellow travelers such as John Reed, Tina Modotti, and a bit later, Katherine Anne Porter, and a host of documentary news reporters invaded the country to experience for themselves the destruction of an old order and the construction of a new one on its ruins. Most often thought of as a modernist writer, Porter crisscrossed the border between her native Texas and Mexico in search of an idealized society she thought would provide her with space to develop her intellectual career as much as it would allow her to find herself. As Thomas F. Walsh sums up the complex and frequently ambiguous relationship between Porter and her utopian vision, "[a]lthough Mexico failed her as the Promised Land she vainly sought, it released her creative energy" (xiii).

Mexico, her Mexico at least, was a catalyst for writing, the source of an effervescent feeling of personal potential, and the space to recover some genuine spark of individual freedom she found stifled in the patriarchal society of Texas. Several decades after Porter left what she called her adopted land of Mexico, she wrote of an intimate relationship with that culture, albeit a romanticized vision of that relationship. At once a source of pride and an enigma, Mexico to her is "this sphinx of countries which for every fragment of authentic history yields two riddles" (Givner 22). The contradictions of everyday life and the underlying patriarchy which so reminded her of Texas are subsumed under the feminine figure of the sphinx whose interior is the darkness that must be deciphered. Both the sphinx and Mexico do not reveal their secrets easily, even after prolonged contact with so-called native informants and with the culture itself. This is an attempt to embody the mysterious and the impenetrable—Mexican society—and like the monument itself provides us with a riddle and a ruin at the same time.

Reed's cinematic version of events in *Insurgent Mexico*, and the diaries that inform it, reflect no less fervor than the journals of Stephens and Catherwood. Half a century later, Reed's wife, Alma, wrote a piece for *Venture* magazine in which she found in a modernizing Mexico the insistent vestiges of that romantic ruin on whose foundations the new nation will miraculously rise. To the U.S. market Alma Reed promises that "[t]he American visitor to Mexico will almost inevitably return home addicted to archeology. Even if he has managed to resist its lure elsewhere in the world, he is likely to succumb in this country, where the ruined indigenous cities are so spectacular . . . A chance visit to one of the many astonishing archeological sites . . . , a chat with an informed guide, is all it takes to produce a sense of involvement in the fate of the peoples who first civilized our continent and who left such enduring relics of their mysterious lives" (156). Such an uncanny experience unlocks some sort of lost connection to a communal past now shared by the traveler confronted by the ruins of his own (forgotten) past. The "unknown and the sublime" of Paz's evocation of the ruin, his sense of combined horror and wonder, echo the Freudian notion of the uncanny. Articulating the process of psychoanalysis as an entry into the "strata of mental life" (193), Freud relates the uncanny experience of a subject to an unexpected encounter with "what is frightening . . . what arouses dread and horror . . . what excites fear, in general. . . . the uncanny is that class of the frightening which leads back to what is known of old and long familiar" (193, 195). The "excitation" of fear, horror, and amazement, for both Paz and Stephens, might be contained in this sense of the uncanny, for the ruin conjures up something in those mental "strata" long repressed but still visible in the glimpse of a momentary trace. Benjamin does not write of the uncanny, yet he might see this same instant as the spark of an epiphany upon reentering an originary aura of an object in decay.

The consumption of geographies—Oaxaca, Chichén Itzá, Teotihuacán, Monte Albán, Mitla, Cancún, Cozumel, among so many officially-targeted places—as a strategy of knowledge has generated both a lucrative tourist industry and a self-satisfying act. As Castañeda writes, these preserved sites and the "truths" (*Museum* 4) they reveal about a culture are, like the Americas for Europeans, there for the discovery or "the rediscovery [as] an individualizing experience of identity with civilization in opposition to cultural other(s)" (*Museum* 3). Ruins confirm presuppositions, present the jaded with "an adventure," and "pose a significant challenge to visit," but their value lies not in themselves but rather in the persistence of the visitor to reach the destination (Coe 1). As Andrew Coe, son of the renowned Mesoamerican archaeologist Michael D. Coe, states in the preface to his recent volume for travelers, "there are other satisfactions. Once I began traveling to Mexico on my own, it became increasingly apparent to me that the ancient wonders of Mesoamerica are not simply the ruins of dead civilizations, but living works of art" (1). These statements would conform well to Benjamin's first and second dicta on the resurrection of the past, evoking personal and cultural memories against the ravages of amnesia. The archaeological model concerns itself with "the salvation and preservation of the objects and traces of the past that modern society threatens to destroy" (Gilloch, *Myth* 13); this is the preserved site in and of itself, guarded and set aside from the hustle and bustle of 'progress' and assured of being unchanged despite all the aspects of modernization around it.

The second dictum admonishes those who would forget the past. This is also assured for the traveler through the establishment of official INAH sites (Instituto Nacional de Antropología e Historia) [National Institute of Anthropology and History]. Both produce the concept of the ruin as a physical place, as a "wondrous" portal to the past, and as "art." It is the dialectical aspect of Benjamin's proposal that is not implemented in either, for a "momentary illumination" can only be garnered by that spark which Benjamin associates with the re-creation of an aura. The aura, for our purposes, is the paradox of Fuentes's example which makes us stop in our tracks and contemplate actively, not passively, the ongoing construction of an edifice. The ruin can lull us to contemplation, mesmerizing us, or it can shake us into activity and critique as Benjamin so desires. Even before writing his monumental (and unfinished) work *Passages*, Benjamin haunts crumbling city streets (for instance the district of Marseilles known to night dwellers as "Les bricks") and the arcades of Paris, not to fall under their spell but to happen on a chance encounter with the spirits of the ruin in order to resuscitate his own past. Like the rubble from the shellfish and oyster stalls of that Mediterranean port city, Benjamin uses mineral images to portray what is left of past activity embedded in the city's alleys. Fossils of previous events litter its streets. For him, they are containers of "shell limestone" and the "mineral hereafter of sea shells" ("Marseilles" 134) rising in monumental display along the trajectory of his walks. Peter Demetz calls these nocturnal descents into the promising urban ruins the scenarios of Benjamin's "sensibilities" (x) since they have the potential to elicit so much from him.

Benjamin's concept of structure as architectural metaphor extends the idea of cultural ruin to an entire project, that of modernity, and to the artifacts produced within the specific time and place under consideration here. The discussion on the problematics of contemporary debates regarding the modern either as a "spent epoch" or as an "unrealized . . . potential" (d'Entrèves 1) will be extended throughout the chapters of this book. The "achievements and pathologies of modernity" (d'Entrèves 1), its splendors and horrors in the eyes of Paz and Fuentes, and its creative potential through confrontation, will serve our argument related to the language, contents, narrative structure, and aesthetics of García Ponce's texts. In these texts, modern times are neither glorified nor entombed as cemeteries of a dead past. Instead, cultural construction and demolition coexist as equal forces, creating something different out of fragmentation and destruction. In his collection of essays entitled *Desconsideraciones*, García Ponce advances the idea that a library shelf may hold the clue to this type of dynamic relationship between past and present, between insider and outcast, and between the world and the text. As he casts his gaze over his personal collection of reading matter, the narrator of "De la ausencia" [On Absence] sees not only titles and spines of books but empty places previously occupied by something. Neither a "spent epoch" nor an "unrealized potential," the missing books are the objects of contemplation and study, holding a relationship even in absence. The narrator thinks to himself: "Todos estos detalles crean un desequilibrio espiritual que determina nuestra relación con el mundo y se refleja en otras pequeñas acciones. Nuestra biblioteca está en continuo movimiento o, como diría Heráclito, en perpetua fluidez. . . . El agujero que dejan los libros prestados nos obsesiona y disminuye la realidad de todos los demás anulando su importancia. Sólo queremos saber cuál es ese libro que tan obviamente falta, que tal vez nunca recuperaremos y quizá nos era indispensable. Así el vacío, la nada, se hace mucho más real que la realidad" [All these details create a spiritual imbalance which determines our relationship with the world and which is reflected in other small actions. Our library is in constant movement or, as Heraclitus would say, in perpetual fluidity. . . . The void that loaned books leave obsesses us and diminishes the reality of all the rest [of the books], annulling their importance. We only want to know which is the book that is obviously absent, that maybe we will never get back, and that perhaps was indispensable to us. In this way emptiness, nothingness, becomes even more real than reality] ("De la ausencia" 2001 14). The metaphor of the library shelf and its holdings, then, can even be a stand-in for the suggestive absences and no-longer-real presences of one's surroundings. Books before our eyes disappear into the search for the ones we can no longer see. Like the layers of silt and debris underlying modern structures, the laws of the collection of books, the desire to fill shelves, and the texts as representations of ourselves all underpin that fluidity of identity we are considering under the aegis of the modern. What better to evoke the modern sense of confrontation than the dilemma of what to do about the visible absences: What are the books (ideas) that are no longer there? Where did they go? What of the faded covers of the books now exposed to sunlight for the first time?

Obviously for the narrator, missing tomes become even more prominent now that they are no longer among their cohorts; both are set into question by this new relationship. If one creates a library only for it to be 'destroyed'—perhaps even 'demolished'—by loaning out material, then what of the tradition of collection to begin with? Any owner of such a collection, therefore, will be a part of the process of making and remaking it, of reviewing its contents and its spaces, of providing new volumes to take the place of the old or, conversely, embarking on a quest to replace the missing with equal volumes. One constructs a library as one constructs an edifice (of cement, of ideas); as Heraclitus is quoted as remarking: this is another venue of fludity and change, of "creative destruction" in the acquisition and dispossession of texts. As García Ponce's essay ends, the narrator remarks on the ultimate question of this situation: is an absence empty or filled with something? He notes, ¿Debe dejar de existir el cuadro [o el libro] una vez que nos ha revelado la pared? Hecho el descubrimiento, ¿no sentimos que queremos tener a uno y otra? Y del mismo modo: ¿esa ausencia llena de presencia . . . no es el motor de una nostalgia irresistible que clama por su presencia? ¿Cuál de las dos cosas debemos elegir?" [Should a painting {or a book} cease to exist once it has revealed the wall {on which it was hanging} to us? Upon such an uncovering, don't we feel that we want to have one just as much as the other? And in the same sense, isn't the absence full of presence . . . the mechanism of an irresistible nostalgia that cries out to be present?] ("De la ausencia" 2001 16). The elements of this essay are reflective of the dilemmas of the provisional relationships of modernity: presence of the past in its absent shadows (the faded outlines of missing books on the wall behind the stacks and related books flanking the empty spaces), the meaning of the wall or even its potential for an aesthetic of the void, the choice to fill the spaces or not, and, in the end, the ineluctable feeling of nostalgia that demands to take over the situation.

In the context of the ruin as text, we have seen that the traveler or observer writes upon the surface of a constantly revised stone (or other material), thereby creating the palimpsestic text. Instead of a whole, the ruin comprises a collection in which the "fragment" (Hanssen 69) is "superior to the harmonies of antiquity" (Benjamin qtd. in Hanssen 70). The "exuberant subjection" (Benjamin qtd. in Hanssen 70) of multiple elements as remainders across the face of the ruin creates a new text, just as in modern times "the work of art [is] a remnant, relic, or ruin left in the wake of the demise of transcendent meaning" (Hanssen 3). The text might be there materially but deciphering it may prove a more difficult challenge. Such a secularization—reflecting the Enlightenment's faith in science and reason—exemplifies for Benjamin "the predicament of modernity" (Hanssen 4).

Now in the text as ruin, I propose that modernity's successes and failures are part of the formal properties of the written text itself, encompassing both structure and content. All of the components of "creativity" and "destruction" contribute to the composition of the 'new' through language, storytelling, and the final product which, paradoxically, is also a part of the great fluid library of Heraclitus. The structures of ruin and allegory, for Benjamin, share a certain power of revelation, despite the "demise of transcendence," for they hint at that previous link now defunct which still manages to survive as a glimmer [*vislumbre*] amid the cultural rubble. "[T]he fabricated nature of the artwork . . . , [and] its character as an artifact" (Hanssen 70) manifest and expose modernity as a construction built of cultural ruin predicated on the fossilized fragments of the past. (This is the narrative of historical coherence reduced to the detritus of the fragment.) Of Benjamin's notion regarding this, Gilloch writes, "The modern [in its constructs and artifacts] reveals itself as ruin. This notion of ruination is rooted in a recognition of the importance of an object's 'afterlife'" (*Myth* 14). The afterlife of both physical ruin and allegorical ruin is inscribed, as the palimpsest mentioned by Castañeda, on building, geography and, now, on discourse. For Benjamin, in an instant the "arcane secret [a work] was believed to hold" can thus be destroyed, and "art's links to the divine place (topos) on which the temple or shrine were formerly built" (Hanssen 78) broken if the trance of archaeological resuscitation is sundered. The cultural present is thus a ruin in itself for it problemizes the link to history and to the past (the third model in Benjamin's schema), the perfect analogy of Jamesonian punctuation and rupture all in one space. What Jürgen Habermas famously and polemically calls the "unfinished project of modernity" (3) duplicates this concept as much as it points to Fuentes's unfinished tower in Mexico City. Both soaring (modern) project and vestigial (incomplete) structure, the tower stands as a monument to itself and to the work of erecting it, but it is also composed of fragments and stands in for the projects of the past as allegory. So modernity as ruin contains "the highly suggestive fragment, the chip" (Benjamin qtd. in Bolz and van Reijen 33) from which life continues to flow.

The two-directional pull of allegory, its reading either as a "subversion of the unifying grasp of systematic philosophy or as a remnant waiting to be redeemed" (Hanssen 83), advances interesting and innovative possibilities for reading García Ponce's texts within this model of modernity's project as it is articulated in the second half of twentieth-century Mexico. A singular reading of the modern toward which, as Jameson puts it, "the so-called underdeveloped countries might want to look forward" as if there were "the illusion that the West has something no one else possesses . . . but which they ought to desire for themselves" (8) is not proposed. Instead, how Mexican visions of tradition and modernity clash in the space of the text may construct a new set of questions regarding this writer, his generation, and the responses of the subsequent five or six decades. The pull of the frequently articulated need for subversion or alternatives and the equal regard for the role of the 'new' meets up with the enchantment of the remnant across the pages of his novels, essays, plays, and art reviews. Benjamin's redemption comes to us disguised as ceremony, but even in what appear to be secular works the writer presents us with allegories related to some lost, sacred sense of the past somehow surviving amid today's world without anomalies. The very ambiguities produced by the collision of these fragments is what Benjamin celebrates in allegory's "excess of signification" (Hanssen 83). The result proves to be an expected clarity that becomes muddled, but muddled in a positive sense, for this is how Giddens's "darker side" of modernity illuminates the "opportunity side" to produce questions about false security and hidden dangers, great risks amid the blind trust of a project (Giddens 7). What by now most Mexicans join other cultures in regarding as "a fraught and dangerous world" (Giddens 10) rests on a number of assumptions which need to be clarified (or revealed through allegory) as myths, especially in light of the everyday violence which has escalated in order to keep stories of progress alive. There is possibly no better rhetorical figure than allegory with all of its convolutions and excesses to approach García Ponce's style and themes and to reveal the obscure recesses of Mexican modernity. The density, accumulated layers, and language and images that fold back on themselves and constitute his texts are nothing if not baroque allegories of the contradictions of the modern in this particular version. These complex tropes and contradictory figures are the sites of further critique and investigation.

The *sexenio* [six-year term] of each Mexican president creates the scaffolding for the construction and implementation of promises made during each electoral campaign by both party and nominee. From the 1920s to the crisis of 1968, the Mexican State seemed to define its role in the modernization of the country as the promoter of a cultural production parallel to material urban development. On the constantly evolving landscape of urban Mexico, each president has inaugurated monuments in the form of public works visible to natives and tourists alike. What Claudio Lomnitz calls "the factory of Mexico's ruins" (212), this emphasis on structures includes the substantial contribution of the federal government to the arts, sciences, and public image of modernization across those decades. Lomnitz writes of the "personal signatures" of these government sponsors as the motivations for their construction, but the same monuments become new ruins in their own right. In keeping with our previous consideration of the ruin as physical construction and as allegorical trope, Lomnitz concurs with the assessment of this double model. He observes that "[a]lthough the discussion of modernist ruins usually brings to mind housing projects, hospitals, bridges, and basketball courts, Mexico's cultural world is also littered with these ruins" (214). We could find ruins not only at sites such as Monte Albán, but also at archaeological parks, the UNAM (Universidad Nacional Autónoma de México), and the Mayan Riviera.These ruins help in the promotion of tourism by attracting dollars and euros. If Octavio Paz grants a "bewitching" quality to earlier monuments, postrevolutionary Mexican writers and artists find themselves within the spaces of even more fascinations and contradictions.

On the one hand, commitment to continuing the goals of the popular Revolution (without interruption, as evolutionary) finds its voice in Agustín Yáñez, Jaime Torres Bodet, and muralists such as Diego Rivera, José Clemente Orozco, and David Alfaro Siqueiros. On the other, those intellectuals who reject the official monumentalizing forces of the State-led construction of modernity emerge as significant counterpoints to the products of the culture "factory," contributing to the "demolition" of the historiographic connection but extending a new vision of a modern nation. One of the pivotal figures taking a critical public stance toward this hegemonic ideology, Juan Vicente Melo, clearly states the motivation of the second group of intellectuals: "Esta generación ha alcanzado una visión crítica, un deseo de rigor, una voluntad de claridad, una necesaria revisión de valores que nos han permitido una firme actitud ante la literatura, las otras artes y los demás autores. Cada uno de los miembros de esa supuesta generación [la denominada 'de medio siglo'] . . . ha alcanzado . . . responsabilidad y compromiso con el arte. No es raro que todos nosotros, poetas, novelistas, ensayistas, campistas, nos preocupemos por la crítica de una manera que, desde hace algunos años, no existía en México" [This generation has grasped a critical vision, a desire for rigor, a will to clarity, a necessary revision of values that has permitted us a steadfast attitude toward literature, the arts, and other authors. Each of the members of that supposed generation {the one called the Generation of the Mid-Century} . . . has reached . . . responsibility and commitment to art. It isn't strange that all of us, poets, novelists, essayists, improvisational performers, are preoccupied with criticism in a way that, a few years ago, did not exist in Mexico] (Melo qtd. in Pereira, *Generación* 128–9). This commitment to something 'new,' something that comes about as a result of a rejection of the official policies of modernization (as understood by the ruling party and its governmental organizations), is the focal point of a collection of intellectuals who find among the ruins symptoms of sclerosis and decay. Instead of pure joyous celebration, which the State sponsors on an almost daily basis in the arts and sports, this generation seems to obey Benjamin's mandate for a dialectical rereading of the ruins.

Composed of writers of the likes of Juan Vicente Melo, Inés Arredondo, Sergio Pitol, Salvador Elizondo, Sergio Fernández, Elena Poniatowska, Vicente Leñero, Carlos Fuentes, and Juan García Ponce, the generación de medio siglo in Mexico is generally characterized by a dedication to several of the fundamental features related to the concepts of history and aesthetics we have been discussing so far. The first shared characteristic is a preoccupation with the future of the postrevolutionary nation as it begins to traverse the uncertain and slippery terrain of modernity with the concomitant question of what to do with the traces and vestiges of a supposedly collective past, and whether they were or are valid for the rest of the century. As ruins are left to fall into ruin, what of culture should be saved and what might be cast aside, what defines the moment in terms of economics, politics, and society, and how does this dialogue with the past? At the forefront of intellectual debates and their edification through literary texts are concerns over the remnants of earlier European cultures, the value of indigenous heritage, and the increasing influence of U.S. culture as the new empire replacing Spain in the Americas. Should the nation and its inhabitants look inward or outward to provide sources for new "splendors" (Paz) for a new nation? Jameson's notion of the modern being a "rewriting" (35) of other stories joins the debate over the mechanisms of social institutions such as monetary funds, the media, banking, the flow of cash and of information and, of course, the institutionalization of capital. The circulation of notions of modernity, ideas and images, and money occurs as older faith (if any) takes on the risks of the new economics and as the security promised by the State to its citizens begins to be conceived by at least some of them as danger. One might look to the Olympic Games and subsequent political repression of 1968, to the government's inadequate response to the victims of the 1985 earthquake, to the stolen presidential election of 1988, or to the defeat of the seventy-year reign of the PRI in 2000. Are these instances of what Schmidt calls "nation building" or "nation destroying" (31)? Is this the triumph of modernity (if we consider it as a singular goal)? Or are these moments punctuated by both endings and beginnings, by the Marxian seeds of a culture's own destruction sowing themselves in different ways? Is reconciliation at all possible, between the global and the domestic, the native and the foreign, or what critic Maarten van Delden refers to in the works of Carlos Fuentes as "the ongoing tension . . . between nationalism and cosmopolitanism . . . [f]or each pole of the opposition simultaneously reflects and resists certain key traits of the modern era" (9)? The "reflection" and "resistance" within the same text or image or ideology present once again the Jamesonian dialectic of periods and renegotiations.

Melo and the others created their own cultural outlets in opposition to the purportedly splendorous Mexican diorama of the sacrosanct values and achievements of the Revolution. In this sense, even the image of the Revolution, and perhaps especially so, becomes a ruin for it is always pronounced as unfinished and each building, statue, column, and amphitheater erected forms part of the monumental project. Modernity and the Revolution go hand-in-hand in this official scenario for both, if we again follow Habermas, are works in progress and goals yet to be met. This is the evolutionary standard across which periodically the nation is asked to stand back and take stock of things before moving on. But, for others, the myth and the "mystique" (Poniatowska, Foreword xi) of the popular uprising earlier in the century against social injustices and the culture of poverty meets the new myth of the modern in a less synchronized form and less coherent continuity. Some of the conduits of cultural difference for intellectuals such as these include the creation of literary supplements to newpapers of mass distribution; the introduction of writers' workshops in public universities; the translation of modern authors from Europe and the United States; the discussion of philosophical thought from sources such as Herbert Marcuse, Georges Bataille, and Theodor Adorno; and the opening of avant-garde film cycles with the participation of both European and American directors, including Spaniard-in-exile Luis Buñuel. All of these cultural structures give voice to a stake in the crucial debates surrounding modernity and its implementation, either in an official sense of "opportunity" or as a darker and more troubling yet equally creative challenge. They do not merely critique the legitimacy of the enterprise of the State, with all of its ceremony and ruinous display, but they also address the issues central to modernity's debates, which Lomnitz concludes to be "[t]he central axis of cultural modernity—which is a productive relationship between science, art, and the constant improvement of the quality of life ('progress')" (214). Just how might such a productive relationship be articulated, especially in terms of economics and culture? How might the promissory tone of emancipation and enlightenment through 'progress' be achieved and what might it take to get there? Who benefits and who sacrifices for the good of all? Gilbert M. Joseph, Anne Rubenstein, and Eric Zolov address the grand narrative about the postrevolutionary era as an evocative tripartite mural composed, beginning on the left-hand side, of President Manuel Ávila Camacho spouting off on the end of earlier anticlericalism, a middle panel filled with the blood of sacrificed students in 1968, and on the right the implementation of neoliberalism under Presidents Bush, Clinton, and Salinas (3). How does the narrative pass from a national economy to a national collapse and how does one tell the story of the parts in-between? We shall address a variety of García Ponce's texts from the 1970s through the early twenty-first century with these inquiries in mind, carefully looking at the related concepts of "emancipation" and "enlightenment," and watching out for living remnants of previous tales as well as new roles for the storyteller.

Addressing forms that range from clothing styles to automobile models, García Ponce writes of the difficult yet provocative relationship between "lo viejo y lo nuevo" [the old and the new] in an essay of the same title. He writes, "Estamos en continuo movimiento. Lo de ayer se aleja y se queda atrás, perdido para siempre, con una rapidez alucinante. En medio del vértigo, viviendo dentro del espíritu de la época, uno no tiene tiempo ni siquiera para volverse y contemplar sus propias estatuas de sal. Estas caen al vacío, destruidas antes de alcanzar forma. Y sin embargo, en medio de la ininterrumpida desaparición de lo nuevo, persiste la nostalgia hacia aquello que, por su misma lejanía, aún podemos recordar como viejo. Apresado en los cambios incesantes, lo nuevo no llega a ser; en cambio, tenemos lo que fue" [We are continually on the move. What happened yesterday fades away and remains behind, lost forever, with hallucinatory rapidness. Amid the vertigo, living in the spirit of the time, one doesn't even have the chance to look back and contemplate his or her own statues of salt. These fall into oblivion, destroyed before they can take shape. And nevertheless, in the middle of the uninterrupted disappearance of the new, a nostalgia exists toward what, owing to its real remoteness, we can still recall as old. Trapped among endless changes, the new never comes into being; instead, we have what used to be] ("Lo viejo y lo nuevo" 2001 19). Caught by the past, one is inexorably pulled toward the future like the image of Walter Benjamin's Angel of History. Despite the urgent desire to move on, something like unwanted nostalgia will not let the spectator be free. The contradictory statues of salt that spring fully formed in the dreaming mind of the individual never come to fruition but never fade away either. Time passes—from Ávila Camacho to Salinas, let's say—but "living in the spirit of the time" each round requires one's complete attention to the horizon of the 'new,' or vertigo will spin us out of control. Jameson reminds us that there is a "distinction between *novus* and *modernus*, between *new* and *modern*. Can we sort this out by observing that everything modern is necessarily new, while everything new is not necessarily modern? This is, to me, to differentiate between a personal and a collective (or historical) chronology; between the events of individual experience and the implicit or explicit recognition of moments in which a whole collective temporality is tangibly modified" (18). The dialectic between "living in the spirit of the time" and taking stock of one's own "statues of salt" enters into Jameson's description of the "personal" intersecting with the "collective" and, often, not having the chance to sort out the relationship(s) between the two. Less a question of the new intruding into the recollection of the old, the disjunction between the two is much more a signal of the modern dilemma than its prescribed outline. Just how García Ponce's narratives will tell this story is the subject of this book.

If we return to the question of the narratives of history, on the one hand, the emergence in Mexico of the Onda [Wave; Being on the Right Wavelength; Being Hip] during the mid-1960s reflects the transcultural influences of popular U.S. music, spoken language, youth fashion, commercial cinema, fast food, and slick media. A change from previous cultural influences, what Carlos Monsiváis terms a move toward "otras vivencias culturales" [other cultural lifestyles, other ways of living] (Monsiváis, "Cultura" 1500), this movement provides the narration of the new and the old with new language, new ideals, new rhythms, and a new economic turn from "la Cultura Universal . . . [al] bienestar de la sociedad de consumo" [Universal Culture . . . to the good life of consumer society] (Monsiváis, "Cultura" 1500). Such cultural artifacts are, then, new to whom: To the society at large as a "vivencia cultural" or to the individuals composing the youth movement? Are these, as Monsiváis sees them, part of a desire to be avant-garde (1500) or do they evoke the dangers and the fears of modernity by dragging with them the baggage of the dark side as well as the side of economic opportunity as Giddens has claimed? On the feet of many young people, the native-made sandals known as *huaraches* made of old tire treads (the ruins of a previous cultural heritage and a modern mode of transport) become a statement of international modernity for some, while they also signal a reconsideration of the old, the past, and the national. The official discourses that recover folklore as the cornerstone of the nation are subverted through consumption into so-called avant-garde indigenous looks (Zolov 257). So the reading of a pair of rudimentary sandals might feed into our idea of allegory and the trope of the modern as well if we find in them a relic of the past cast into the role of the present by both the State and the so-called counterculture group.

Unlike the youthful writers of the Onda who look northward for totemic forms of transnational movements and groups which can be appropriated for other uses and other places, García Ponce does not find the only signposts for alternative nation-building there. Rather, he picks up the dilemma of the two-in-one, the period and the continuation of the modern, in his vision of Mexico's present. In the same essay "Lo viejo y lo nuevo" he examines the aesthetic of uncontrolled urban development in Mexico City and finds two ruins coexisting: "Lo viejo reaparece contaminado por lo nuevo, intentando ser nuevo, y esto mediante la inmediata aceptación, como elemento integral, de uno de los rasgos más característicos de nuestra época: lo gratuito" [The old resurfaces contaminated by the new, trying to be new, and this is done by means of the immediate acceptance, as if it were an integral element, of one of the defining attributes of our time: superfluousness] ("Lo viejo y lo nuevo" 2001 22). The gratuitous appearance of old and new pretending to be innovative, whether on the facade of a building or on the feet of an adolescent, does more than create an avant-garde aesthetic; it points out incongruities but it also calls the attention of all spectators to the consumption of the image. The first Spanish meaning of the word *gratuito* is "free," but the cost of exhibiting these images and ideologies is much more financially oriented than 'without cost' would lead us to believe. In cultural terms, nothing is free. Inhabiting that very problematic space where modernity pitches its most fervid battles for cultural and economic control, García Ponce fills a Mexico City of the imaginary with phantasmagoric signs of past and present in constant collision. In that nightmarish space of opportunity (for some) and danger (for others) he finds remnants of European discourses and American narratives left over from previous encounters hiding behind facades of new nationalist rhetoric and new youth culture. The boulevards of that megacity, its sports complexes and tourist Zona Rosa, its television studios and *discotecas*, all appear in dream form on the pages of his novels. From their whirlwinds emerge characters on ritual display caught up in the pageantry of modernity and, more often than not, trapped by it. If the modern is the moment, then more are asphyxiated by it than those who found the air to be clear in 1959 with the representation of the same city by Carlos Fuentes. The ceremonial centers of Teotihuacán might be emptied of practitioners, but new sites abound infused with remnants of other societies and other cultures obeying their own new rites. These spaces and their architecture are the monuments to many of the hopes of the twentieth century; these are a combination of the mundane and the uncanny which allegorically open up the cityscape into its contradictory fragments. Mexico City is the stage on which the allegorical story of the new Mexico will take place and García Ponce turns to for it most of his fictional settings. Even if characters return to the provinces, drawn by the survival of old myths, they inevitably must repay the sins of these departures and live once again in the city.

We might now view this as the second shared characteristic between García Ponce and other writers of the generación de medio siglo: a vision of the metropolis as the privileged space of modernity, whether seen as "pathology" (d'Entrèves 1) or as celebration or, sometimes, as both simultaneously. While not all of his narratives are set completely in this venue, Mexico's capital forms the crucible for the working through if not the working out of modernity's deep-seated tensions. If Benjamin considers the French poet Charles Baudelaire the figure that gives "voice to the shock and intoxication of modernity in Paris; . . . as the lyric poet of the metropolis . . . who [sought] to give voice to its paradoxes and illusions, who participate[d] in, while yet still retaining the capacity to give form to, the fragmented, fleeting, experiences of the modern" (Gilloch, *Myth* 134), then we may now look to García Ponce as the Benjaminian or Baudelairean 'poet' of the Distrito Federal. Just as in the nineteenth century Parisians dreamed of themselves as inhabiting the great new imperial capital of the modern world, and just as they saw something of the hero of that world every time they looked in the mirror, so Mexico City is transformed in the twentieth century into modernity's ruins filled with both the mundane and the uncanny, with loss and expectation.

Populated with ghosts, disembodied voices, and crumbling architecture, García Ponce's narrators' Mexico cannot be placed on a map. This is not the Mexico of the tourist guidebook, but it certainly contains the remote echoes of the Romantic wanderer, the archaeological explorer, and the utopian dreamer. It also functions as an allegory of the entire nation-building process, and is composed of problematic and intersecting relationships among many disparate elements. The city provides for García Ponce a kaleidoscopic background for his novels, essays, plays, and short stories between the 1960s and December 2003 (the time of his death). The characters in his fiction wander through urban spaces, landscapes of memory, literary spaces (in their homage to other authors and other fiction), and spaces of the psyche in search of some sense of subjectivity and roots amid the ruins of change and innovation. If they live during a time of feeling the pull of the modern, then they fall into García Ponce's critical space of encounter between the new and the modern, the individual and the collective, the period and the rupture. These figures embody not cold, distant, remote observers but are, like Baudelaire before them, fiery, tortured, exuberant, and even celebratory—souls seeking bodies that will not fail them in their desire to experience all of the anomalies of modern life. Like the coexistence of the BMW and the Volkswagen on the streets of the capital, the bathing costume and the briefest bikini on the beaches of Acapulco, the *antiguas casonas* [old mansions] and skyscrapers on the Paseo de la Reforma, the human body and its constructs are the only set on which this challenge can play out. Set against the excesses of urban allegories, García Ponce's characters are both subjected to the rituals of modernity and are subjects of the same. As such, they are the true heroes of the modern age in that, like Benjamin, they fall into the purview of critique and not of nostalgia. Benjamin writes of such individual subjects that these survivors are "the true subject[s] of modernity . . . [for] it takes a heroic constitution to live the modern" (qtd. in Osborne 81). Given the fact that there is no return, what remains, if anything, is individual redemption among the ruins. As García Ponce sees it, the risk and the danger of this newness is that entropy comes quickly, the "modernos edificios . . . se hacen viejos de inmediato, amenazando con convertirse en ruinas" [modern buildings . . . age immediately, threatening to become ruins {almost as soon as they are built}] "Lo viejo y lo nuevo" 2001 22). He cites Walter Benjamin's desperate attempt to "salvar lo muerto, trayendo lo viejo a la vida otra vez, con la esperanza de que mediante esta operación se conservara su esencia humana" [salvage what has died, bringing it back to life again, in the hope that through this operation its human essence might be preserved] ("Lo viejo y lo nuevo" 2001 20–21) not as a temptation but as a danger. If individual as well as collective life is characterized by constant change, then there is not a permanent essence to resurrect. Yet the hope of finding oneself amid the ruins may be the true object of this operation.

Let us focus for a moment on the figure of the Ángel de la Independencia [Angel of Independence] at the heart of Mexico City as an icon of Mexico's path toward modernity and, as an allegorical figure, a ruin of that very movement toward some general vision of 'progress.' Situated near the crossroads of two symbolic boulevards—Paseo de la Reforma and Avenida Insurgentes—and overlooking the Zona Rosa, this androgynous gilded figure looks out over the vast extension of the urban landscape and has been a mute witness to earthquakes, floods, strikes, demonstrations, political repression, monumental traffic jams, and raucous celebrations of soccer victories. It has been an eyewitness to the spectacle of modernity played out at its feet and to the phantasmagoria of daily violence which accompanies the spectacular. This angelic form echoes Benjamin's Angel of History in that it sits astride the allegorical ruins of past and present, from its perch on the column, casting its gaze outward and upward toward what used to be, but which has been covered over with the veneer of utopian dreams. Far more than the statue of salt alluded to by García Ponce, the angel is solid and, except for brief falls from its pedestal owing to the trembling of the earth, fairly permanent on the horizon.

So often referred to as an angelic figure, this metaphorically fallen angel (perhaps even demonic, for it has been cast into the thick polluted atmosphere of the largest city on earth) can be anthropomorphized as Benjamin has done to Paul Klee's painting *Angelus Novus*. The painted image Benjamin examines turns our gaze to this statue as a witness to history. Seen as decay that is constructive, the producer of debris that marks a simultaneous building up, the origins of the pile on which the angel sits: "The Angelus stares open-mouthed at the pile of rubble that human beings have left behind them in history" (Bolz and van Reijen 42). Astounded at the enormity of the ruins, perplexed by the whirlwind that drives it forward, the angel remains at the crossroads, agape yet seemingly powerless to respond. If the angel is mute, however, García Ponce breathes life and voice back into this allegorical monument to independence, aesthetics, and maybe even progress amid the melee of the modern. It is imbued with a narrative voice not bereft of paradox, criticism, and irony. The observer's gaze is swept upward by the force of the floating angel's golden brilliance atop the pillar; the city's gaze is oriented in the same direction if we consider the pull of 'progress' and modernity in terms of lofty, celestial goals. But again we find the duality of the image, for if one looks skyward, one is propelled loftily forward even as the second allure is a downward fascination (à la Paz) with the earthly, flesh and blood, bricks and mortar, and steel girders of modernity's constructions. As the Zona Rosa has fallen into decay, now deemed by jaded inhabitants the Zona Negra [Black Zone] for all the political corruption that has led to its demise, and the drugs and crime associated with its geography, the angel can now turn 180 degrees in search of miracles. On the opposite side of the avenue from the previously Pink Zone, just across from the crumbling movie theaters, condemned nightclubs, questionable bars, and cheaply decorated Pizza Hut storefronts, lie the new Bolsa de Valores [Stock Exchange], banking centers, mercantile headquarters, and glass skyscrapers erected as signs of twenty-first century Mexico. The State never ceases to dream, even as the city collects the remnants and fragments of former fantasies-turned-nightmares on its public face.

CHAPTER TWO

The Storyteller's Ruins

In David Scott's examination of "political presents and . . . reconstructed pasts and anticipated futures" (1) in the nations of the Caribbean basin, he points out the urgent need to avoid viewing modernity as a single point or goal in the future, as "the larger developmentalist narrative of modernity" (113). In contrast, he underlines the fact that a more culturalist reading of modernity is a "kind of acculturation story, the story of innovation within adaptation" (113), leading to multiple visions of the modern and alternative views of how (or why) to strive for such objectives. As one might surmise, this movement would involve the construction or "invention" (113) of alternatives to dominant systems. Such a view implies a reconception of modernity in opposition to another image. The implication is that there are two differing strands of narrative involved. As Jameson sees this, it is instead a symptom of a "political discursive struggle" (9) over the implementation of a free-market system of economics or the reliance on some sense of 'native' alternative. As he concludes, "adversaries of the free market . . . can only be classed in the negative or privative category of the unmodern, the traditionalist" (10). Rather than invent new terms for the internal elements of the polemic of modernity, let us instead open up the term to all of the periods and breaks of the dialectic in the Mexican context. Not a conscious decision but an ideological remnant, what story to tell and how to tell it come into focus within the larger arena of incipient capitalism and social change. One cannot ignore the conditions in which Mexicans will make their lives in order to find the variables between action and restraint, between choices and limits.

Between 1932 and 2003, the duration of García Ponce's life, seven decades of "electoral enthusiasm . . . and sincere disillusionment" (Gutmann, *Meanings* 164) occurred, public politics and private desires collided, the concept of legitimacy was on trial at every turn, the rituals of democracy played out or were thwarted, myths rose and fell, popular culture vied for power with elite culture, regionalism and the urban center continually clashed, screen actresses became elected congressional delegates, the Olympics came and went, immigration rates rose to record levels, tourism peaked and waned, privatization took over real estate, politicians and their friends became richer, the model of *ejido* agriculture all but disappeared (except at limited and publicly-televised moments), women banged on empty casseroles in the streets, the PRI was defeated at the polls to make way for the PAN (Partido de Acción Nacional) [National Action Party] as an opening to the new, Marcos and the Zapatistas emerged from the jungles of Chiapas to resuscitate the utopia of a long-dead revolutionary leader, and the social project of the Revolution survived in discourse if not always in practice. As practiced by the undefeated ruling party for seven decades, politics as an industry in and of itself began to be challenged by what Jameson has been sustaining all along: capital. The narratives of authority and of authoritarianism met the narratives of neoliberalism and of the liberation of the free market. The tilt toward determinacy regarded as a fixed part of the former—State, local, familial rule—met up with the more indeterminate, reaching a crisis in 1968 and again in 1988. Schmidt refers to this disequilibrium as "a less than almighty state" (37), but for our intents and purposes it can also signal the break and period of the modern.

If we were to map out García Ponce's early life according to his own words we would encounter a "porosity" (Gilloch, *Myth* 66) between memory and event reminiscent of Benjamin's writings on his own relationship with the city of Berlin. Rather than walls—the backyard "bardas" (García Ponce, "Mi última casa" 43) of piled up stones dividing the family property in Yucatán from the next family's plot of land—separating the two spheres, memory and desire intersect in the story line to produce dual narratives as 'city-like.' The dense networks of streets and alleyways are like the knotted, intertwined threads of memory which feed into the written text. "The open spaces . . . are like the voids and blanks of forgotten things. Lost times are the overlooked places" (Gilloch, *Myth* 67). The work of remembrance is, like modernity, dialectical. Places and events do not inhabit separate spheres, but rather coexist in the recollections of the narrator, frequently casting the irrecoverable moment in time as a space instead. Throughout García Ponce's narratives, half-preserved and half-forgotten, half-lived and half-invented episodes dot the landscapes and surround the characters, one of which he himself often becomes. Benjamin begins and ends in the city, yet García Ponce's version of the city is informed by stories woven from earlier personal history in the provinces and coexisting with issues confronting all of Mexico. His early days in Yucatán cannot be recovered in a more literal sense, much as Mexico cannot *really* propose in any viable way a return to some traditional past, some moment before conquest, some red-letter day when the Revolution was 'won.' All of these are cast into narrative structures of gain and loss, evoking euphoria and misery in the very act of narration.

Allegorical in form, and often fragmentary, the narrative structures of his fiction, essays, and short stories are more urban labyrinth than open field, a combination of archaeological strata, involuntary memory, and cityscape. Just when a storytelling voice seems to be stringing together a chronological sequence, or so one might hope, readers are presented with rupture and discontinuity. Allegory functions to produce this, to throw the sight of the unexpected into the eyes of readers, to interrupt the flow of discourse, to uncover the bizarre amid modern amnesia. In the face of the struggles between a vision of the nation as uninterrupted tradition and the nation as innovative, modern, and cosmopolitan, perhaps it is to be expected that narratives such as these reflect those same problematic encounters. At these intersecting places, the whole of "truth" (Castañeda, *Museum* 3) meets the ruins of critique, and Benjamin's model of dialectical archaeology (the excavation of sediments of the historical and the personal) kicks in. If the project of the State is to solidify the supposedly singular social and economic structures of modernity inside the facade of national history, then one would have to rummage around the ruins of culture to unearth the contradictions artificially binding them together.

In the ceremonies evoking his childhood memories, García Ponce explicitly clarifies that what he revisits are remote instants and fragmentary sites. When he recounts life before the D.F., he says that it is "la experiencia que hubiera deseado tener, la experiencia que imaginé" [the experience I would have liked to have, the experience that I imagined] (Ruffinelli 24), not a solid and complete life story. A parallel to an "idealized monument to the image of [a nation's] dreams" (Bruce-Novoa xii) could not be further from his imaginary recollections. A monumental structure cannot be built to last from the bits and decaying remnants of a past history, since the monolithic story on which it might stand does not hold. From his experiences as a Boy Scout on an expedition to the ruins of Uxmal, Chichén Itzá, and other tourist sites of the peninsula, García Ponce eschews narratives of glorious structures in decay and heroic acts of surviving the insects of the jungle to focus on his grandmother's burning of ticks, on the sounds of nature before tourism arrived, and on the deeply fascinating but equally terrifying waters of the sacrificial *cenotes*. As he writes, that "más que cualquier ruina" [more than any ruin] ("Infancia" 21), his experiences of the landscape take precedence. He recounts what we might consider a momentary break and period of modernity seen both through the eyes of the adult in the city and those of the child in the provinces. The Ferrocarriles de Yucatán [Yucatán railway] is a perfect example of the economic and social ferment in Mexico's encounter with modernity. As he retells his own childhood, this innovation in transportation is narrated in two ways. The first is through the youthful game of placing bottlecaps on the rails to be crushed, forming thin disks of metal. The boys then made holes in the centers, strung the disks on string and swung them at one another in mock battles. Dividing the world into friends and enemies, they sought to vanquish through pain: "se trataba de cortar el hilo al contrario, con lo cual el disco podía cortar al enemigo" [the goal was to cut the string of the enemy, so that the {freed} disk could cut him {to bits}] (22). The fact that this so-called game was prohibited by all of the families involved only made it more attractive to the boys. Forbidden games lead to hidden ones, and readers may not be totally surprised to find that "lo practicábamos religiosamente" [we practiced {them} religiously] (22). While the nation appeared to be absent, it was merely hiding behind the innocence of these adolescents in all of the 'freedom' and glory allowed by their class.

The second aspect of the railroad system is the narrator's deployment of its use as a symbol of the modern against the highways of the 1990s that run parallel to its now-abandoned tracks. Immediately following the look back at the innocent games of the bottlecaps, the narrator turns to his travels on the railroad to and from Mérida and his attendance at a Marist school. The trip to Campeche lasted seven hours and, even though it began a two-month summer vacation from classes, it was filled with other types of emotions that included the walk to the station and the sight of the steam emanating from the locomotive. He reviews in detail the route of the train and the final destination: home. His recollections of this modern system—modern for the times, at least—include the Poeta del Crucero [Poet of the Crossroads], who composed verses and limericks for the students who passed through, the food sellers on each town's platform, the soot that filled the passengers' eyes, and the now-disappeared orchards and *henequén* plantations. If he does conclude that "todo es inolvidable" [everything {about it} is unforgettable] (23), and if much of what is in his story no longer exists, then his journey is truly a modern one of periods and breaks for it reconnects with a story whose thread has long ago run out but which lives on in his memory.

As his memories come to a provisional close, the narrator breaks off to turn, in the subsequent piece, to "Otras voces, otros ámbitos" [Other Voices, Other Places]. But García Ponce has already experienced another period and break: an encounter between his parents over his father's infidelity led to an imposed reconciliation mediated by the Marist fathers and mandating the move of the entire clan to Mexico City. The rupture had little to do with economics as far as the family was concerned, or with the federal politics of land reclamation, yet it led to a different narrative perspective from the vantage point of the urban space in which new social and economic stories were already being configured. At the age of twelve, García Ponce was absorbed into the burgeoning metropolis and found that this was "mi destino" [my destiny] (24), moving from the known to the unknown (as Mexico moved from the past to the future), leaving behind recognizable faces and places to resurrect their vestiges in his recollections in the big city.

At mid-century, the urban intellectuals of García Ponce's generation confronted a world filled with what Juan Bruce-Novoa calls the "solidified, if not ossified" (x) postrevolutionary aesthetic traditions of the Mexican State. Paradoxically allowing for the inclusion of numerous voices, even as it promoted a single narrative line around which a national image might be constructed based primarily on past glories and splendors, the State created a "mystique" (Poniatowska, Foreword xi) about itself that is reflected in the public works of art it subsidized and promoted. As Joseph, Rubenstein, and Zolov write, "[t]here is a historical narrative about Mexico after the Revolution that everyone knows" (3). It takes shape in murals, buildings, and frescoes, in sculptural traditions of the Mexican School, whose vision of nationalism petrified images for all to see. But for those in dissent, those "who desired new answers for the future" (Bruce-Novoa xii), those children of wealth and privilege who felt constrained by the single narrative thread of this univocal history being monumentalized in stone and stucco, that type of seamless storytelling was a thing of the past. But even as they mourned its passing, the overwhelming desire to narrate haunted the pages of their texts. Caught on the horns of a dilemma, these young writers and artists looked toward a variety of sources and inspirations both inside and outside the borders of the nation.

In a changing Europe, Benjamin has seen the role of the storyteller in similar terms, "since the capacity to remember one's tale and the ability to narrate it unproblematically have vanished in the modern epoch" (Gilloch, *Myth* 69). For him, the aura of the storyteller is broken by the advent of modernity when the narrative glow no longer possesses the teller, the listener, and the contents, when "the gentle flame of his story" ("Storyteller" 109) flickers and sputters instead of burning on. So while García Ponce finds in fiction that both teller and narrative are cultural ruins at this point, that by having been usurped and cast into the official role of nation-building they have lost their auratic energy, he does see in poetry, in the *cronistas* of the nineteenth century, and in historians, especially humanists such as Alfonso Reyes and Octavio Paz, a place to "ganar el tiempo perdido sumergiéndose en esas realidades" [recover the time lost by submerging oneself in those realities] ("Autobiografía" 504). The "time lost" in prose fiction is recovered, in a Proustian way as the quote suggests, through the potentials of a new poetics and/or a new sense of historiography. Storytelling is the site of the "rising up" of the new State but, for the opposition, it may entail a "falling down" (Castañeda, "Aura" 452) into a degraded form from which it may once again arise, but now with an aesthetically different and critical role than before. (One might find an echo of the notion of ruin here.) No longer "bewitching" in fascination, as Paz sees in the splendors of the pre-Columbian ruins, the duality of the image brings forth the "exaltación y desamparo" [exaltation and abandonment] ("Autobiografía" 503–4) García Ponce revisits in his essays on his early days. As previously stated, allegory offers one way of exploding the singularity of modernity's narrative into the breaks and periods of involuntary memory.

Born in Mérida, Yucatán in 1932, García Ponce spent most of his childhood in that city, enjoying all the comforts that his connection to the Barbachano family could offer. A mestizo son of a Spanish father and a Mexican mother, whose privileged family lineage was referred to by inhabitants of the region as "la casta maldita" [the accursed caste] ("Autobiografía" 506), he grew up within the walls of a hacienda that protected him from the rest of society's evils and whose enclosed spaces were filled with photos and mementos of an illustrious past. The same walls that were built to keep the family line together functioned to keep out all sorts of social, economic, and political influences. Any intrusion into that separate space was considered an invasion by external forces. So President Lázaro Cárdenas's expropriation of private property during the 1930s, in an effort to bring land and wealth into a more egalitarian structure as dictated by the tenets of revolutionary discourse, reduced the family's holdings to a few buildings.

As García Ponce 'remembers' those moments, "los hacendados sólo se quedaron con el casco y las máquinas"[the landed property owners were left only with the shell and the machinery] ("Infancia"16), effectively enclosing the storyteller within personal ruins. What once was an elegant country estate turned into crumbling debris, the facade marking its former luxury. I place the word 'remembers' in quotes since, as Benjamin reminds us, narrating no longer adheres to chronology, linearity, or progress, but rather to the labyrinth, the spiral, and circularity. Around the memories of those ruinous past glories, García Ponce constructs new tales in which his own life is just a fragment among so many others, "a life, incidentally, that comprises not only his own experience but no little of the experience of others; what the storyteller knows from hearsay is added to his own" (Benjamin, "Storyteller" 108). The fact that he calls his home a "casco" or shell of something formerly whole, implies from the outset that García Ponce writes from the inside of the ruin which both inspires and "horrifies" (Paz, once again). His characters often gaze through windows toward an outside world that seems to mark time in a different way, as if in imminent collision with the spaces of the interior. The collection of short stories entitled *Cinco mujeres* [Five Women] is filled with such references, and the opening pages of *Personas, lugares y anexas* contains a sketch by García Ponce that portrays a tiny writing desk, sheaves of paper, and an inkwell facing his grandmother's window, filled with plants, through which the onlooker is positioned to gaze alongside the writer (12).

In his texts there is a constant and convoluted interplay between presence and absence, between the material and the phantasmatic, between the recollection of the past and the mystery of the future. If Carlos Fuentes's metaphorical image of Mexico City is summed up in the halfway hotel, the structure rising and falling on the urban skyline, then García Ponce's familial abode is even more unsettling. Lapsing into decay, it is a visible symbol of another time and another story, one which is rapidly changing under the impetus of the State. On the other hand, the construction phase of the building reverts to the imaginary alone for there will be no more additions or innovations to the hacienda; it is at a mournful standstill. Only in the narrative mind of García Ponce can it be evoked as a remnant worthy of recovery: the scars on his body provide the starting point for such stories for they bring back bits and pieces of the house's structure where he has suffered some physical or mental trauma—a stairway here, a banister there, a front door, a balcony, a bedroom, a hallway. But at some point stories fade into remoteness and decay; they cannot be followed to their beginnings or to their endings; they are Benjaminian sparks which then flame out. García Ponce writes of such recollections:

> Ahí todo se borra. Otra imagen u otro recuerdo: Jorge, mi primo, juega fútbol con sus amigos . . . mientras [mi hermano] Fernando y yo los contemplamos . . . Nadie nos invita a jugar. . . . Sentimientos de envidia y de inutilidad de la riqueza.
>
> La Villa Aurora está en un barrio apartado, entonces. Tiene un amplio jardín, patios interminables. . . . En ella estamos retratados sentados en los escalones. . . . Otra imagen: una fotografía de mi abuelo junto a una palmera real rodeado por la vasta familia. . . . Y luego, como en los sueños y en las películas, todo se borra en una súbita disolvencia con respecto a la Villa Aurora.

> [That's where everything gets blurry. Another image or another memory: Jorge, my cousin, playing soccer with his friends . . . while {my brother} Fernando and I watch them . . . No one invites us to play. . . . Feelings of jealousy and of the uselessness of being rich.
>
> Villa Aurora is in a separate neighborhood then. It has a large garden, endless backyard. . . . In the photograph we appear seated on the stairs. . . . Another image: a photo of my grandfather next to a royal palm, surrounded by his vast family. . . . And then, like in dreams or in movies, everything fades away in a sudden dissolve as far as Villa Aurora goes.] ("Infancia" 15)

Figures inhabit an architecture of dreams and memories in his story, fragments like ghosts that peer out of fading facades. They seem to be material and ethereal at the same time, their faces distinguishable yet elusive. Like the past, the narrator comes and goes, consuming "the wick of his life" (Benjamin, "Storyteller" 108) in the telling of his tale. He attempts to evoke an aura of authenticity in a story that is unsustainable in a traditional sense of beginning-middle-ending. It starts in mid-feeling ("sentimientos de envidia") and it ends in the erasure of the image in the fadeout. The 'reality' of his grandfather is evident to him in the quantity of progeny surrounding him, yet he too goes the way of the Villa Real. Both dreams and movies are composed of fleeting chiaroscuros destined to evaporate into thin air as one awakens or as the lights go on in the theater. Time, wear, erosion, transformation, and all other factors that produce the ruin are at work here.

Once displaced to the metropolis in 1945, García Ponce and his family could conjure up the walls and buildings of their homestead, and their narrative past, only through photographs and by retreating inside the subconscious. Benjamin explores the "scars" on his own unconscious mind from events and disruptions like García Ponce's (Gilloch, *Myth* 69), relegating them to the imagined space enclosed on one side by the forces of consciousness and, on the other, by "the fragmentary, disparate data of the *memoire involontaire* . . . , the principal traces of a person's past to survive the rigors of the modern epoch and the demise of conscious recollection" (Gilloch, *Myth* 69). Caught in the middle, García Ponce's narrators are spurred by sounds, smells, and sights of the city to stir up flashes and traces of the past from the depths of the rubble. Their version of the world never ceases to be a melancholic one built on the faded and cracking images that live amid glorious festivities of the 'new.' There is very little sense of continuity in these texts; instead, there is a continual punctuation of them by staccato endings and beginnings. Where might it all lead? That too is an unknown.

In his autobiographical writings, García Ponce claims to have found pleasure in reading as an escape from the everyday life of his neighbors and of the factory workers on his father's *henequén* estate. The pleasures of such activities are in some ways the allegories of a class system in ruin, a class structure that forms one of the building blocks of the edifice of his own (and Mexico's) past in transition to a future of capitalist fantasies. Tarzan and Jane, the archetype of tales of 'civilization and barbarism,' formed a centerpiece of García Ponce's youthful readings. Perhaps reading about the 'salvation' of European culture from the clutches of the natives and the happy-ever-after myth were precursors of García Ponce's later preference for things European over artifacts and products of indigenous Mexico, as they also may be indicators of a felicitous harmony missed in national projects when they exclude such 'outside' influences. Can there be a happy ending if a nation resides only amid its own unpoetic ruins? Or is there poetry to be found in some different sense than a Romantic escape (either Benjaminian nostalgia or archaeological visitation)? In some cases, both cultural traditions—the high and the low—are the objects of his parody and of the allegorical encounters among cultural breaks embodied in the texts.

At the age of twenty, García Ponce embarked on a journey of exploration that built on his earlier interests and that filled the void—another *casco* or shell like the architectural one left in the wake of Cárdenas's policies—left by the departure from Yucatán with new discoveries which informed all of his subsequent texts and invoked the "porosity" between event and narrator that Benjamin explored in Berlin. In what García Ponce frequently calls the greatest mistake of his father's life, he was sent on a mission of self-discovery from which he refused to return for an entire year. His fascination with the cultures and literary works of the European continent was so complete that he postponed reintegration into his family and national scene for over a year. Upon his return home much later than expected, he unearthed the ruins of his grandmother's library of European classics as the visible site of broken connections between Mexico and the Old World. Fragments of the cultural past represented by these works called up a sort of "involuntary recollection" (a Proustian yarn in which remembering and forgetting were woven into the same *memoire involontaire*) of missing pieces from his own past as told by other storytellers. He picked up the numerous volumes and picked up their tales as well. Embedding them in Mexican society once again, García Ponce experienced something akin to the shock of the urban setting described by Benjamin, an experience of discontinuity that both attracted and repelled him for the trauma and "horrors" (Paz) it evoked. Already melancholic the first time around, with his appropriation of them the stories acquired an additional tinge of loss even as they function as narrative monuments to those moments and memories.

His relationship with the burgeoning city was one of potential dialogue; as the voices in the library spoke into his ear, he heard other voices around him that contradicted and challenged any singular telling of a tale. None of them was adequate for the storyteller, since even the cultural building stones in clear view are like ruins "which stand on the site of an old story" (Benjamin, "Storyteller" 108). If we consider Benjamin's schema of "mutual recognition and illumination" (Gilloch, *Myth* 13), however, the idea of self-recognition is now made problematic. Instead of finding himself in the cultural sediment of the nation, García Ponce began to look around and see nothing but piles of debris. If "[t]he task of the archaeologist is to dig beneath the surface of the modern city and the modern sensibility it engenders, to unearth the evidence of past life and the shocks that have become lodged in the depths of the unconscious" (Gilloch, *Myth* 70), then our storyteller retrieved only chips and shards that piled up at his feet. Rather than facilitate encounters with others, García Ponce's narrators are imbued with an experience of place, with "the sites of our encounters with others and ourselves" (Benjamin qtd. in Gilloch, *Myth* 67). The architecture of the city, its half-built high-rises and planned communities such as Ciudad Satélite [Satellite City], are officially touted as monuments to a forward-looking State, but felt by narrators as localities for jarring the memory into storytelling. The narrative voices of his urban fiction thus form part of the strata of the process of coming-into-being of Mexico City in its modern guise and are, conversely, what Laura U. Marks calls the "indexical traces" (227) of the generations inhabiting it. Each layer of the city, each rereading of a work of fiction from the family library, sets off "chains of associations" (Marks 227) for García Ponce's narrators. His texts are structured around repeated episodes of incursions into spaces that "disinter" (Gilloch, *Myth* 70) events and experiences buried inside the personal and the collective history of the adult. An archaeologist of sorts, Benjamin delves into Berlin's hidden layers; García Ponce digs up the labyrinth only to find that there are more questions to what he unearths than answers. Like the very streets of Mexico City, the lives of his characters are continually *en obras* [under construction].

As a vocation, literary studies were not part and parcel of the professional goals for someone of García Ponce's social and economic status; reading was a pastime but not an occupation. But it became not merely an occupation but a preoccupation for García Ponce as he rescued the fragments of European culture cast aside by nation builders as constructive elements for his vision of the so-called new Mexico, adding them to the mix that began to settle as contradictions and anomalies came to the surface. As Monsiváis writes of this generation of intellectuals in Mexico, "[f]rente a la Historia, la alternativa es otra suprema totalizadora entidad, la Cultura" [when faced with {the narrative of } History, the alternative is another supremely totalizing entity, Culture] ("Cultura" 1497). Monsiváis points out very clearly the switch in register from an official narrative of nation-building stories linked together across a historical continuity and seen in harmony all the way to the horizon of the future, to another all-encompassing master narrative of Culture. Contrary to European intellectuals of the moment who witness the decay of old empires in the Old World as loss, García Ponce uncovers in a 'lost' European past residues of cultural energy for the future alongside the contemporary immersion in popular Mexican and U.S. cultural artifacts. His ruins, then, are composed equally of provincial haciendas as monuments to institutionalized power, a traditional class structure, old money, and an Old World epic while he finds around him new discourses of political power, State centralization, rapid urbanization, economic projects, cultural contamination by U.S. enterprises such as Sears Roebuck, the invasion of Hollywood spectacles into Mexican theaters, and the rise of movies starring the character Cantinflas. A break in chronological narrative structure reflects these profound and conflicting cultural encounters, as does the use of allegorical characters and situations. García Ponce tells his readers that this change is, for him, a personal one; Jameson would defend its ideological base.

> [n]o sé si en este aspecto puedo hablar en nombre de mi generación o sólo a título personal, pero en mi caso, el paso de la costumbre de gozar de la literatura a la necesidad de estudiarla, el descubrimiento, obvio y sin embargo desconcertante, de que si iba a escribir escribiría en México y sobre lo que yo conocía y deseaba expresar, llegó unido al reconocimiento de una profunda ruptura. El escenario, por ejemplo, de las novelas que admiraba se extendía desde San Petersburgo hasta Nueva York, pero jamás tocaba México.
>
> [I don't know if in this regard I can speak on behalf of my entire generation or just for myself, but in my case, the step from the habit of enjoying literature to the need to study it, and the discovery, obvious yet disconcerting, of the fact that if I was going to write I would do so in Mexico and I would write about what I knew and what I wanted to express, came in tandem with the recognition of a profound break. The settings, for example, of the novels that I admired, ranged from Saint Petersburg to New York, but they never had anything to do with Mexico.] ("Autobiografía" 503)

In the transition from pleasure to "necessity," from storytelling as enjoyment to storytelling as challenge, the rules regarding the literary text demand that readers delve among the residues contained within and not merely glance at it for enjoyment, edification, or national glorification. The sense of "discovery" that to write in Mexico would imply discomfort and agitation—the combination of "exaltación y desamparo"—cohabits with the narrator's recognition that a chasm between his own desire and the national political culture has yawned. In spite of the fact that some critics have seen mass culture in the 1940s, 50s, and 60s as a "bridge between the traditional and the modern, between *lo mexicano* and the American Dream" (Joseph, Rubenstein, and Zolov 11), there is no such facile connection for García Ponce between inside and outside the nation, between what is native and what is 'other,' between discourses of the past and new media culture; nor does he represent official discourses on either side of the "American Dream." The metaphor of the bridge would not seem to work for either Benjamin or García Ponce; the fluidity of its construction—perhaps akin to Fuentes's high-rise—and the reading of its destination do not hold for all those who tell the story. There is no such dream in easy terms: like the figure of the ruin, the dream can be a fascinating hallucination. In addition, the definition of "*lo mexicano*" is ambiguous in any case. If the definition lies in that old storytelling tradition, it has certainly fallen into decay for narrators seeking other tales and finding greater ironies. Despite the confession that it would be indiscreet for him to enter into any details regarding his parents' move to Mexico City in 1945, García Ponce concludes that "[m]i relación con la ciudad de México, más allá de la historia, es estrictamente personal" [my relationship with Mexico City, beyond history, is strictly personal] ("Otras voces" 26). There are no bridges to anywhere but inside the ruinous labyrinths of the narrators themselves, and they as frequently lead from past to present as they do from material city to internal images.

As links between the bourgeois culture of Mexico and the aesthetic traditions of the Old World were not suppressed but celebrated by writers such as García Ponce, the intellectuals' place of birth becomes mere coincidence. Destinies and fortunes for writers or artists are bound to other places and other cultures, not those found right outside their doorways as if in isolation from the rest of the world. Personal histories, family sagas, and the quest for the modern all belong to a vision greater in time and space than their immediate surroundings. Octavio Paz has pointed out as much in his essay "Will for Form." Of Mexican history and culture he writes, "Two civilizations have lived and fought not only across its territory but in the soul of every Mexican. One is native to these lands; the other originated outside but is now so deeply rooted that it is a part of the Mexican peoples' very being" (3). It is that second, insider-yet-outsider, cultural model which appealed, and continues to appeal, to a large number of artists and writers who envision their aesthetics in broader, more international cultural terms and who find the function of the text to contain more critique than nostalgia, celebratory enhancement of history, or mere archaeological remembrance. This contestatory cultural exchange based on raising the ruin as monument to more than an insular past is what Carlos Fuentes terms the "hidden history" of Latin America or its "unfinished business" (*Buried Mirror* 311). Fuentes adds to the layers of inquiry related to the historical rise and fall of Mexican cultures by questioning whether the political, cultural, social, or economic factors of this nation can be united to "finish" the business of Mexico's modernity, or whether this is an impossible task doomed to failure. García Ponce, while in the throes of feeling both "exaltado and desamparado," comes down on the side of construction marginally winning over destruction. Perhaps one way of dealing with *desamparo* [the feeling that one has been cast adrift] is *exaltación* [being excited or fired up] at the loss and not merely numbed.

After 1950, the social realism of the old masters of the Mexican School of both literature and the plastic arts was subject to widespread attack by new generations of artists who questioned their filter of a historical vision.[1] Their "zeal for Modernity," as Monsiváis terms it (79), was to force a revision of the encounter between the oldest and the newest traditions, to question the immediacy and inevitability between historical past and cultural present. The other Mexican painting, in particular that done by Rufino Tamayo, was to become one of the sources of inspiration for intellectuals who seek aperture and not closure. Although he belongs to the same generation as the "Three Masters" (Siqueiros, Orozco, and Rivera), Tamayo's identification as an aesthetic "synthetist" (Lucie-Smith 112) and eclectic stylist distance him from the immediate (monolithic) national context. The polemic between generations extended to a particularly acerbic verbal attack by José Luis Cuevas against Siqueiros, and the young painter's admonition to the rest of his cohorts to look beyond the *cortina de nopal* [cactus curtain] to renew and revolutionize the national aesthetic. In an era of muralism and stardom, Fuentes writes of art in Mexico as having

> always been allied to mythology. Whether creating a stone pedestal for the worship of the earth goddess Coatlicue, a gilded temple honoring Guadalupe, a novel defending the underdog or a mural recalling the

> heroic past, the Mexican artist has seldom been able to act outside the demands of the all-encompassing myth. The artist in Mexico after the Revolution identified with a rediscovery of the lost myths and, up till the fifties, saw his duty as a patriotic guardian of local traditions and the national character. ("New Wave" 128).

As the State continued to produce the urgent need for recognition of the nation, and as it continued to invest in public monuments, "[m]yth was resurrected with a vengeance." As it fell into decline, however, more and more violent actions were needed to keep it alive in the public eye. Fuentes clarifies that the nationalistic movement was "only a stage in Mexico's cultural development" but in an attempt at self-perpetuation it became "repetitive, chauvinist, picturesque, and finally degenerated into self-caricature" ("New Wave" 128). What from the vantage point of the late 1960s he sees as the New Wave is akin to what we have been calling García Ponce's contestatory vision. Fuentes cites the artist Cuevas yet again about what is to be found among the riches of the cultural ruins behind the murals: "Death, prostitution, sickness are part of the Mexican tradition, so my paintings are sad. But I do not have to live in sadness, only be its spectator" ("New Wave 131). I do not intend to imbue García Ponce's texts with a sadness that is not there, much as I would not include them among the traditions of nostalgia that Benjamin overcomes with critical vision. Nevertheless, Cuevas's tinging of "tradition" with darkness instead of bright lights revokes the celebratory tone of State modernity and puts in its place a need for more of the resourcefulness of *desamparo* than of *exaltación*. The "spectator of sadness" is the vision of the melancholic and, more importantly perhaps, of the modern.

An art exhibit entitled Confrontation of 1966 exemplifies this engagement in that it pits the works of the Mexican School of previous decades against the alternatives proposed to be explored by the painters Cuevas, Manuel Felgúerez, Vicente Rojo, Fernando García Ponce (Juan's younger brother), and others, whose paintings embody the spirit of the modern in the arts and whose aesthetics address a market of international tastes. Art critic Marta Traba, for whom the promotion of this generation is a touchstone of her career, describes them: "No longer content with passive storytelling, they gave standing to more indirect and symbolic modes of expression, advancing to the limits of art without specific meaning" (84). Aside from the hint that nonrepresentational art would be some step beyond the social realism of previous decades, Traba offers a clue to the consideration of the generación de medio siglo as an avant-garde unbound from traditional realist or mimetic representation. In literature, we might think of what we have examined as a new role of the storyteller and a new form for the tale.

Their challenge to and transgression of the norms of social realism and the mural panels of the story of the nation's emergence into modern times is posited in radical changes to literature as well. The possibility for this confrontational climate in Mexico is distinguished by art critic Edward Lucie-Smith as owing to, somewhat paradoxically, a cultural environment open to discussion. Until the tremendous collapse of the civilized facade of the national edifice in 1968, "[t]he best publicized debate about the future of the visual arts took place in Mexico, for two reasons. One was that the régime had remained stable, and open expression of dissent was possible, no matter how much heat it generated. The other was that Mexico was the home of Muralism, and there was thus something tangible against which to react" (112). So it is that Muralism, the movement institutionalized by the postrevolutionary State, served as the rallying point for an oppositional aesthetic. It did not disappear but, like the structural ruins before it, was built upon and refurbished. Like the ruins of ancient Rome, whose limestone blocks were recycled into newer structures, and like the pyramid of Cholula, which provided stones for subsequent Christian temples, Muralism furnished the raw materials for other artworks. The same can be said for the Novel of the Revolution and the narratives which follow and respond to it. The populist clichés that form the underlying structures of those novels are the targets for writers such as Juan Rulfo and Carlos Fuentes who begin to demythify the icons of the Revolution with the icons of Modernity. Social realism is confronted with psychological dimensions of characters, and chronological stories of triumph come face-to-face with stream-of-consciousness narratives and the suggestive and allegorical "porosity" of the city. These reactions were spurred on by the *desarrollista* [developmental] impulse of the presidency of Miguel Alemán (1946–52) which opened up once and for all a dialogue with aspects of modern culture inside the borders of the Mexican nation. Such a policy of embedding an image of modernity in the shapes and forms of 'development' is found in Alemán's promise to every citizen: "Un Cadillac para cada mexicano" [A Cadillac for every Mexican] (Gutmann, *Meanings* 178). The equivalent of President Harry S. Truman's patriotic pledge of "two cars in every garage" (never mind the chicken in every pot), this statement binds economic progress with cultural acquisition. Moreover, the objects to be acquired represent the pinnacle of economic success in postwar United States. How does this jibe with postrevolutionary Mexican politics? On the one hand, it conflates culture and economics; on the other, it does away with what Monsiváis has called the discourse of History. It does not take much analysis to see the period and break of this moment.

As critic Armando Pereira summarizes, Mexico City in the 1950s bustled with change and 'progress': "[La ciudad] estaba estrenando su modernidad: cafés, teatros, cines, librerías, restaurantes, los cuales eran un punto de encuentro obligado para todo aquel que demoraba sus ocios nocturnos por las calles iluminadas y bulliciosas del centro" [{The city} was debuting its modernity: cafes, theaters, movie houses, bookstores, restaurants, all of which were an obligatory point of meeting for all those who spent time during the leisure hours of the night along the bright, noisy streets of downtown] ("Sobre" 6). Pereira's words suggest the imagined communities of the flâneurs of Paris and Berlin, those individuals wandering the urban labyrinth in search of evocatory images and personal stimulation of lost recollections. As Benjamin writes of the flâneur's environment, "[t]he street becomes a dwelling for the *flâneur*; he is as much at home among the façades of houses as a citizen is in his four walls. To him, the shiny, enamelled signs of businesses are at least as good a wall ornament as an oil painting is to a bourgeois in his salon. The walls are the desk against which he presses his notebooks; news-stands are his libraries and the terraces of cafés are the balconies from which he looks down on his household after his work is done" (*Charles Baudelaire* 37). The challenging and varied strata of street life are the iconic symbols of a Mexican modern, and nightlife provides García Ponce's characters with spaces for encounters. The clubs, *tertulias*, literary circles, and round tables that exist in abundance give rise to an effervescent intellectual community that is woven into the mental images that García Ponce and his narrators carry with them from childhood and from literary readings. The Centro Mexicano de Escritores [Mexican Writers' Center] gave financial and collegial support to many of the generación de medio siglo, although García Ponce, perhaps unsurprisingly, rejected the fellowship it offered him. The lack of surprise follows the writer's critique of all such institutionalized aesthetics in favor of a personal one, even if this proposition itself is evidently problematic. The *Revista de la Universidad* [University Journal] of the UNAM (Universidad Nacional Autónoma de México), as well as the *Revista Mexicana de Literatura* [Mexican Journal of Literature], offered young writers an open forum for new ideas; each was headed at one time or another by García Ponce. In his promotion of fellow dissidents, a group was created that was seen by some critics as a *mafia literaria*, a pejorative assessment of their tastes for the foreign and their propensity toward a closed community that resembled a private club. The contradictions of a rejection of one forum for another are evident. What the so-called mafia managed to accomplish, among numerous other innovative projects during the decades of the fifties and the sixties, was the translation of works by writers from the United States and Europe whose works had been unavailable in Spanish until then. In the face of a celebration of the popular by some, others unearthed storytelling traditions from other cultures as raw material for new compositions. García Ponce translated the works of Herbert Marcuse and Cesare Pavèse for this project.

Mexican literary critic Margo Glantz coins the terms Onda [New Wave] and Escritura [*Écriture*; Pure Writing] to distinguish two of the important directions taken by the generations of writers in Mexico, first during the 1950s and 1960s, then into the 1970s. In a now-classic 1971 essay on the multitude of aesthetic tendencies layered among the cultural folds of the era, Glantz studies Gustavo Sáinz and José Agustín as examples of the Onda. In novels such as *Gazapo* [Young Rabbit or a Misprint] and *De perfil*, [In Profile], she roots out a series of characteristics that create a profile of these texts as sites of rebellion against inherited social values. They include "el imperialismo del yo" [the imperialism of the self, the focus on the I] (91), a new sexual morality (95), the acquisition of a critical political consciousness and, above all, the rescue of the language of the streets as the expression of a new subculture. Popular speech, rock and roll, the Spanglish of border cities, and the slang of an incipient drug culture are the resources to demythify what is deemed the dead world of 'literary' language along with the stories it has to tell. As a reaction to what is considered stultified language, or a nationalistic idiom aimed to codify values and mores into a timeless vernacular (as in the novel of the Revolution, or in the writings of Rulfo, Yáñez, etc.), writers of the Onda infuse the written text with testimonies to the orality of the moment.

The Onda aims for the ears of the reader to produce an imagined auditory experience as it recovers the speech of the rapid-fire slang of the streets; it is an experience written on the page but oriented toward performance through its phonetics. But on the other side of the coin, Escritura writers shift the focus to the page itself as a canvas on which to renovate language and storytelling in other ways. Rather than the solid, immovable surface of the epic mural, the page holds open a space for experiments in narrative structure and deconstruction. Language is not merely a vehicle for communication but an end in itself as it loops around and piles meaning upon meaning in a baroque manner. Such a concept of narrative as the terrain of linguistic innovation using, of course, the ruins of other texts, and not as the mass communication of slang subcultures, tackles the vision of the Onda head on. Glantz concludes that this aspect of Escritura denotes the confrontational mode of that movement lacking in the Onda. She writes that this negates the potential power of the Onda, in that "la negaría en la medida en que el lenguaje de la Onda es el instrumento para observar un mundo y no la materia misma de su narrativa. Onda significaría en última instancia otro realismo, un testimonio, no una impugnación, aunque algunas novelas o narraciones de la Onda empiecen a cuestionar su testimonio" [it would negate that movement in as much as the language of the Onda is the instrument for observing a world and not the very substance of its narrative. In the end, the Onda would mean another realism, a testimony, not a challenge, although some of the novels and narratives of the Onda might begin to question its testimony] (108). Another level of realism atop the social realism of previous decades would, for her, not imply a challenge to the accurate or 'realistic' portrayal of historical events. The palimpsestic text would be insufficient for critique and would leave behind vestiges more of accord than of disharmony, as if one layer were connected to another in some logical or reciprocal progression. Benjamin's revelatory spark or flash of recognition on the photographic plate of the unconscious ("Berlin Chronicle" 56) is thus forged into a whole rather than a collection of superimposed sedimentary fragments. In the end, the potential power of deflecting and reorienting representation that language might hold has to be unleashed through other, more disruptive means. Benjamin's calling on allegory as excess to "spell an end to all systematic and universalistic conceptions of history" (Hanssen 68) directs us toward the linguistic and cultural structures exploded in all directions by García Ponce as he digs among inherited tropes for new, and often frustrating, combinations.

The Escritura cult of the text includes the presence of "an imaginative, symbolic reality," a disinterest in linearity or chronology as formal elements, a hybridity or crossover of genres, and the "replacement of the omniscient narrator by multiple or ambiguous narrators" (Duncan 9). The written word dominates the text as both tool and subject, message and messenger, in a ritualistically repeated evocation of a world grounded in and on the page. Mimetic realism has no place. Language is used to theatrically or pictorially cast tones of light and darkness, replay stage entrances and exits, exhibit a certain static quality of images (as archetypes), or reproduce the slow pan of the cinematic camera in order to give the reader/viewer access to a interior panorama. The role of the writer, then, is as a "facilitator" (Duncan 26) to visually expose the contradictions inherent in linguistic representation. Situating the act of writing outside obvious connections with social reality, García Ponce challenges the reader to forge links to the cultural ruins in and with which the text is produced; he will not provide them himself. Threatening to explode in many directions at once, the linguistic sign sprouts more like telltale shoots from shrubbery than from linear root. As García Ponce makes clear:

> El terreno de la novela es ese terreno de la libertad absoluta en el que ninguna regla social, ningún mandato moral, ningún principio de ninguna especie detienen el curso de la narración . . . [Los] dos elementos fundamentales [para realizar la tarea de imaginar o inventar posibles imágenes del ser humano] son el cuerpo y el lenguaje. El cuerpo porque es el único garante legítimo de la realidad del individuo en un mundo dentro del que todo sentido de la realidad, toda posibilidad de coherencia, se ha ausentado. El lenguaje porque sólo él puede establecer la comunicación entre la vida del cuerpo y la conciencia de esa vida, porque nacido del cuerpo le permite contemplarse a sí mismo.
>
> [The terrain of the novel is that of absolute freedom in which no social rule, no moral mandate, no principle of any kind deters the course of narration . . . {The} two fundamental elements {to carry out the task of imagining or inventing possible images of human beings} are the body and language. The body because it is the only legitimate garantor of the individual's own reality in a world in which all sense of reality, all possible coherence, has disappeared. Language because it is the only means for establishing communications between the life of the body and the individual's consciousness of that life, because, born of the body, it permits that body to contemplate itself.] ("¿Qué pasa?" 147, 153).

While the concept of "absolute freedom" is more relative than absolute if we consider the text as part of its social context whether the writer denies it or not, the flow of the narrative to do and undo stories appears to reflect once again the building that is under constant construction in Carlos Fuentes's essay. Language is the construction material of the edifice of the text, as it enters and exits the body that produces it. In the process, the human body itself comes into being as an edifice as well, as a construction of language as much as the written text is. Each facet of this movement from inside to outside, each step of this transformation calls on previous residues of linguistic acts to forge new topographies mirrored in the final product. García Ponce's words offer evidence of the "porosity" we have explored in Benjamin's cityscapes and their wanderers, a sense that between the body as text and the word as text there are infinite, pervasive, and secret connections. By "communication" García Ponce implies less the fundamental nature of language than its latent or concealed power of revealing secrets from the personal life and experiences of the narrator. Such a reduction to communication would devalue the potential potency of language, especially in its use of metaphor and allegory. This is a fundamental proposition of Benjamin's view of what constitutes a "sacred" text, and not necessarily only the sacred Scriptures. Any and all texts may contain "the magic formula" (Rosen 153) for the reader, they may be taken as sites for "contemplation, for meditation, incantation, for a form of understanding that evades intention, author's as well as reader's" (Rosen 154). To distinguish only its communicative ability is to impoverish language; it is capable of much more. Although García Ponce does not directly write of the sacredness of the literary text, the rituals and ceremonies of his storytellers perform powerful acts of narration that make the reader take them as incantations and not just words.

What Glantz refers to as the "Byzantine" style (106) of his texts sets García Ponce's characters among the complex and convoluted linguistic ruins of cross-continental and cross-cultural narratives; they appear and disappear from view, they dissolve into obscure borders or outside the frame. Their language seems to weigh on the page for its honeycomb of relationships and secret dialogues that come forth from the recollections of the narrators. Sentences and phrases run on with little or no interruption to their train of thought or observation, indicative of their link to involuntary memory and not conscious crafting. Readers encounter characters and scenarios in excess. In the multiple and repeated reiterations of the same scenes from different perspectives, language acquires the sound and phrasing of incantation and not the quick burst of communication of the Onda's everyday colloquial slang that evaporates into the stories of the streets. While Duncan has found a certain similarity between Fernando del Paso's novels and Diego Rivera's frescoes in their dual allusions to Mexican society and politics, as well as in their incorporation of pre-Columbian mythology into a totalizing scenario of historical events, García Ponce's novels evoke instead a static quality of isolated ahistorical phenomena even when the setting appears at first glance to be recognizable to the reader. Even in the vast historical genealogies of *Crónica de la intervención* [Chronicle of an Intervention], the one novel with more than just passing reference to a historical epoch, there are only tableaux of congealed images, not lucid and systematic pieces of a coherent panoramic puzzle. Posed or frozen moments have been extricated from larger contexts and imbued with symbolic meanings. The only key to these has to be excavated from among the cacophony of all the narrative voices. And even then, the "key" is only suggested in scattered and disconnected form; the shifting scenes, panels, or moments in the labyrinth must be articulated by each reader. In this manner, Duncan's notion of "hybridity" or "ambiguity" emerges as the blending of visual images and linguistic signs. And Monsiváis's vision of the demise of History's discourse is sustained.

Even though they share the same avenues and boulevards filled with buffeting crowds, swift pace, intrusive commerce, and ubiquitous billboards, the Onderos and the Escritura writers do not equally share the modernizing experience. The transformation of the city is, for the first group, an integration into the 'greater modernity' of America and a chance to show off membership in consumer society in the "contact zones" (Joseph, Rubenstein, and Zolov 16) of, for instance, the Colonia Roma, the Zona Rosa, and the Zócalo. For the second group, the city is a "mnemonic device" (Gilloch, *Myth* 173) for recalling half-forgotten moments and half-ruined relationships. Neither Benjamin nor García Ponce pauses to lament the changes in the city, but both find in its fleeting moments of contact, not leisurely repose, but opportunities that respond to personal sentiments of loss and gain, of darkness and light. The calmness of previous storytelling narratives makes way for metropolitan magic and the "deceptive facades" of architecture and urban life. Characters read circumstances provisionally, they do not attempt to solidify what they see into a whole. The city becomes for Benjamin and for García Ponce alike "a theatre, a labyrinth, a prison, a monument, a ruin" (Gilloch, *Myth* 170). Stories play out, they fade away, and they reappear in other guises across novels; they are not relegated to one text and they do not seem to end when the printed page does. This is not to affirm some sort of disintegration of the avant-garde while tradition remains unblemished and in absolute power. Instead, it is my contention that the social, aesthetic, and political terrains of the 1950s and decades after are unstable and fluid. Otherwise, the cultural production of the Onderos as much as that of the Escritura writers would have long since disappeared into the commercial sediment of the PRI or elsewhere in official rhetoric. Benjamin's desire for critical engagement and not archaeological visitation or nostalgic reconstruction has many facets in the formative decades of Mexican modernity. The organizing motifs of the State allowed for the coexistence of dialogue, at least for the moment. Funds and resources from previous investment in the countryside were reallocated after the Revolution brought all of these contentious forces together in the capital city. Without an overarching meaning to it all, however, Mexico City turns into an allegory of the nation's greatest triumphs and failures.

Over the course of the five decades between the 1950s and his death at the end of 2003, García Ponce increasingly burned the wick of his storytelling at both ends. Like Benjamin's Janus-faced Angel of History who looks backward as he is catapulted by the forces of modernity into an unknown future, his narrators glance outward as they increasingly become aware of their inner turmoils. Both facets of their story are joined through the subjective consciousness of the characters who, rather than situate themselves within some external linear narrative, create labyrinthine dialogues with it. Daniel Goldin remarks of this dual process that such characters "[prefieren] internarse en los oscuros meandros de su propia conciencia, siempre acechada por la fuerza del inconsciente, e indagar en las innumerables posibilidades de las relaciones intersubjetivas" [{prefer} to penetrate the dark labyrinths of their own consciousness, always threatened by the {obscure} forces of the unconscious, and to inquire into the countless possibilities of intersubjective relations] (7). The dark recesses or secrets of the individual, and of the imagined reactions by others, turn into obsessions and neurotic fascinations (with all that 'fascination' implies for Paz.) These repetitive returns and compulsive reiterations are the paradigms of "una visión cada vez más íntima" [more and more of an intimate vision] (Sefchovich 179) that signal the return of the private and the repressed regions of human activity to the space of literary representation. The mimetic goals of social realism should not be applied to these experiences on the page for they lie at the core of baroque excesses. What has been taken for either hidden or "repressed," a marker of social control or normativeness, is the site at which García Ponce concentrates his sometimes surprising and unexpected excavations. What is revealed about the recondite forces of behavior contributes to a series of allegorical encounters and gestures as both the result of the social construction of identity and the potential for turning it against the society responsible for its formation.

The watershed year of 1968 is a particularly profound moment of political rupture that brought to a head an already long-eroded confidence in the State's projects for the nation. While journalists such as Elena Poniatowska and Carlos Monsiváis,[2] and filmmakers like Jorge Fons, and others, have documented the violence of the decade of the 1960s as part of a vaster panorama of political and social upheaval, García Ponce manifests the schism in a different emotional and aesthetic form. The internalization of layers of innocence and disingenuousness cohabit in his narratives from the sixties and beyond, turning the crisis in society into a storytelling impetus. The cliché of crisis in Mexican society, rather than forming an overt reference to massacres and student repression, is for him another type of repression from whose depths images might be culled. On a psychological level, violence plays out in the encounters between fascination and horror with what one ultimately chooses to do and what might impel an individual to act in certain ways. This is reflected in ruined relationships, and in relationships in ruins; in decaying settings for societies in transition; in an impetus for control through the exercise of violence (where other types of control have been lost); and in the ambiguous forces that alternately push and pull a (male) character to compensate for patriarchy's loss with narratives of constraint and excess. The preference for European novelistic accounts of family epics, empires in ascent, and the virtues of the head of the household are understandable in this context, for the 'awakening' of narrators at the sight of blood running in the streets of the city needs to impel them elsewhere for storytelling if the documentary impulse is insufficient or co-opted. There are so many versions of State-sponsored violence that the psychological ramifications become a venue of alternative expression and are shocking in their own right.

At a decisive moment in modern Mexican history, President Gustavo Díaz Ordaz (1964–70) returned to the discourse of the Revolution as a justification for the State's suppression of worker-student political coalitions, and he appealed to the utopian legacy of that time as his basis for taking action. But it was the brutality of his repression of the middle class urban professionals that signaled an end to the so-called miracle of modernization. The often awkward, but essentially continuous, combination of political stability and economic growth achieved by Mexico between the 1940s and the 1960s inclined many in Latin America to point to the nation as a model of development. But the crisis of legitimacy in the government when faced with popular protests changed this optimistic view. It revealed the authoritarianism hidden underneath the layers of modernization as the tactic necessary for the national project. The silencing of opposition was institutionalized, and fissures appeared in the so-called miraculous transformation to modernity. The youth of the country defied this authority in its traditional forms—these have not changed with the 'miracle'—and proposed to look at history in other ways. The administration of Luis Echevarría that followed (1970–76) proposed a democratic opening of the Revolution's legacy, not with the intent of questioning its foundations but of updating the forms of its implementation. This built a new facade on the edifice of the modern, but did not answer the questions left over from the previous decade.[3] José López Portillo (1976–82) inherited the same preoccupations about the conflictive relationship between the hopes of the past (solidified or "ossified") and the realities of the present. To these was added the complication of the discovery of vast oil reserves on Mexican territory. A new optimism was born of these factors, but it still left open doubts about the road to yet another 'new' Mexico. When called upon to give a balance sheet of his administration, of its accomplishments and failures, López Portillo used the term "chiaroscuro" (Aguilar Camín and Meyer 213) to describe the ambiguous nature of those years. He saw the assets and liabilities of his term in office as either spots of light (which we might see as modernity), or as shadowy areas (Aguilar Camín and Meyer 213–14) akin to the obscure forces of 'horror' that Paz finds accompany an almost uncanny fascination with the new.

In this manner we come full circle to Fuentes's cityscape of ruin, with the persistent construction and reassemblage of scaffolding and girders, the rusting of projects, and the gaze directed toward the open horizon as both a place on the globe and a social goal. The edifices of the State include not only those made of cement and rebar, but the human bodies that build them and that find their own stories amid their walls. How these constructions are made viable to live in, how one finds a voice to represent experience, how the body is viewed "variously as a machine, a prison cell, a glory, or a plague, a beauty or a beast" (Krell 4) are part and parcel of the ruins of this particular modernity. Plans and elevations aside, spaces of the city acquire an uncanniness of the ruin (Krell 7) that García Ponce mines in his quest for bringing back the aura of the storyteller. When even the ruinous vestige is no longer invoked as unfamiliar (unheimlich), wonderment and pleasure have been absorbed into a totalizing official discourse of forgetfulness. Beyond the mere pleasure principles of Freud and (later) Marcuse, "such a turn [toward homeless bodies and inhuman constructions such as Tlatelolco] invariably takes us [elsewhere]: it implies a loss of mastery, a failure of control, and an openness to the uncanny" (Krell 7). The uncanny sparks recognition like the streets of Berlin do for Benjamin. The body of the narrators is political by implication, but it is also part of Cartesian geometry, and most of all for García Ponce, is a lived body. The living body perceives its surroundings, engages in activities and projects (as does the social body of the State) but, as Krell reminds us, "it [is] also a prime instance of *extravagant expenditure*, . . . in the ecstasies of orgasm and sacrifice. If the hyper-Nietzschean thought of Georges Bataille is 'against architecture,' it is so only in order that we learn to spell it new as *archeticture*" (7). In brief, this play on words reorients the idea of construction (architecture) from the technical (Krell calls it the tec-), the building, toward the hidden sources of design and construction (the tic-). This is what he means by ecstatic, and it is what we have been calling the excessive, the baroque, and the fascinating.

To bring forth the shift from rigidity and the ruin as construct to multiplicity, fragmentation, and the ruin as a constellation of possibilities, we return one last time to Benjamin. As his narrator converts time into space (Sontag, "Sign of Saturn" 389), as he strolls amid the ruins of Berlin, as he projects his awareness of facades and portals onto their very stones, he "merges his life into a setting" (Sontag, "Sign of Saturn" 390). The fusion of body and city, the 'tic-' of an ecstatic moment, creates the basis for a different storytelling. García Ponce's characters penetrate their surroundings as they themselves have contributed to the formation of part of the (cultural) architecture they inhabit. These are not facile relationships, nor ones that are static; on the contrary, only the formal elements of ritual, ceremony, and compulsive repetition adequately address them for the telling of the tale outside the artificial boundaries of containment (mimesis, realism, celebration, documentary). Sontag concludes that "Benjamin's recurrent themes are, characteristically, means of spatializing the world: for example, his notion of ideas and experiences as ruins. To understand something is to understand its topography, to know how to chart it. And to know how to get lost" ("Sign of Saturn" 390). The spatial is the projection of the forces of building up and knocking down on the cultural monuments one finds strolling around the city (the double drives of construction and destruction), or for that matter around the photographs of the family in its millenarian hacienda. Equally so, the meandering through linguistic and aesthetic monuments to a certain turn of narrative creates a notion of spatiality as time settles into layers. Knowing the streets perhaps produces the Onda or documentary texts; but it also sparks the getting lost in the recesses of the mind that García Ponce revisits and refuses to erase. Among the last few short prose pieces of his collection of essays entitled *Personas, lugares y anexas* is one entitled "Celebración familiar" [Family Celebration]. Focused on the recollection of an event which included the entire extended family, this piece evokes every attendee as it simultaneously laments the passing of each one. It ends with a last mental glance at what could be called the fading photograph of the celebration. While the original moment indeed sparks the memory and the writing of the text—as the city streets do for subconscious labyrinths—what remains of the day is a garden filled with people now deceased who live on in the ruins of memory. The narrator's last words are: "En estas páginas están todos vivos en el jardín y poco a poco las sombras caen sobre nosotros"[In these pages everyone is alive in the garden and little by little the shadows fall over us] (141). There is no real photograph of the event; the image is an internal recollected one. The shadows are indicative of time's passage, for such a darkness cannot fall across the frozen image of a photo. One can only chart the ruins of the past by means of such evocations, and one can only make them live over and over by ritualized encounters.

CHAPTER THREE

Monuments and Relics, I

MELANCHOLIC COLLECTIONS

The collection of drafts, notes, and sketches Benjamin worked on at the same time he was planning his monumental work on the Arcades Project carries the title of "Convolutes" or sheaves of writings dedicated to a wide variety of topics. Composed of short essays and prose fragments oriented around multiple motifs and themes, and presented from various and distinct points of view, these writings are structured as a montage (Eiland and McLaughlin xi). Items such as the poetry of Charles Baudelaire, urban Paris, painting, spectacle, beauty and the transient, and modern manners in general are the centers of his constellations which spin out in multiple directions with only the writer's observations at the gravitational center to hold them. As the translators of his Arcades Project into English conclude, "the montage form—with its philosophical play of distances, transitions, and intersections, its perpetually shifting contexts and ironic juxtapositions—had become a favorite device in [his] later investigations . . . this ostensible patchwork as, de facto, a determinate literary form, one that has effectively constructed itself (that is, fragmented itself) . . . would [surely produce] significant repercussions for the direction and tempo of its reading, to say the least. The transcendence of the conventional book form would go together, in this case, with the blasting apart of pragmatic historicism—grounded, as this always is, on the premise of a continuous and homogenous temporality" (xi). Intersecting at different angles, and then splitting apart into constellations of meanings and experiences, these "convoluted" texts could be referred to as "blinks" of an eye (Eiland and McLaughlin xi) or fragments and discontinuous pieces of thought, rather than a cogently presented linear argument. Like Benjamin's own apprehension of the city in all of its excessive modernity, the entries in these notebooks and sketches—much like the Arcades Project that is, finally, left behind—respond to a way of perception and a counternarrative structure.

If such texts can be seen from the point of view of the visual arts—as blinks in our eyewitnessing of events, and far from historiography in its traditional form—they may also be superposable and fragmentary fossils of cultural perception. Remnants of daily life as lived by the taker of notes therefore acquire an "afterlife" (Eiland and McLaughlin xii) long after the gaze of the spectator has moved on. They are not articulated around formal relations of literary narration nor coherent epic stories. Rather, the framework of the montage, much as it did for Sergei Eisenstein and other filmmakers of the early twentieth century, split historical chronologies wide open. For Benjamin at least, this allowed for the infiltration or "vislumbre" (Paz) of secret, powerful, hidden, and forgotten moments and affinities to seep through into discourse.

Given the innumerable different angles from which each splintered nucleus or "convolute" is approached and addressed, these notes are perfect examples of the Benjaminian concept of the baroque allegory as "a structuring of the antithetical feeling for life" (Bolz and van Reijen 33). Depicting much more than what is seen at face value, allegory is the container of antithesis, the holder of the ruin. Gilloch writes of the power of allegorical figures for Benjamin as they reveal "the apparent or surface meaning [as] a veneer which conceals . . . . One narrative appears disguised as another; it is a palimpsest" (*Myth* 135). Meaning is elusive, but the profane world of the everyday comes to mean anything and everything, not merely the quotidian details one finds on the surface of places and events. The tension that holds together the subjects and the forms of the "convolutes" is cited by Benjamin as the force of the melancholic gaze. The capacity of the melancholic vision to produce art (vision, genius) is its contradictoriness and its richness; it is "the precondition for brilliant breakthroughs of petrified systems of order" (Bolz and van Reijen 33). While the object, scene, or memory remains behind, petrified in the allegorical fragment on the page, dead in some way to the forces of history, it can now paradoxically evoke meanings in multiple directions since it has been wrenched from its limiting context. And here we have come full circle to our trope of the ruin, for "[t]he allegorical, melancholy gaze must reduce the world to rubble" (Bolz and van Reijen 33) to build it up in innovative form from the shards of the past. One particular nucleus for these fragmentary texts is the allegorization of the bourgeois world as an image filled with degraded ruins from which new visions and readings may spin off. This is part of the architecture of the trilogy of works written by García Ponce between 1982 and 1989, although Benjamin's desire to redeem society from such decadence is not exactly duplicated by the Mexican writer. The urban archaeologist with a twist, García Ponce digs around amid the rubble, not always with the intent to move beyond, but to redeem in an alternative sense even if it is only through phantasmagoric revelation. What survives is the evocation, the movement, if not always the redemptive end.

The first in this trilogy, the novel *Crónica de la intervención* [Chronicle of an Intervention] (1982) is the centerpiece of a series of panels around which stories are articulated in shifting and 'convoluted' scenarios. The three texts—*Crónica*, *De ánima* (1984), and *Inmaculada o los placeres de la inocencia* [Inmaculada or the Pleasures of Innocence] (1989)—while interconnected, function as the remains of unstable, allegorical tales whose details and perspectives frequently contradict one another. In this way, the three pieces suggest the "indirect and symbolic modes of expression"(84) we have seen Traba indicate in the response of artists and intellectuals as they distance themselves from the realist narratives of previous decades. They also reaffirm a certain aspect of the personal, "private" (Rama 180) vision of language and art that responds to quirks and angles of perception, not to tenets of composition or limits of being embedded in coherent and logically fluid structures. We might recall García Ponce's own words as he reflects on the task of writing against social rules and moral mandates: "El terreno de la novela es ese terreno de la libertad absoluta" ("¿Qué pasa?" 147). The freedom to compose from the elements of social decomposition and the liberty to reconsider the novel itself as a 'convoluted' form, and not the chronological, organic edifice of former times, are the impulses for his fictions. In the three novels, the "afterlife" of images, characters, relationships, and the cultural constructions themselves cuts across artificial divisions as it provokes and challenges the reader to encounter bodies and linguistic signs as if for the first time. Allegories of the social and the cultural rework the ruins into new structures.

Reminiscent of the sketches of Benjamin's notebooks in relation to the tremendous Arcades Project, *Crónica* indicates a shift away from the shorter narratives of earlier years even as it retakes some of their preoccupations and twists them into more complex passages and rituals. Critic Juan Pellicer uncovers in this text the fragments of all that has come before in the life and artistic production of the writer. He sums up: "En ella [la novela] cabe toda su obra en el sentido de que consuma la recreación de todo un mundo de relaciones y correspondencias que el autor había emprendido desde su infancia. Aquí se representa aquel desdoblamiento que propició su primera lectura; se acaba de crear un mundo donde la realidad y su imagen, la vida y el arte, se vuelven irónicamente intercambiables. Aquí también se usan prácticamente todos los mecanismos narrativos que se encuentran en las otras novelas y cuentos" [All of his work fits in it {the novel} in the sense that it is the consummate recreation of an entire world of relations and correspondences that the author had begun since childhood. Represented here is that doubling begun with his first readings; {here} the last touches are put on a world in which reality and its image, life and art, become ironically interchangeable. Here as well practically all of the literary devices found in the other novels and stories are used] (38). There is little reason that irony should be found in the substitution of art for life, or image for reality, since García Ponce's own words reflect the building blocks of narrative as the human body and the language it produces (and which, in turn, produces it). His reference to these sites as "legitimate guarantees" of an evacuation of the rules of realism from the text would favor the idea of art or representation as the only communicative action. There are no other tools to forge the rubble of the material world into allegorical fragments than these two sources. And, we must remember, mere "communication" does not fulfill the desires of the Escritura narrator. Something more must be conjured up out of the depths of the subconscious and of the social imaginary.

In *Crónica* one of the first ways in which we recognize that we are facing an encounter with the allegories of cultural ruins that inform and embody contradiction is the word "chronicle," used as a relic of epic tales, from the times of the Conquest to the modern European tomes by Heimito von Doderer (*The Demons*) and Robert Musil (*The Man Without Qualities*). In his allegories of a Viennese bourgeoisie on the brink of disaster as World War I approaches, Musil uses the convolute of decay and ruin as the centerpiece for a narrative fraught with impending doom. Not focused on historical event in the sense of outside narrative, the writer instead turns the tale inward and truly convolutes and twists it into an internal (and infernal) dialogue. In his review of a recent biography of Musil, Stefan Jonsson remarks on this turn away from historiographic prose: "His narratives spiral downward from the daylight world of bourgeois conventions into the night of madness, the negativity of disorder, criminality and war . . . Crimes without identifiable perpetrators, events without visible cause, historical shifts without agency—Musil's works are inquiries into the multiple determination of human action and social change" ("Citizen" 131). The downward spin into the maelstrom of darkness and so-called values gone awry parallels García Ponce's narrators' descent into the "casco" or shell of Mexican society, finding themselves surrounded on all sides by madness instead of reason, disorder in place of coherence, and violence rather than rational discourse. Not content to offer the reader just one aspect of these scenarios, however, García Ponce makes all of these contradictory forces coexist.

The liberation of crime from the criminal, of events from history, propels the reader into that "free terrain." The ruins of the Austro-Hungarian Empire are the free-falling whirlwind into which the "man without qualities" of Musil's novel of the same name is drawn, just as García Ponce thrusts the reader into the jaws of Mexican modernity. In *Crónica* a similar sense of foreboding and melancholia is recreated through the evocation of the atmosphere of the days preceding the social and political disasters of 1968 in Mexico. If the Angel of History faces the collapse of the empire created by Austria-Hungary in the first instance, in the second it is gathered up in the storm produced by the fall of the PRI's national project into a bloodbath perpetrated on its own citizens.

Another vestige of imperial fantasy gone astray and old regimes in decay feeding into the convoluted labyrinth of *Crónica* comes from the cultural vestiges of Europe as well. García Ponce has written an extensive essay on Austrian writer Heimito von Doderer's novel *The Demons* in which he emphasizes the embedding of the personal within the historical as an "exceptional" quality of Old World work, one which the Mexican novelist aspires to emulate. This "exceptional trait" appears as part of the subtitle of García Ponce's essay in which he writes:

> Heimito von Doderer no trata de escribir una novela histórica; sin embargo, su gran novela hace historia en el campo del arte y en el de la historia a secas mediante el recurso de darle más importancia al arte de novelar, a sucesos particulares, seres y acciones, que a la historia en sí misma con excepción del hecho histórico central. Así, por ejemplo, aunque la acción las incluye en el largo tiempo que abarca, no se narra nada concreto de las dos guerras mundiales más que un encuentro de caballería entre cosacos y austriacos al principio de la primera y este combate es descrito, en un restorán especialista en guisados de ganso en un pueblo cercano a Viena, por un antiguo sargento a dos obreros que lo escuchan fascinados.
>
> [Heimito von Doderer does not try to write a historical novel; nevertheless, his great novel makes history in the fields of art and history per se by means of the technique of giving more importance to the art of storytelling, to specific events, people and actions, than to history itself except for the historical event that forms the core. So, for example, although included in the long historical trajectory covered by the text, nothing concrete about the two world wars is narrated save an encounter on horseback between Cossacks and Austrians at the beginning of the first, and this combat is described, in a restaurant near Vienna specializing in dishes made with goose, by a former sergeant to two workmen that are fascinated by his tale.] (*Ante los demonios* 10).

The 'long view' of history recedes into the background of von Doderer's narrative and the core (like a relic of former events and relationships) becomes the intimate, personal story that takes up fragments at will, including dinner conversations and regional menus. Like Benjamin's allegorical montage of cultural debris, von Doderer's narrators find a fascination with the afterlife of momentary encounters and chips of experience. To cover a historical period of a nation such as Mexico, then, García Ponce does as von Doderer has written, moving back and forth through decades and centuries, finding multiple ramifications of purportedly singular historical events, and using many voices to tell the story. Narrators look outward at events, then inward to capture their effects on individuals in a tapestry of narrative fragments that cannot reproduce a solid result since the project that gives rise to them—the incorporation of the Mexican nation into the international economy of modernity and its products—does not itself get resolved.

In *The Demons*, von Doderer's central historical event is the burning of Vienna's Palace of Justice on July 15, 1927. The remains of historical discourse in *Crónica* are the moment of repression of the student movement in Mexico City two weeks before the inauguration of the Olympic Games in October 1968. In the first case, flames consume "Justice" and, in the second, bullets silence dissent. This suggestion of the realm of the public sphere intrudes on, but never replaces, the convoluted strands and layers of personal stories woven in and around the text. As critic Gonzalo Martré proposes, *Crónica* and other novels related to the events of that year "se impregnan intensamente de *la atmósfera del 68* por lo que permiten que el movimiento flote en ellas con su presencia distante o con la repercusión del recuerdo" [are intensely saturated with *the atmosphere of 68* which allows the movement to float in them with a distant presence or with the repercussion of memory] (36). Albeit never mentioned by name, the circumstances and participants in the narrative are clearly recognizable as part of Mexico's modern history, with shifting pairs of couples from various social classes representative of those social and economic origins. Any identification beyond a first name or as a member of a particular fictional family dissolves into the phantasmagoria of the nightmare that functions as an allegory of contradictions: modernity and repression, youth and tradition, language and silence. Thus reoriented, the characters' behavior is conditioned by and responds to the historical events which surround them, adding levels of depth and complexity to their thoughts and acts, as well as implying connections between the microcosm of individual history and the macrocosm of the history of the nation, without spelling out the way in which this may come about. What Benjamin contemplates as the veneer of the modern is thus stripped away to bring to light the paradoxes underlying layer after layer of social pretense and ruin. Faith in modernity as the power to subjugate nature and culture to human mastery breaks down into debris and rubble when "wielded by a callous, indifferent humankind in its arrogant domination" (Gilloch, *Myth* 90). Reason, science, art, and technology at the service of modern society disintegrate into forces of violence and death seen in the blinks of the eyes of the narrators. Underneath the facade lie the crumbling shards of cultural promises and the dying embers of bourgeois dreams. The construction of the State's centralized and monumental edifice is built squarely on the sacrifice of its future intellectual pillars.

The fluid narratives of García Ponce's novel contain numerous versions of private tales that belong to characters who are forced to become active participants in the struggles against the official policies of the Mexican government, for their lives are disrupted and convoluted by their plans for the nation. The personal and the political seemingly merge into one chronicle, calling on the account from the perspective of the individual rather than the official, supposedly collective, version of the story. The Onderos might look to the street interview or the documentary (or docudrama) to find a genre appropriate for the contents of the text. For García Ponce, Escritura at this juncture sends us instead inside the skin of the characters and the recesses of their psyches.

THE MOVABLE BODY OF THE TRIPTYCH

An integral part of a narrative triptych of which *De ánima* and *Inmaculada o los placeres de la inocencia* form the complementary panels, *Crónica* therefore posits a movable story whose pieces are not solidified into the gesso of a mural. Rivera, Orozco, or Siqueiros demonstrate on walls, palaces, and government buildings that the story of the emergence of modern Mexico from the conflicted rubble of its past could be fixed on a surface for all to see and recognize. One supposes that this means one is recognizable within the story these murals have to tell: each member of the nation can see Zapata, scenes of the Revolution, popular movements, or workers brigades as part of their own coming-into-being. But for García Ponce and the generación de medio siglo, this story is not so easy to tell, and its images have afterlives that the founders and promoters of the nation might never envision (or might repress). What does each inhabitant of the megalopolis live on a daily basis that connects to the murals? Together, the three complementary components (the three novels) suggest a geometric construction capable of being disarticulated and rearticulated according to a personal reading of the image. Rather than the pieces fitting neatly together under the "will for form" that Paz uses to entitle his essay on Mexican art, the form itself embodies the message of disruption. That is to say, the tensions holding reasonable discourses together are evoked as the palimpsestic surfaces on which constantly new creations can form and seep through. The mystery that surfaces from these three texts embodies García Ponce's prolegomena about the fate of the act of writing—a vision of the breaking of the limits of the text, the act of *écriture* itself as a form of transgression, writing (and deciphering or reading) as a revelatory process.

Besides the appropriation of the narrative fragments of European crisis and decay, another aspect of revelation in an allegorical order of the texts, one also controversial and challenging, is García Ponce's exposure of those closed systems of social thought which attempt to define and entrap the declared 'moral truth' about sexual identity. Ambiguous and unstable, voices and actions emanate from the lived and sexually charged bodies of characters to add to the montage of the novels. It seems appropriate, then, that this writer chose the triptych as the preferred form of representation of such shifting and mobile stories. The tripartite or multifaceted retablo storytelling panels (ruins of a popular folkloric tradition elevated to the structure of the narrative text) are repositioned and transposed, opened and shut, hidden or displayed, according to the needs of the storyteller. They are deployed as prompters for the articulation of a narrative line adapted to each retelling and to each audience, one may assume, depending on the tales being told and on the spark that ignites the act of retelling. The afterlife of an image might at one point come to life and at another might be hidden in the depths of the closed panel. Not dead, but only dormant, such images can revive at any time and provoke the germination of another story. Proust's involuntary memory, or Freud's recollection of concealed strata of repressed memories come to mind as we approach García Ponce's texts to sift through their porous contents. So one should not be expecting to find the realism of a testimonial novel (à la Elena Poniatowska, for example) among these pages. But as the urban center—the site of all modern strife—is conjured up in bits and pieces, like Benjamin's Paris of the nineteenth century, "the home of the mundane and the routine . . . [becomes] the site of the extraordinary and the macabre" (Gilloch, *Myth* 148). Mexico City for García Ponce's characters holds all the fascination and horror that Paz finds in the early explorers' chronicles and that Stephens and Catherwood come across in Sayil or Kabah or Uxmal. The monuments of antiquity along the crushed stone roads of Yucatán hold, for the romantic voyagers, secret stories and hidden narratives in their earthen material. At first just a path that disappears into the horizon, the *sacbé* [white gravel pathway] acquires a dual significance for the cultures that would be vanquished by the Spaniards. Legends regarding the couriers that traverse the trails from gulf to central plateau, carrying messages from chiefs to other chiefs, are signs written on the bark of trees but also signs of impending doom and dark, ruinous events to come (Stephens 2:77). So the avenues of Mexico's capital city carry traffic and commuters, but they also carry hidden meanings and secret relationships within the minds of those whose bodies form the masses of the cityscape.

Although Deleuze and Guattari's use of the word "assemblage" (in *A Thousand Plateaus*) covers the explosive images of composing and decomposing implied here, their reference is not immediately connected to the aesthetics of painting, but rather to the idea of constellations and groupings in the constant "becoming" and shifting of human identity. Benjamin uses the "convolute," Eisenstein the montage, Adorno the constellation, and Deleuze and Guattari add to the allegories of structuring and restructuring. Their notion of the arranging of actors on a theatrical or film set, the ordering and reordering of the composition of a text (or scene or recollection) in a perpetual state of passing from one layout to another is reminiscent of *Crónica* and of the collection of panels to which it belongs (Deleuze and Guattari 306). The concept of "assemblage," then, might well be used to describe how the triptych is put together around a series of images or themes, how the pieces or elements therein may be moved to reconstitute other versions of stories, and how the contents and appearances of the images vary with each new position. The mural is a whole; the triptych is a Benjaminian monad or plethora of transient ruins and, best of all, it "is never what it appears to be" (Gilloch, *Myth* 170).

An artistic tradition originating in late medieval European religious cultures, especially those of Spain, Italy, and the Low Countries, the retablo presents an ornamental and elaborate view of the world stylized to the point of repetition. Placed above and behind the altar, these vertical panels consist of an assemblage of scenes focused around a principal figure such as the Virgin Mary, a particular saint, or the passion of Christ. They narrate fragments or episodes, in a more or less formalized manner, related to the life of the character or personage in the center of the body of the retablo and can be rearranged at will by the storyteller. Framing elements such as wooden strips, gold leaf, and sequencing (the articulation of a narrative, then an effigy, another narrative, and another effigy) maintain the gaze of the observer within the general space of the retablo. Fixed within some sort of material borders or edges, the retablo or triptych is nevertheless convoluted since it spins out in the multiple directions of individual storytellers. Judith Sobré has noted, in a commentary that corresponds interestingly to the allegorical layering of García Ponce's texts, that the individual paintings within these works "can be broken down into two components, narrative and symbolic" (167), with certain figures depicted as having attributes which distinguish them easily at first glance but which set in motion varying tales about them. The narrative elements flank the allegorical, grasping at the afterlife of the image which becomes the raw material for the construction of endless new fragmentary episodes. Shifting juxtapositions and startling contrasts bring into focus objects and interpretations perhaps unseen and unexpected until the shifts occur. What Benjamin sees as the "actualizing" (Eiland and McLaughlin xii) of images, of ephemera, embeds faces and things in momentary positions just to be lost again when the perspective of perception changes. Nothing survives intact because even the concept of permanence that "intact" suggests is not viable for the ephemeral ruin. (Pieces of a construct might remain, but not the entire edifice or cultural reading of the tale.)

Following the structure of the retablo as a palimpsestic surface with relics of previous stories peeking through the veneer, one might well consider the collection of fragmentary incidents composing *Crónica* in terms of the events of recent history as the underlying yet ghostly frame within which allegorical figures appear and reappear. They are distinguishable to a reader familiar with the traces or vestiges of similar characters across the three texts of the triptych: from *Crónica* to *De ánima* to *Inmaculada*. While it is the case that retablo figures have often served "as earthly manifestations of the miraculous and the divine" (Rountree 2) for believers who use them to represent a relationship with a divinity, in the narratives of García Ponce such a tradition becomes personalized as the ceremonial reenactment or "assemblage" of episodes related to lost human relations. The stability of a recognizable narrative—humans and divinities, for instance—disappears into an absence. The worship of the erotic encounter as the moment of greatest revelation produces the central image of "woman" in the flesh as the object of veneration, as a lived body capable of evoking hidden images from the past for the (mostly male) narrators. The categories of divine or sublime, and material or human, conflate on her body. The imagery of the retablo might invoke the traditional use of pictorial means to convey a message to an audience unable to read the story in written form; but in the case of García Ponce the words themselves function on a different level for an audience whose previous exposure to linguistic portraits sparks new meaning in these images. The suggestion of a popular form (the retablo) transposed into an intellectual text breaks apart the singularity of each and proposes an allegorical reading of both image and text itself. Far from univocal historical discourse, *Crónica* explodes into different directions as it picks up discarded objects from the landscape of the city to rework them in new, intuitive relationships at the will of the narrator. What is revealed is less about the circumstances (history) than about the narrator himself (as a story of subjectivity).

One of the principal sources of García Ponce's use of women as the centrally-placed and interchangeable figures in a trilogy of works is the comparable series of novels by Klossowski, *Roberte Ce Soir* [Roberte This Evening] (1953), *The Revocation of the Edict of Nantes* (1959), and *Le Souffleur* [The Spirit] (1960). Although these novels were originally published separately at intervals of several years, together they form a collective opus entitled *Les Lois de l'hospitalité* [The Laws of Hospitality]. Republished later as three-works-in-one, the first novel is recast in this complete edition as the center of the triptych, given the fact that the character Roberte occupies the primary space in each of the three narratives; she is the central figure of his panels. In the case of García Ponce's trilogy, it is the novel *De ánima* which functions as the center, occupying the middle space of the three works. Although the female characters may vary in name from one novel to another, from María Inés to Mariana to Paloma to Inmaculada, they all share certain characteristics and these, in turn, stimulate the response of recognition in the reader and the spark of intuition in the narrators. As the nucleus of numerous convolutes, they are fundamental catalysts in the male characters' search for themselves, by awakening fascinating and uncanny episodes lost among the ruins of the psyche.

In this aspect, García Ponce's narrators embody one of the core contradictions of modernity itself: the containment of identity on the surface of the body. Tamar Garb writes of the gendered body of the modern in these terms: "Modernity produced its own image of the body. According to the dictates of science and philosophy, modern men and women were expected to look [certain ways according to] a preordained set of distinctions that were rooted in biology, decreed by nature and endorsed by the complex organization of sexual and social behaviour which characterized modern society. . . . Appearances testified to the maintenance of a social order" (11). Therefore, any rupture in the perception of such lived bodies would construct a new edifice atop the ruins of the old. In the predominance of the male gaze, even if interrupted and fragmented as events intrude on it, García Ponce's narratives project fantasies of masculinity on bodies that, outside the text at least, are in the midst of radical change. Modernity's struggles for control over the human body, whether in discourses on biology or societal norms, underlie and sometimes overlay the masculinist discourses' endeavor to prevail despite the counterforces of rebellion. That women might attain some form of freedom from social restrictions and speak for themselves is neither part of the discourse of modernity allowed to flourish here, nor is it part of male fantasies. Rather, women are no longer a Freudian enigma but a key to unleashing the secrets harbored inside men. Elena Poniatowska describes the implied author "Juan's" (García Ponce's) representation of this dilemma of the modern: "Juan es la mirada más joven, la más libre que le sea a uno posible conocer. Las mujeres fueron su coto de caza, su propiedad privada, su posesión, su campo de batalla, porque las batallas de amor son de exclusividad y Juan siempre anduvo de pleito" [Juan's gaze is the youngest, the most liberated that one may find. Women were his hunting grounds, his private property, his possession, his battlefield, because love's battles are unique and Juan was always looking for a fight] ("Jardín" 3a). Let us make certain that we agree we are referring to "Juan" as a character and not as an author here, and as the dynamic behind the creation of so many conflicted narrative voices. Political battlegrounds cede to those of eroticism in his triptych.

Women as the battleground of modernity is a trope of the Surrealists (Dalí, Magritte, and Picasso come to mind) and not just of a singular Mexican writer of the second half of the twentieth century. Threatened by the forces of modernization, first in Europe and then in the Americas, masculinity sought refuge and pitched its most fervent opposition in and across human flesh. In officially sanctioned murals after the Revolution, women are shown as *soldaderas*, commanders, cooks, teachers, mothers, and even politicians but their portraits end there. Even if they belong to a revolutionary aesthetic, these images cloak women in conformity and recognizable social forms. Now, when they populate the fantasies of those who gaze on them, when they conform to expectation that has become part of the internal structures of masculinist discourse, this turns the battles from the field to the mind. It does not mean in any sense that they are over and done with; it does imply that all of the contradictions of convention are erected in the mind's eye as ruins of exterior forces. The Revolution is over but the struggles rage on. If they were resolved in some way by García Ponce's narrative voices, then modernity would be complete. But this is not possible. Ending this essay with the statement that his last "woman" was death, Poniatowska's words reveal how the contradictions permeating Mexican culture over the last half century continue to survive amid the cultural debris. Garb concludes her introduction with an affirmation of the potential power of the modern: "It is the capacity of the imaged bodies of modernity to articulate dominant social relations while managing sometimes, to expose or erode them" (14). If "exposure" comes about through the texts of the Onderos, can the forces of "erosion" be a way to refer to what is revealed in Escritura? I wish to underscore the word "sometimes" in Garb's quote, for it is not a rule of thumb that the modern comes down on the side of alterity or that erosion is the result. Poniatowska herself, with a substantial number of documentary texts as evidence of her desire to unearth the ravages of modern times, is a good example of this dilemma. Her article commemorating García Ponce's winning of the Premio de Literatura Latinoamericana y del Caribe in 2001 ends with these comments: "Y nosotras, las mujeres de México, a las que a veces nos duele hasta el aire, necesitamos decirle como [Manuel] Acuña el de Rosario que lo adoramos, lo queremos con todo el corazón y que nuestra primera y última ilusión es besarlo como las locas que somos y seremos hasta nuestro último suspiro" [And we, the women of Mexico, who sometimes suffer with every breath, we need to tell him {Juan} like {Manuel} Acuña does in his poem {Nocturno a} 'Rosario' that we adore him, that we love him with all our heart and that our first and last illusion is to cover him with kisses as the madwomen that we are and we will be until we draw our last breath] ("Jardín" 3a). Granted, these words are pronounced on the occasion of awarding a prize to a man relegated to a wheelchair, ravaged by illness and facing imminent death. On the other hand, however, the hyperbole of the statement addresses in baroque fashion an allegory of the vision of women that covers the pages of García Ponce's novels and stories. The contradictions of social and erotic battles have not ceased despite all of the splendorous monuments to modernity built across the nation over the past fifty years.

In the introduction to *De ánima*, García Ponce acknowledges the influences of Klossowski and Jun'ichiroTanizaki on his aesthetics, as he has noted elsewhere in the cases of Pavese, Musil, and von Doderer. If we return to the "transcendence of the conventional book form" in Benjamin's convolutes, with discontinuity as the motivating force of composition, García Ponce's praise of the hybridity of Tanizaki's and Klossowski's texts is quite reminiscent of such principles. Sheaves of fragments, collections of diaries, and remnants of events all get grouped together artfully and artificially among the pages of the text. García Ponce writes that the borrowings are both personally pleasurable and aesthetically useful.

> He pedido prestada para escribir esta novela [*De ánima*] la óptica que utilizaron Pierre Klossowski en *La revocación del Edicto de Nantes*, [y] Junichiro Tanizaki en *La llave*. Independientemente del placer que me produjo intentar repetir una forma que me seduce, el uso del diario intercalado de una figura masculina y otra femenina, que dan su diferente visión de sucesos idénticos o muy semejantes, me era indispensable para contar la acción que los hace existir de una manera que mostrara su verdadero sentido.
>
> [To write this novel I have borrowed the optics {lens} used by Pierre Klossowski in *The Revocation of the Edict of Nantes*, {and} Junichiro

> Tanizaki in *The Key*. Aside from the pleasure it gave me to try to repeat a form which {personally} seduces me, the use of the intercalated diary by a masculine figure and a feminine one, each of which gives a different vision of identical or very similar events, was indispensable to me in order to narrate the action which makes them exist in a way that might reveal their true meaning.] (9)

Aside from the suggestion of what Rama has already referred to as the private or "intimista" (180) aspect of García Ponce's texts—what the author calls here the narrative form which seduces him on a more personal level, a seduction reminiscent of what has been eliminated from the social realm—his reference to the contrastive gender-related visions of events as well as the need to find an appropriate vehicle for the revelation of some "true" or hidden meaning offer the first step in the articulation of allegorical narrative. We find here, then, a hint of the porosity between society and individual subject that characterizes all three novels.

Since the three pieces of a triptych, or the multiple panels of the retablo, face outward side-by-side in a pattern of images, one may observe an intertextual dynamic among them with regard to the representation of and reflection on the women whose tales are told in what Rama has called García Ponce's "relatos visuales" [visual stories] (180). Once again, as is true in the case of previous texts, it is the female characters which connect and convolute the tales joined together in this narrative. And it is also true that the retablo tradition has not died but has survived and flourished in the popular devotional images of contemporary Mexico. In this form of representation, while the painter of the piece may not be known, his or her relationship to the subject matter portrayed is certainly clear since he has left behind traces of his interpretation of figures and events. Let us recall Jonsson's assessment of Musil's narratives and their representation of "crimes without identifiable perpetrators and events without visible cause" as we ponder the retablo's afterlife. The crimes and events exist; their authors have vanished. So it is with the stories of *Crónica*: historical events and criminal acts, intense emotions and complex relationships have come and gone, leaving behind monuments of a sort. As Castañeda reminds us about Maya ruins as runes, "the artifacts are mute when narrated into visibility, but not silent" (1996 156). The ventriloquizing voices of *Crónica* decipher meanings and invite the reader to inscribe others onto the interfaced layers of the narratives. Though not the tourist guidebooks substantiating the fables of archaeological sites, García Ponce's texts do offer reinventions of cultural monuments as ceaselessly repeated moments of revelation. The

Onderos make the stones of the streets speak; García Ponce and the Escritura writers give voice to the sedimentary levels of the unconscious.

To discuss these and other aspects of *Crónica* within the ruins of modernity, we must excavate the thirty chapters the text contains to unpack their obsessive return to numerous variations on the same story. Akin to the narrative scenes of the retablo and its complex strata of discourses, recollections, struggles, conversations, and reinventions, this text emphasizes ritualized connections between the act of storytelling and the interrelated pieces of the puzzle made up of equal parts erotic life and faintly-traced historical milieu. Repetition, mirrored scenes, and a constant return to the same temporal moment over and over, eliminating historical discourse, are the structural elements on which the novel is based. Among these shifting sands, the reader is cast into a world in which it is difficult if not impossible to find a solid place to stand. As Krell puts it, "[w]e no longer dream of structures of thought and knowledge in the way Kant dreamed of them, searching madly for (and failing to find) the bedrock on which to construct a Tribunal of Pure Reason" (92). Glimpses (Paz's "vislumbres" once again), snippets, chips, and the odd narrative phrase are to be found, but attempts to reconstruct a cultural dwelling will depend on the reader and on what each portion of the narrative summons up.

Of the relatively few critics who have written at any length on this work, several have noted the role of doubles and repetition that might suggest some sort of structural circularity or doubling.[1] To take this general observation one step further, I propose to call the relationship of the first chapter of the novel entitled "Con Esteban" [With Esteban] to the last—whose title is exactly the same—a mirroring. The opening line of the novel, part of an interior monologue of the character Esteban as he remembers an intense physical and spiritual experience with the now-dead Mariana, a figure of the past in ruin herself now, appears again incorporated into the closing pages as an attempt to return to the same intimate moment. Yet these are not merely stagnant doubled episodes but narrative walls that loosely contain the interior spaces wedged between them, with Esteban and Mariana suffering tremendous losses along the way. Pellicer summarizes the beginning, saying that with the first few words "el lector queda instalado, por decirlo así, en la mente del protagonista Esteban. Se trata de la evocación de un evento y de la impresión que éste produjo en [él]" [the reader settles into, as it were, the mind of the protagonist Esteban. What we find is the evocation of an event and the impression it left in {him}] (110). In between what intervenes are all of the tragic social and political events of 1968 in Mexico. When we are narratively placed "con Esteban" the first time, he is a different character from the Esteban we find at the end or, if we read his episode as a convolute, his recollection of the event just shifts and never finds an absolute version; the same is true for his friend Mariana whom he recalls in both fragments. Layered in between the narrative beginning and ending, the reader finds a chorus of voices which contribute charged particles to the complexity of the overall narrative puzzle and create shadows around the characters, almost like the framing panels of a retablo. These choral groups include reiterated appearances by six voices, including Anselmo; María Inés; Fray Alberto; doctor Raygadas, an omniscient narrator, a nameless, bodiless spirit which inhabits a space outside the everyday historical world of the characters; and Mariana and Esteban themselves. The polyphonic fragments also consist of the confessions, diaries, letters, and dialogues of numerous other characters, and the clinical reports of psychologists and psychiatrists about the mental state of Mariana, María Inés, and other characters. These narrative modules affirm the stories circulating around the allegorical characters whose lives return in obsessive repetition, the medical establishment, the church, a man, a woman, and several anonymous citizens make up the social allegory that confronts the forces of evil embodied in the State's repressive organisms. The remembrance of Mariana's words, "Quiero que me cojan todo el día y toda la noche" [I want to be fucked night and day] (*Crónica* 9, 1099), returns as an echo within Esteban's unspoken thoughts, setting up a face-to-face encounter between the beginning and the ending of the narrative around the afterlife of their relationship. If the physical relationship is not longer feasible for she is dead, then the words remain as a melancholy lament that marks the loss.

Significantly, it is to Mariana's words and not his own that he journeys back after his nightmarish experience in Tlatelolco where she loses her life. Mariana is converted into an iconic ruin beyond her material self, much like the evocative religious figures of the triptych. She now represents an almost uncanny link to past events since her ghostly image haunts the psychological landscapes of those who survive, unsure as to why the fate of one is not that of the other. Directly, the external circumstances have taken their toll on Mariana's life since they have ended it. There is no doubt that her physical life has been terminated abruptly in the streets of the city, but she lives on as an after-image. Indirectly, Mariana has had just as great an impact on Esteban's psyche as the events around both of them and it is through her that he attempts to sort out their significance for himself. As a melancholic storyteller, he desperately looks for a way to reconstruct what has been lost, as Hanssen notes of Benjamin's turn to minerals and stones, by "turn[ing] his gaze toward earth, . . . [toward] the coldness of stone, matter, or inert mass . . . the melancholic remain[s] bound to abject matter" (160). In order to find what he seeks in Mariana—the dead, the relic, the remnant, the afterlife of matter and debris—as a Benjaminian storyteller, Esteban (and us, "with him") must rummage among the rubble into which all is degraded. Mariana is resuscitated in his mind expressing her personal desire for liberation, but the events occurring around her (really, around them) reflect just the opposite: they unveil the brutal repression of a society in the throes of confronting recycled myths of national identity and subsequently being denied the freedom to do so. Both Mariana and Mexico suffer the consequences of such a desire: the "quiero" [wish] expressed in both episodes of the novel echoes longingly throughout the pages. By the end, it is merely a vestige of a desire, a wish unfulfilled, an enigma left in the subjunctive and unresolved.

Therefore, we might suggest that circularity may not be the best description of the textual structure. Instead, the concept of a ruin displayed in the grotesque reflections of a distorted mirror might serve us better (pace Valle-Inclán and his *esperpento*). As characters seek to find their own images within the rubble of the narratives of modern culture, but are confronted with the disruptive forces of allegory and not realism (mimesis), even the concept of recognition and the figure of the self are dismantled. For Benjamin, allegorical readings of images and constellations of them "expos[e] a fissure between nature and signification" (Hanssen 68), thus canceling out the circularity since representation no longer reflects but spins outward into new layers and even greater piles of debris. Decay, decomposition, and dissolution come between a character and his or her image. The allegorical structure of the baroque is exuberant and fascinating, not harmonic or circular in the sense that it merely reproduces some previous thing. Esteban or Mariana, even as they long for endurance and recognition, become reiterated others. Although one might posit the end of meaning in a dead Mariana, for García Ponce's narrative voices she forms a powerful Benjaminian ruin to which they might return obsessively, perhaps as compensation for an impossible social return to innocence.

The title of the novel *Crónica* indicates an important discrepancy between the multiplicity of images revisited in the text itself and the insinuation of a purely linear structure by those for whom perhaps there never was an "intervention." The suggestion of an official version of events, ones with putatively logical precedents and consequences, is interrupted by the "intervención" of the private, *intimista* accounts of García Ponce's characters into the official narrative stream of the history of the 1960s. The opposite is true as well since this is the first time García Ponce anchors his characters in the mire of history and in its power to scar those caught up by the intrusive forces of politics. Previous tales have been constructed around a time without event, whereas *Crónica* embeds characters in the afterlife of historical event. The ultimate product, both in its formal structure and narrative content, is a textual discrediting of a singular, linear version of events in favor of constant intrusion and, in the words of Gliemmo, "la representación de un mundo a dos" [the representation of a world split in two] (17). In other words, the personal and the political disrupt or interrupt at any time into the realm of the other. As one is built up, the other comes to destroy and rebuild from the ruins, which then produce fossilized vestiges of previous fragments. Fuentes's allegory of the construction of a high-rise as an indication of the nation's modernity offers us a parallel once again in that each part of the world split in two is really a fragment of a process and not a product. Political life and psychological life contain remnants and survivals from which the storyteller may glean material for new constructions. Simultaneously thrown backward and forward, human beings are the stuff of new orders and of vestiges of the old. Fields of ruins do not only inhabit the outside world, they are scattered across the inner world as well.

In *Crónica*, what might be traditionally divided as intimate stories and political events are both articulated around several axes of synchronic and diachronic meaning. These axes include challenges to ideas and traditions of conservative provincial life when bourgeois families emigrate to urban centers and refuse to cede their old myths to the promissory discourses of modernity. They also center on the frictions which evolve among the members of three generations when power struggles ensue over political and social ideologies as well as over the preservation of a certain economic status. A third axis is oriented around issues of class divisions between the wealthy Gonzaga clan and their hired servants. These issues are not always presented as conflicts per se but also take the form of the adoration and obsession of the 'have-nots' with the supposed aesthetic perfection of the upper classes, in particular the fetishizing of María Inés's body by the family chauffeur Evodio Martínez. This obsession leads him to kill the husband of his object of desire, although the novel never makes it completely clear whether the murder is done in the name of the lower classes, in the name of a jealous suitor who can never have María Inés for himself, as an act of madness, or perhaps as all three. In any case, the class conflicts supposedly resolved by the triumph of the Revolution survive in the ruins of familial relationships and the declaredly untouchable body of the bourgeoisie. On the other hand, the bourgeois family, as might be expected in light of the traditional conflicted relationship between rich and poor in Mexico, retains an image of the working class as a horde of elementary beings on the margins of humanity holding fast to their bodily needs and appetites. María

Inés is the sublime body of fantasy; lower-class women are portrayed as animal bodies surviving on instinct. It is telling that in this novel the only cases of incest, the ultimate taboo of any modern society, are committed by brothers and sisters among the servants of the Gonzaga household.[2] The reason? Even among the ruins, inside the shells of expropriated haciendas and overgrown plantations, beauty still attracts beauty, at least in the fantasies of characters whose world is on the verge of losing its mythmaking powers. (Let us recall Fuentes's 1967 essay on the rise of The New Wave and the increasing violence needed during the 1960s to perpetuate that mythmaking function in the future vision of the nation.)

The structure of *Crónica* presents the reader with the narrative representation of two vertical panels which depict the complex and unstable relations between the wealthy in their provincial glory and their subsequent life in the city, and the poor in the same two settings. No class occupies its own panel separate and isolated from the other, but instead crosses over onto both sides, the point of articulation of their identities being their shared geographical space rather than just class as such. In city or in countryside, class divisions subsist even as discourses of modernity promote democracy and change, progress, education, and prosperity. Class is the more permanent function of social identity for characters despite geographical change or narrative panel position. García Ponce's reminiscences triggered by his family photographs hint at this debris of the past. Even as his narrators lose prestige and privilege in the construction of a future Mexico, the photographic images both reassure them of their origins and hint at having to mourn being cast out of traditional social prominence. His lament over being excluded from soccer games carries a critique of modern society in which wealth is of little value (when others are rising in social class). What to do with these changing relationships is a dilemma inside and among many of the characters of *Crónica*.

In *Crónica*, the underclasses carry with them the primitiveness of the land and their relationship to it into the urban setting, as if they were condemned from birth to the violent 'nature' they exhibit in their actions. One explicit example is to be found in the story of Ramiro Morales, formerly a pig farmer and avid hunter whose expertise in slaughtering the animals for market is put to use when he becomes a soldier in the Mexican army and is ordered to massacre students in the streets of Mexico City in October 1968. His so-called blood lust is transferred from swine to human beings as naturally as he moves his family from the provinces to the capital in search of a better job. The essential excesses of his actions in the fields, the streets, and the bedroom (he is the incestuous partner of one of the servants in the Gonzaga house) are encapsulated in the following passage from Chapter 28

"Dificultades imprevistas" [Unforeseen Difficulties], which charts the reactions of the government soldiers to their encounter with the demonstrating students. The State's confidence in its own modernizing mission produces a blindness with regard to what its citizens might be thinking about such changes, and with respect to the extremes it requires of them. The narrator recounts the tragic event of the invasion of the UNAM and one soldier's emotions in one unified episode.

> Ramiro, que durmió durante todo el largo trayecto desde el cuartel hasta la Universidad y podía confesarse a sí mismo que luego había pasado algunos momentos divertidos amenazando estudiantes, persiguiéndolos y golpeándolos si tenía oportunidad con la culata de su fusil y ametralladora, se sentía ahora de nuevo un tanto aburrido . . . , paseaba con su metralleta al hombro por los corredores de una de las Facultades . . . , sin perder al mismo tiempo la remota esperanza de encontrar algún estudiante rezagado y gozar con su posible temor y su sorpresa en el instante en que lo apuntara con su metralleta.
>
> [Ramiro, who slept during the entire long stretch from the barracks to the university and could tell himself honestly that he had later spent some enjoyable moments threatening students, running after them, and beating them when he had the chance with the handle of his rifle and machine gun, now felt a little bored once again . . . , walked up and down the halls of one of the schools with his weapon on his shoulder . . . , at the same time without losing the remote glimmer of hope of finding some student left behind and of delighting in the possible fear and surprise created at the moment when he aimed his gun at him.] (996–997)

The physical and mental sensations he experiences are the links between before and after, the glue between the provinces and the city, with the ruins of one life put at the service of something else. The voice of Ramiro himself holds the two pieces together, much as the intimate feelings of his own power and control over the external historical events (being part of them as if he were an agent in their plotting which as a soldier, of course, he is not) link the two fragmentary narratives. While surrounding, threatening, and sacrificing the 'enemy,' he feels the same as when he used to close the corral gate on the piglets in order to use his knife on them, slit their throats, and send them off to market to be sold (1021). Even as the federal government works to keep classes in separate spheres of the city, encounters such as these are frequent and unavoidable. They reveal the hidden relics of the past that refuse to disappear behind the facade of modern buildings, television studios, tourist hotels, and centers of higher learning. Class warfare, racism, and a patriarchal State battle it out on the streets of the city as a monument to the future. Rubenstein addresses this clash between monuments to the past and to what is to come.

> In choosing where to dig and place electric lines, which streets to pave, where to build new government office buildings, how to site new avenues and highways, and especially where to construct the huge, modern, new campus of the National Autonomous University, the government supported and encouraged an enormous change in the organization of the capital city. Mexico City's commercial and artistic hub moved rapidly southward, aided by all the new infrastructure the government provided, and leaving the center of the city to a combination of historical monuments and poor people's housing. The government left the central barrios to molder, neglected, while it rapidly met the needs of the richer and better-connected citizens who had settled themselves up just to the south. Those left behind understood this process well, as newspapers and magazines depicted the elites' daring adaptations of the antique structures of Coyoacán and the sleek modernity of the new colony called Narvarte. (223)

This transformation of the metropolis is merely the setting for the emotional and psychic crises and transformations of the characters of *Crónica*. Set amid the crumbling ruins of the city's center, visible just outside the glittering splendors of the Zona Rosa, they come and go from daily activities and return to their own familiar spaces.[3] The campus of the UNAM, first a showplace for the democratization of education, becomes a battleground between the classes artificially separated by State decree, but meeting on the same grounds to protest. From the construction of a museum of sorts to enlightenment and modernity, complete with the artistic recollection of the past in the mosaic walls of the campus library's murals, the university's afterlife is that of decay and ruination. The site of promise and of loss, the UNAM struggles along with over 300,000 students, constantly reiterating its mission even as educational goals fall by the wayside. Perhaps the "intervention" of the title of the novel can be extended to include an intrusion on the city's landscapes aside from the military intervention into the students' protests. In what Pellicer calls "un país marcado por las contradicciones" [a nation marked by contradictions] (167), he finds the same space of cultural debris as in that of a "país ficticio" (an imagined and imaginary nation) (168) and a ruin from the past that refuses to decay into nothingness once and for all. García Ponce's narrator remarks on the same ironic juxtaposition: "En el subsuelo subsiste el pasado indígena y en el subsuelo, con cada vez mayor certeza y siempre bajo otro nombre, deben realizarse todas las operaciones públicas" [In the subsoil the indigenous past subsists and in the subsoil, with increasing certainty and always called by another name, all of the public works have to take place] (318). One cannot speak of bedrock in the case of Mexico City, for its underground is lake bed and not granite, allowing a slow descent over decades. But the subsoil is an allegory here for the rootedness of monuments to historical moments and social projects. The indigenous past cannot literally always be there visibly, but it certainly can be resurrected and rebuilt in archaeological sites dedicated to the preservation of some modern (if uncanny) memory of it. The indigenous subsoil, then, brings forth an allegorical figure upon which each observer may write a story and on which the tropes of the battle for the nation play out. As far as modern constructs go, Fuentes's take on their scaffolding as the sites of modernity's struggles includes public works (as spectacles of progress) as well as private reconstructions.

CHAPTER FOUR

Monuments and Relics, II

LET THE GAMES BEGIN: PUBLIC SPECTACLE AND VISUALIZING THE RUIN

In his essay "Otras voces, otros ámbitos" [Other Voices, Other Places], García Ponce revisits the terrain of his youth, on the level of both physical uprooting and psychic disturbance, in an effort to narrate the periods and breaks in his own life which have left remnants of images in his memories. He begins with the early days of provincial life, those of his grandparents before electricity arrives in Yucatán, and moves through his travels, his education, and the upheaval of the family's move to Mexico City. Perhaps signaling even more than he consciously acknowledges, his narrator fills paragraphs with phrases related to a single general question: "¿Qué futuro nos esperaba?" [What future awaited us?] (27). Although he refers essentially to a particular change of address and a specific point of arrival (that "siniestra ciudad" [sinister city] which will overwhelm his senses for a long period of time), readers may also see this as a more open doubt regarding the individual as well as the national days ahead. The narrator recalls what is being abandoned: "Atrás quedaba Mérida, mis familiares, sus vastas casas con pobladas huertas, sus calles conocidas, su segura civilización" [Mérida was being left behind, along with my relatives, the enormous houses and dense orchards, the familiar streets, the security of {a known} civilization] (27), while what lies ahead is mysterious, dark, unfamiliar, and above all, small.

The paradox of the sentiment of smallness evoked by the soon-to-be colossal city cannot go unnoticed; it would appear to be the result of the weight of the past resting on, and even obliterating, the lightness of the future. His memories of arrival disappear and fade away, with the new geography overpowering the concept of time and abolishing all notions of objectivity and observation. In a combined moment of "descontrol" [lack of control] (28), "nostalgia" (36), and "melancolía" (37) the narrator ends the essay with a paragraph dominated by exclamation points. What he finds he needs to exalt in this way is the feeling of "Cuántos cambios!" [How many changes!]. (37). The short passage is similar to what Benjamin's understanding of the French capital is in the decade of the 1920s. In his study of the urban arcades, Benajmin moves from cityscape to dreamworld, from material architectural structures to "thought-images" (Gilloch, *Walter Benjamin* 91). The alterations refer as much to the change from rural to city life as they do to how the metropolis looks different every morning under the aegis of a government building itself a future. While García Ponce's narrator laments the fading of his family's faces in the memory portraits he desperately tries to sustain, he evokes a different feeling toward the new people and places he lives among now. These include, of course, neighbors and classmates and *novias*, but they also include the face of politics. It is notable that even as President Miguel Alemán supported the construction of civil institutions, and with them the construction of edifices to house them, García Ponce recalls a more personal aspect of this historical moment. As a student in the Instituto México, a Marist school for boys, García Ponce witnessed an annual soccer game with a rival school, the Colegio México, noting that these were both male only, and that no private schools for girls existed within a wide radius of his institution while there was a sister school of the other. His conclusion is a "thought-image" of presidential politics, related to the fact that Alemán's son studied at the Colegio México, and that he was privileged as no others were. Internalized and recalled much later, the comparison becomes a personal recollection of the city: "Ahí estudiaba, lo digo como prueba de que nuestros políticos siempre fueron mentirosos sobre su fe en las instituciones civiles, el hijo del presidente Alemán, Miguelito. Quizá como hijo del presidente él tenía todas las novias que quisiera; yo sólo puedo afirmar que mi primer amor en México estudiaba en el Colegio Oxford y no me hizo caso nunca" [Miguelito, the son of President Alemán, studied there. I say this as proof that our politicians were always untruthful about their faith in civil institutions. Maybe as the son of the president, he had all the girfriends he wanted; I can only affirm that my first love in Mexico {City} studied at the Colegio Oxford and never ever paid attention to me] (32–33). An invisible young man in a bustling metropolis will necessarily have to cast his eyes upon people and events around him as if from a dreamworld from the very beginning.

Memories of provincial life for the wealthy are reduced to recollections once their ranches, plantations, and haciendas have been left behind for the resources and glitter of the metropolis. All of this transformation takes place in the modernizing schema of the social and economic structures of the Mexican nation, commencing in the 1950s and continuing through the 1960s and after. Both young and old in the Gonzaga family in

Crónica idealize the mythified past as a space of genuine family relations (ones now lost and only evoked in memory), a close attachment to long-held family values and lands, and the traditional practices of religious piety in accordance with the tenets of the conservative church.[1] Of course, this recollection becomes problematic when the family enters the (allegorical) gates of Mexico City. If the chauffeur Evodio Martínez and his friend Ramiro, the farmer-turned-soldier, are figures emblematic of the lower classes, the high social strata filled with so-called wealth and sophistication are personified by Esteban and his cousin-by-marriage, José Ignacio Gonzaga. Very early in the novel the reader is made aware, through narrative comments and asides and the characters' own monologues, that the relationship between the two men—Esteban, the artist and reclusive photographer more interested in aesthetic matters than economic success, and José Ignacio, a secure and respectable businessman in the Mexican community—is not distant and remote but runs deeper than what is seen at first glance. In point of fact and kinship, these distant cousins have in common the figure of Tía Eugenia, a Gonzaga on her mother's side whose deceased husband was part of Esteban's family as well. Later on, we discover that their female counterparts—José Ignacio's wife and Esteban's lover Mariana—are interconnected besides, and that their stories parallel one another until a singular (but provocative) moment of intersection occurs. In the private chapel of the Gonzaga family, during the First Communion of José Ignacio's two children, Esteban is witness to a moment of confusion as well as of revelation. Invited to be the official photographer of this critical ritual moment in the life of the family, Esteban captures through his camera lens the figure of a woman standing next to his cousin. The woman appears to be not a double of Mariana, but Mariana herself. The eye of the camera is in the process of creating a monument to the family's future but, at the same time, apprehends the afterlife of an image of the past. From this point on, Esteban's perception of the identity of these two women blurs: Is it one woman who projects an aura (shades of Carlos Fuentes's novella *Aura*) and thereby creates a Gothic mystery? Are there two women so similar that they confirm a female archetype by their mere existence? Since Esteban does not yet have the power to unravel this dilemma, nor have access to both women in the same place at the same time, he is left with only the traces of their appearance. These residues are the pictures he snaps at the communion, the artistic representation of their physical and material existence, a bit of the debris of outside life reconstructed and fixed on paper.

It is José Ignacio Gonzaga's wealth that establishes a bridge between the upper classes in the countryside and the modern world of industrial tycoons and State power visibly concentrated in the city. His is the sort of wealth that belongs to the so-called respectable traditional rural families and which, according to official government ideology, is the prime mover capable of shifting the country toward modernity. An essence of 'good taste' is the signature of the everyday life of José Ignacio and his exemplary family. As the narrator concludes in a moment of revelation for the character Evodio, who is in search of a job: "En él estaba de pronto toda una realidad" [All of a sudden he {Evodio} saw in him {his future employer} an entirely new world] (71). José Ignacio acquires the status of a revelatory figure here since he is not merely a man standing before Evodio but the 'convolution' of an entire narrative history that extends in two directions, toward both the past and the future. The expectations for this new world of opportunity hold true not only for the individual in search of employment but for the nation as a whole. This extended family, whether in their haciendas in the country or their urban mansions flourishing in the suburbs, is presented as the 'natural' inheritor and receptacle of 'good taste' and genuine values, much as Ramiro appears condemned to the cycle of violence and brutality connected with his poverty in some 'natural' way. The Gonzaga mansion in a secluded area of the urban metropolis—colonies such as Narvarte or Coyoacán mentioned before—becomes the utopia of harmonious space eventually disrupted by the arrival of the irrational forces and barbarians such as Evodio and the rest of the servants with what is considered their inherently grotesque behavior and attitudes. Their rudeness, lack of formal education, insatiable sexual appetites, and general lack of 'good taste' intervene in the bourgeois family chronicle in crisis—another level to the suggestive phrase "crónica de la intervención"—and put an end to its story with the murder of José Ignacio. Not as facile a tale as it appears, this allegory of a national tragedy has many convolutions before it reaches this end.

As an eminent and worldly industrialist, José Ignacio becomes more powerful, and his reputation inside the nation's elite is enhanced when representatives of the federal government formally invite him and his close associates to join the commission in charge of coordinating what in official code is known as the "Gran Proyecto" [Great Project] (329). This commission has been formed and appointed, it seems, to plan, promote, and control from its inception the international spectacle referred to (euphemistically) as the "Festival Mundial de la Juventud" [World Festival of Youth] (329), otherwise revealed in the narrative to be the Olympic Games of 1968 held in Mexico City and its immediate environs. The campus of the UNAM, that monument to Mexico's world-class status and to the demolition required in order for it to be completed, is one of the central venues for these games. Postponed until October owing to social unrest that, paradoxically, takes the government by surprise (we need only recall the chapter entitled "Dificultades imprevistas" [Unforeseen or Unexpected Difficulties], these public ceremonies are dedicated to the visible representation of modern Mexico on display for all to see. Streets, facades, sports stadiums, elaborate housing, and a city decked out in ostentatious display, all reflect the official code of conduct for foreign eyes to witness. To comply with the government's wishes, José Ignacio eagerly accepts the official request and organizes his entire personal administrative team around the project. Therefore, his private family life (and fortune, it goes without saying) and his public service to the nation are intertwined through this group of appointees who create a tight, closed network of intrigue, hysteria, and opportunities flowing around and through him. Such a network is reminiscent of the structure of the novel itself as it weaves together a number of narratives from different perspectives around the figures of the Gonzaga clan, Mariana, Esteban, and others. It also provides an allegory of the process of modernization. The result is a collection of fragments in a landscape of ruin in those two senses set out by Castañeda: construction and destruction.

Throughout the chapters of the novel dedicated to the preparations for the Festival, one cannot fail to perceive in the contradictions between official language and the narrator's voice a sense of the spectacular and the carnivalesque in the words of the State and its pet project. To create an aura of good taste, a patina of national cultural values, spectacles for the masses are fabricated by the committee with the help of Esteban's photographs, which are appropriated and given captions to promote the required spirit of the unified nation. In the words of a foreign representative of the committee (whose incomplete linguistic command of Spanish is reproduced in the text), "tenemos la obligación de crear un imagen {sic} de algo que no existe todavía" [we have the obligation to create an image of something that doesn't {even} exist yet] (331). (Why an English-speaking member of the committee would be consulted to begin with signals one of the ironic remnants of cultural traditions that look northward for advice and validation.) This "something" which will be created through the *de*formation of the glossy images captured on film by Esteban for José Ignacio and his colleagues to use as propaganda is a ruin of the future, a vestige of the moment that will be mechanically and, for them, unproblematically produced and reproduced. How images are read, their potential for appropriation by any number of individual and social forces, and their subjective freezing of moments of historical reality all come into focus in the center panel of our tripartite narrative with the photographs of Esteban. In other words, the entry of the nation into modernity is represented here as a masquerade, a failed project from the very beginning due to the endemic social problems that cannot be resolved and the so-called atavistic tendencies of the country's population. The photographic images can be used to promote a future "something" as long as they are interpreted in a self-fulfilling way, as long as they fulfill their official function. Both José Ignacio and Evodio are tied to their roots, even after their feet leave the soil of their native lands. Each of their narrative panels shows the story behind the facade, the players without their masks, the tenuousness of the thin veneer of 'good taste' and modern, democratic culture promoted in literary and visual images to lure outsiders to the spectacular Festival. The mixture of national monuments isolated in time and space by Esteban's camera and the promotion of youth and health in the bodies of the athletes set to compete, looks inward (to the nation) and outward (to the international community of 'like' cultures) to produce the perfect recipe for modernity, or so the public is told in the chronicle of the Festival's proposed activities through posters, flyers, newspaper articles, and political speeches.

If García Ponce clearly attributes to the family saga of early twentieth century Europe one of the models underlying the construction of *Crónica*, the politics and aesthetics of representation suggested by the episodes dealing with Esteban and photography eerily evoke the Nazi propaganda films of the 1930s. Perhaps the most famous of them, Leni Riefenstahl's *Triumph des Willens* [Triumph of the Will] (1934), relies on ritualized expression and grandiose panoramic gestures to overwhelm the spectator and, one supposes, bring him or her into the ideological fold of fascism. As Kaes writes of this film, "In *Triumph of the Will* (generally regarded as the archetypal fascist film) cameras are constantly in motion, circling and moving, creating a compelling energy in the highly composed spaces around formations of masses of people, *animating even buildings and monuments*. . . . Images such as these have become part of the public memory in Germany" (5; emphasis added). As buildings and monuments are reanimated through the manipulation of the photographer, and as the camera lens ceases to be invested with that traditional objective function attributed to it before modernity's critical eye intervened, private memories fade and crumble into debris as "public memory" erects a monument to a singular version of events.[2] This goal of giving life to spectacular national monuments as visible evidence of the narrative of modernity corresponds to what Esteban's camera is to do for the Festival. When he is sent out by the Organizing Committee into the streets of the unnamed metropolis to take pictures of architectural wonders, statues, and vistas (with and without human figures), the result is the animation of these landscapes as participants in the larger history of the nation.

While documentary film is the medium used to promulgate the idealized images of Hitler's rise to power, the photograph is the vehicle of choice in García Ponce's depiction of the government's approach to the Olympic Games as lived by his narrators. The use of a medium which, since its invention, has been granted an inherent truth value as a mechanism of technology capable of offering unmediated and therefore authentic documentation of events, immediately calls into question the concept of authenticity itself. With the intervention of the photographer's gaze, the artifact created, whether photograph, film, painting, or written text, is made relative to a moment and a use value. There follows the concept of the leader, in this case Mexican president Gustavo Díaz Ordaz, as a human being whose countenance, rhetoric, and gestures are reduced and stylized into a grotesque monument as well. The process of creating the photographic image allegorizes the revelation of the Project's leader as a figure highlighted in the depths of chiaroscuro. As such, he is touted as part of the ideal landscape of the moment of triumph captured in the scenes of the Olympic Village as yet another part of the nation's inexorable historical advancement toward modernity's arches. In other words, in the brochure photo, the president becomes an authentic monument in the vast panorama of historical markers among which he appears. He promotes all of the ceremony of the moment, but he also casts a shadow on the success of the Project by enforcing its goals through repression and violence.

What Kaes calls an "arsenal" of images (17) addresses the paradoxical fate of two communities in *Crónica*. The first group is the national audience, one part of which is composed of the already-converted (bourgeoisie) and the other made up of those who see this type of media propaganda as just another skirmish in the long ideological battle with the manipulative State. The second group is the community of international spectators which has to be convinced that the forces of law and order have everything under control so that the Festival can go on as planned, the games being the crowning achievement in a long history of public accomplishments. The glossy photographs are used to tell the official story, as opposed to the narrative *crónica*, by weaving convolutions around what the eye focuses on as a series of images belonging to one single national narrative. In this way, the photos are similar to the panels of the retablo. They might stand alone, but they acquire added significance when articulated around a central tale to which each contributes and from which each takes new life. And captions are added to the photographs by the State in case the viewer does not interpret the images 'correctly.' So the visual image is charged with a Benjaminian spark of storytelling, now envisioned especially as the catalyst of discrepancy and contradiction.

The bureaucratization of the arts, as well as their use to legitimate the State's vision of historical events, is at the heart of García Ponce's novel.

The myth-making capability of the photographic (or cinematic) image is what is employed by the committee to "create what doesn't yet exist": the idealized, imagined future nation. (But one might well ask what the model of that vision is. Is modernity a copy of an 'original' akin to the mechanically reproduced photograph, or is there a Mexican modernity responding to more than emulation?) For the purpose of such imagining, the present is not enough; vast expanses and layers of cultural ruins must be recycled. Remnants of other times and other spaces must instead be shown as part of an ongoing process, tied to the past and to the future through—in the best of circumstances—a particular figure or event that then becomes a stand-in for that myth. In Riefenstahl's Germany of the 1930s, the events are in part the spectacle of the Congress and its rallying behind Hitler. But her later works, "Festival of the People" and "Festival of Beauty" (1938) which together form the film *Olympia*, insinuate even closer ties to the celebratory preparations in which Esteban is involved. Rather than a sports documentary on the XI Olympiad in Berlin, as she had been requested to do, Riefenstahl directs a two-part work reflecting what Ott calls the "epic nature of the games" (166). They condense all temporal narration into an excessive, larger-than-life presentation on stage. Focus and technique take the place of storyline in these films; lenses, editing, and lighting effects contribute to the montage of events portrayed. When Ott refers to the opening shots of the first part of Riefenstahl's film as "unfolding like a massive tapestry" (172), one gets the same idea as the plan of the committee in *Crónica*. A "tapestry" or montage of monuments is collected in a single brochure, linking elements of past and present to suggest the future outcome: a "triumph of the will" of one beautiful and homogeneous nation coming together to celebrate the Festival. The ironic twist of García Ponce's text is that it uses the genre of the novel to break open the narrative and permeate the cracks in the image of the "triumph." The Festival of Youth will provide the battleground on which "youth" in and of itself becomes the body of the enemy for the State.

In Chapter 11, panoramically entitled "Grandes perspectivas" [Grand Perspectives] and ironically suggestive of the idea of great expectations for the nation as well, the narrator recounts the cultural and historical origins of such a climactic moment in order to reveal its place within a continuum of masquerades by so-called barbarians. This narrative is a bitter portrayal of the nation's colonial past replete with class struggles, conflicts between indigenous peoples and European invaders, and the *criollos'* wars among themselves. At no point does the nation seem to be able to come to terms with its internal problems; different historical eras appear and disappear like a succession of apparitions which leave behind nothing but empty monuments and vast panoramas of devastation and decay. Governments come and go, each leaving the legacy of a cultural icon in public recognition of its six-year term, but these images stand in the place of real social or economic achievements. Through Sor Juana Inés de la Cruz and Octavio Paz, and through María Félix and Elena Poniatowska, the State has proclaimed Mexico as belonging to feminism, to intellectual history, to a world-class cinematic tradition, and to transparent politics (by recognizing a documentary writer and journalist). Yet the gestures correspond more to a recovery of the past for political reasons and to a nostalgia for belonging in general that comes and goes from public view with each successive presidential term.

Such markers of historical moments are the very same subjects of Esteban's photographs, captured for yet another appropriation and circulation of cultural images for questionably honorable official ends. The triumphant moment of the Olympic Games, a tremendous governmental investment to create an image of progress and modernity, is commemorated in stamps, brochures, and other consumer-oriented paraphernalia. How the notion of progress becomes one of consumption and the marketplace is an ellision that fills the novel. Yet, as *Crónica* reveals through the voices of the multiple narrators, these mass-produced "monuments" to a single moment are really allegorical references to endemic political violence which periodically tears the nation apart instead of moving it in a communal and positive direction. In spite of a strong desire to institutionalize what are seen as revolutionary changes fought for and won at various critical times in the history of the nation, it is made evident in the narrative that "jamás nada duradero se ha realizado" [nothing lasting has ever been accomplished] (318), in the words of the principal narrator. Seen from this perspective, this nation appears devoid of a genuine spirit (à la Nietzsche), a nation which continues 'progressing' almost despite itself just because there is a sense of inertia carried forward by the rhetorics of modernity. It is caught up in a kind of blind and unconscious force, one which continues to "avanza[r] siempre hacia adelante" [always move forward] (318). Taking this vision of culture presented in *Crónica* as a panorama of history as nightmare—as a coalescing of fascination and horror—seems to point toward what Horkheimer and Adorno argue in *Dialectic of Enlightenment* to be a modern version of sacrifice necessary for the nation to achieve the touted "modernity" (55). Alongside the ritualistic games of the Olympiad, that sacrifice occurs in the Plaza de las Tres Culturas of Tlatelolco. Another site of ruin, this public housing project is constructed and dedicated to masses of middle-class workers in the city. Yet it also has in its subsoil a Franciscan church whose steps are barely visible and an Aztec pyramid peeking out amid the high-rises. It has a duplication of the pyramid form in its modern architecture, with the three-sided figure rising into the skyline housing El Ministerio de Relaciones Exteriores [The Ministry of Foreign Relations]. There is little doubt that this is the site of Adorno and Horkheimer's sacrifices to modernity since what is erected on the dual ruins of conquest and conversion becomes the altar to so much more bloodshed in 1968.

The layered structure of the narrative fragments opens fissures to reveal other relics incorporated into tales of Mexican modernity. In "Grandes perspectivas," the mention of the royal House of Hapsburg, its intervention into the politics of "the country" (which here remains unnamed), and the execution of its emperor in front of a firing squad sent by the president of a liberal government (318), recalls the emperor Maximilian and his later removal by the forces of Benito Juárez. Later on in the novel, one of the floating narrative voices reveals that the scene described above is actually taken from a series of paintings by Édouard Manet and not from a direct source of historical narrative itself. In other words, the reader does not witness the encounter between Juárez and Maximilian as a fictionalized version of a chronicled historical event, but as a narrative "assemblage" of the dramatized figures evoked by a French painter. Although the titles of the paintings are not specified in this novel, from the descriptions they correspond to *The Execution of Maximilian* Versions I, II, and III. In a sarcastic reference to the relationship between a country's tragic history and the outside witnesses to it (or precipitators of it), we read in *Crónica* that "El suceso [la ejecución] inspiró incluso a grandes artistas extranjeros" [The event {the execution} even inspired great foreign artists] (318). What does violence "inspire" among the citizens of the nation?

The news of the execution, which reached Europe by telegraph, led the French artist to sketch the composition on three very large canvases as a major contribution to the Paris Salon. While there was on display in the 1867 Salon an oversized painting celebrating the French victory at Puebla in 1863, Manet's rapid response to the news of the execution was to ready three canvases dedicated to what Wilson-Bareau says is an event "greeted with universal horror and condemnation" (38). However, the universality of this reaction might very well be placed in question as far as García Ponce's presentation is concerned. And we already suspect that horror is always accompanied by fascination as well, as Paz reiterates.

Manet's three versions of the same scene, a triptych in its own right, painted over the years 1867 to 1869, belong to what are referred to as his history paintings. In each of the subsequent visions of this execution, Manet "[picked] his way through often conflicting evidence in order to sharpen the impact and meaning of his image[s]" (Wilson-Bareau 61). Focusing in on the aspects most pertinent to his overall project, Manet's versions of events scavenge among the debris of historiography to choose what most evokes his personal confrontation with the "horror" of the event. (As an artist, but also as part of French society, he is doubly marked in this respect.) The process of focusing in on emotions, details, and sentiments of nationalism or power does not necessarily nor logically lead to the same conclusion for all involved. An examination of this process leads Neil Larsen to conclude that "[i]n Mexico the event itself retains a strongly symbolic cultural and political connotation, but outside Mexico one might almost speak of the event of Manet's painting as having displaced and supplanted the spectacle of the execution proper" (32). So we might conclude that Maximilian's execution becomes an allegory of the nation and not a monumental representation. Larsen goes on to discuss what he calls the modernist interpretation done of this painting by Georges Bataille in conjunction with the same historical theme of execution as represented by Goya in his painting *Las ejecuciones del tres de mayo* [The Executions of May Third]. Bataille's conclusion that, contrary to Goya's version, Manet's work functions "[t]o suppress and destroy the subject [of history]" (Larsen 33) is of obvious interest to the reader of García Ponce, for the tragedy of the loss of the subject of (Mexican) history—what is left in the fragments of narrative voice—is the centerpiece of *Crónica*. Art supplants life (history) in the European reception of Manet's version of this scene. In the particular case of García Ponce, this event appears as just one in a series of national fractures and failures which point up the image of tragic masquerade as the key to the personal histories belonging to the storytellers. The Manet paintings are monuments to such moments of tragedy, but they do not take the place of the historical events that inspire them as interpreted by those who live among the ruins of the society in question.

A curious point of intersection exists, however, between the painter of the execution scene and the narrator of the same events later on in *Crónica*. Manet, the very figure of the flâneur in Paris and always the painter of images of modern urban life, nevertheless included political allegories in his works. In one specific instance, Wilson-Bareau refers to an early lithograph by Manet that shows a large crowd gathered to celebrate the launching of a balloon owned by Emperor Napoleon III, a figure of modernity and progress at the time. The print is an ironic comment on the celebration of the emperor's official birthday in 1862 as a masquerade of national pride and unity while concealing the defeats suffered in Mexico that same year. As the balloon rises, the attempts to expand empire collapse. The same may be concluded about the scenes evoked in *Crónica*, since the State's proclamations of unanimous support of the Olympic Games hide the violent scenes of repression needed to give the public appearance of peace, progress, and modernity. The manner found by García Ponce to represent this obscure and concealed political dimension of his narrative is allegory; the same is true for Manet. Hanssen examines Benjamin's emphasis on "the dialectical potential of allegory" (67), the representation of which we find in both Manet and García Ponce. We might conclude therefore that allegory's opening up onto "a landscape of death and devastation" (Hanssen 68) functions to pry open the discourses and monuments of modernity for the eyes of the narrator (and the reader, by implication). Neither canvas nor bound volume can contain the excesses of allegory or its possible convolution of the storyteller and his tale.

A second case of intersection in the novel is the spectral figure of Gustavo Díaz Ordaz, president of Mexico during the decade of the 1960s, whose government is responsible for the massacre at Tlatelolco. His semblance appears in the novel tagged with the epithet "la calavera sonriente" [the laughing skull] (1023), both a caricature of his physical appearance and a covert reference to his intimate connection to the forces of death. As an allegorical figure, he ties the narrative to those landscapes mentioned above since "death" is responsible for the "devastation" one must excavate from allegory. The epithet is a coded reference to Díaz Ordaz, which appears in newspapers and other publications of the time. Such a figure, once again extracted from a specific historical moment but reiterated in a kaleidoscope of narrative fragments, becomes a specular marker of tragedy. The student killings ordered by the government, and the media silence afterward, almost fade into the background as the "laughing skull" takes center stage and moves its jaws. The drama of the moment is distilled into the reduced gestures of this figure as mask and as performance. Describing the representation of people and conflicts in baroque theater, Benjamin looks toward the prince as the greatest figure of a tension between hope and despair. Of the melancholic prince he finds, as Bolz and van Reijen remark, "The prince is seemingly the most powerful but at the moment when he is expected to make a decision he reveals himself as being absolutely powerless. An unbridgeable chasm opens up between ruling power and the capacity to rule. The absolutist prince, who carries cruelty against his opponents to extremes, knows that he himself will fall victim to their cruelty in the end" (32). Although Benjamin uses Golden Age theater of Spanish dramatist Pedro Calderón de la Barca and German baroque theater as his sources, it is not difficult to extend these words to Díaz Ordaz as the allegorical prince of the PRI [Partido Revolucionario Institucional or Institutional Revolutionary Party] that has given the death blow to revolutionary hopes by institutionalizing them into official policy. The power of the prince lasts only as long as his constituents agree to overlook what is happening in favor of the masks of modernity. But when that "unbridgeable chasm" widens, the only way to cross it is through violence and death (after all, he is the living death figure). The absolutism of the prince and his cohorts (now in the Mexican State and not on the Spanish throne) can rule only through extremes if the revolutionary promises of democracy have all but disappeared. The image of revolution itself in this context becomes the greatest tragic figure because its promises (equality, freedom, democracy) and its failures (force and irrationality) are two halves of the allegorical image that open up to reveal nothing but contradictions that destroy in order to survive.

The allegory of the figure of the *caudillo*, [the leader or the dictator, in modern times] has a long history in literature from Spain and Latin America. One cannot help but be reminded, for instance, of Ramón María del Valle-Inclán's classic representation of the Latin American dictator in his novel *Tirano Banderas* [The Tyrant Banderas]. This work, one of the author's *esperpentos* from the late 1920s, takes place in an imaginary Latin American nation whose characteristics are an emblematic compendium of the languages, politics, and history of a great number of countries in Latin America. The figure of the dictator Santos Banderas, otherwise known as the tyrant, uses planted informants to uncover traitors among his citizens. When a demonstration occurs and these informants incite a riot, the resulting jailings and political repression are traces remaining in the scenes evoked by García Ponce; they are as psychologically devastating in *Crónica* as they are in *Tirano Banderas*. Of the image of the dictator, Smith writes "Santos Banderas . . . is at the very center of this novel, affecting in arbitrary fashion the lives of everyone in the country he dominates. He is not an extrovert, sybaritic dictator with a love of fast living; instead, he is ascetic, choosing to reside in a former monastery, prudish, pedantic, and mentally unstable" (130–131). The same traits are condensed into the figure of Díaz Ordaz, the "smiling cadaver," who ends up spending his days closed up in the National Palace in Mexico City after the 1968 debacle. A common popular reference to him in this situation is "el solitario de Palacio," the solitary man in the palace. Far from a self-indulgent tyrant, the presidential image is one of auesterity, abstinence, severity, and denial. The masses do not have to take revenge on the tyrant as Benjamin suggests will inevitably occur in tragic drama; he perpetrates the victimization on himself by withdrawing into a self-destructive death-in-life.

The first book of Valle-Inclán's novel is entitled "Ikon of the Tyrant," a reference to descriptions equating Santos Banderas with wooden-like humanoid figures. In some passages he is described as a mummy, and his head is reduced to the form of a skull without human flesh. García Ponce uses synecdoche to reduce the Mexican president to a puppet or a fleshless human skull, exaggerating the prominence of Díaz Ordaz's teeth and glasses to create a monstrous allegory of evil. Both writers embody the fascinating and horrific notion of death in these figures. García Ponce's intention seems to be similar to that of Valle-Inclán: to open up grotesque and phantasmagoric spaces that have pervaded the psyche of the nation's inhabitants and to allow the allegory to reveal all of the traumatic cultural debris therein. In the words of Jérez Ferrán, "la visión de la historia . . . que se proyecta en el *esperpento* [es] un reflejo . . . grotesco y distorsionado" [the vision of history . . . projected by the esperpento is a . . . grotesque and distorted reflection {of events}] (116). García Ponce likewise "projects" a semblance of crumbling and ruinous politics onto the countenance of the mask of death: the nation smiles as its foundations crumble. René Avilés Fabila, author of the novel *El gran solitario de Palacio* [The Great Solitary Figure in the Palace], which is based on what he calls an allegory of the grotesque figure of Díaz Ordaz, confesses that among the books he read in preparation for the writing of his novel is Valle-Inclán's *Tirano Banderas*. The earliest of the narratives about Latin American dictators he finds (followed later by *El señor presidente* [Mr. President] by Miguel Angel Asturias, *Yo el supremo* [I, The Supreme] by Augusto Roa Bastos, *El recurso del método* [Explosion in the Cathedral] by Alejo Carpentier, and *El otoño del patriarca* [Autumn of the Patriarch] by Gabriel García Márquez), Santos Banderas is, chronologically, the lowest stratum of these images to be recalled and resuscitated, perhaps obsessively, as Avilés Fabia prepares his own text. Avilés Fabila says of the character embedded in his novel that he does not intend him to stand alone as a monument to some sort of sporadic interruption of violence into the harmonious passage of history. Instead, he finds a pattern established that has created resounding echoes in the minds of citizens whose lives have been brutally affected. Subjects of this violent nation suffer not only physical scars and lesions, but psychological wounds as well. And rather than a 'reasonable' or logical progression from past to present, history is distorted by them into a compulsive series of violent acts underlying the official discourse of a collective modernity. Avilés Fabila writes:

> Yo concebí el libro como un amplio mural. No se trataba solamente de hacer una crónica novelada del 68 ni un testimonio, mi intención era repasar los cincuenta o sesenta años de Revolución y ver en qué había terminado: en una lamentable parodia. Y algo más: equiparar todos los gobiernos 'revolucionarios' con las tiranías latinoamericanas. Crear a un dictador eterno al que cada seis años lo transformaban dándole una nueva apariencia y un programa distinto.

> [I conceived the book as a broad mural. I didn't just want to write a novelized chronicle of 68, nor a testimonial; my intention was to go back over the fifty or sixty years since the Revolution to see what it had turned out to be: a lamentable parody. And something else: I wanted to compare all of the 'revolutionary' governments with Latin American tyrannies. I wanted to create an eternal dictator who, every six years, was transformed {on the surface} by giving him a new appearance and a different program.] (101)

The evocation of the Mexican sexenio, the farcical election and re-election of interchangeable members of the PRI at the reins of the power of the State, is the scenario for the 'democratic' choice of the dictator as the vehicle of the nation's imagined future. (In other words, the tragic drama that Benjamin watches on stage is performed every six years in Mexican politics.) The parallels among the texts of Valle-Inclán, Avilés Fabila, and García Ponce would appear evident in the constellation of their narratives around the axis of a grotesque authoritarian figure whose grimaces celebrate decay (in the shape of national projects). Despite the allusion to the figure of the tyrant engraved on the mural of Latin American history, we might take it up as just the starting point for psychological repercussions within the characters created by García Ponce. Like Avilés Fabila, his intention is not to give testimony to some historical event or situation. García Ponce plumbs the sedimentary backwaters left by seemingly eternal dictatorships not only to unearth the fossils of damage and ruin produced by them, but also to find what his own family epic has lost over the intervening years.

DUST, LINT, DARKNESS: MODERN CREATION AND ITS REMAINS

Benjamin's *Trauerspiel* [The Origins of German Tragic Drama] oscillates between a sublime, winged (perhaps even angelic) side to melancholy and the earthbound, telluric, tectonic part of the mixture inherited from antiquity but filtered through the thinking of the humanists of the sixteenth and seventeenth centuries. The "dialectical nature of melancholia" (Hanssen 159) fascinates him, as the dialectics of allegory have done so before. Cast for him as competing spheres of animality and spirituality, "the Trauerspiel study wavered between a benign and base version" (Hanssen 160) of the coldness and the flaming genius contained within a single figure. The predicament of melancholy varies in his writings from an early turn toward the medieval to, as the part most applicable to our discussion, a later positive spin on the melancholic "through . . . an immersion into the matter of objects [that] could salvage the potential of things" (Hanssen 162). Such objects—stones, minerals, earthly material—enclose contradictory forces in their very substance (as petrified by the passage of time and the pressure of geology). The image of the semi-precious stone embedded within the barren, cold exterior rock (Hanssen 162) might serve us to describe and examine the representation of the contradictory impulses of modernity equally embedded in García Ponce's novel, in the houses, stones, gates, and walls of Mexican architectural ruins. The gaze of the melancholic narrator, for Benjamin, is the only way into that rock; turning it into ruin is the first step in its critique.

Turning their gaze on the intelligentsia such as Esteban, Anselmo, and Fray Alberto, but on those who belong to the working classes as well, the narrators of *Crónica* perform a splintering of the rock to reveal its core as well as the outer layers that have been chiseled away. Taking the nation as an archaeological ruin of sorts, to pry the innermost (secret) angelic dimension from its mineral enclosure implies going back and forth from external objects and events to internal phantoms. Both the inhabitants of industrial zones on the outskirts of the modernizing, spectacular metropolis, and the wealthy families that remain in seclusion behind the protective walls of their estates are targets of the excavators' tools. One way in which the angelic and the demonic, the mineral and the precious, are represented by García Ponce's narrators is in the dialectical interplay between light and dark, hidden and exposed, glimmering ("vislumbrante") and abject. Much of this is architectural in nature, and some is specifically projected on the architecture of the body.

The luminosity and obscurity of chiaroscuro effects used to portray the mansion of the Gonzaga family aestheticizes their remoteness and withdrawal into a series of tableaux, while the residents of the sordid interior of the Martínez home—with its permanent smells of beer and cigarettes—are depicted as dark figures in a thick atmosphere. This obscure enclosure houses the lives of human beings, but it also is an allegorical figure of the ruins of modernity. Industrialization produces luminescence and, as by-products, rubbish, refuse, litter, dregs. If we cannot directly call the human inhabitants dregs, we can see them living among the residues of the promises of the modern nation as an allegory for the darkest aspects of that very project. In this makeshift abode, human beings are reduced to the level of dust and lint, the fibrous material that remains behind as the most visible trace of the process of production of rags and stuffing for a variety of uses. The Martínez family members are covered with lint; it fills their eyes and ears and thickens the air so as to impede breathing. They will never be able to afford the cotton cloth that results from these processes, but they are condemned to live among its ruins. There is no status lower on the social scale than to inhabit the kingdom of lint. This abject situation conditions their perception of everyday life, the aspect most central to the narrators. Benjamin's Paris as represented in the Arcades Project focuses on the telluric aspects of the metropolis, focusing specifically on the fog and the rain clouds overhead and the intrinsic connection between weather and melancholic boredom. Moving on, however, he observes that the rain falls as dust, settling atop the arcades (monuments to the economic and cultural forces of modernity) and this dust is, of course, one of the allegorical figures he deploys to be able to write on the city. This dust, in turn, infiltrates every corner of buildings and rooms to accumulate underneath beds and chairs, settle on plush and contaminate with debris even the most luxurious new upholstered furniture of the bourgeoisie. No one escapes the sediment of industrial production and economic 'progress.' As silt on the external surface of objects, dust also permeates history and the psyche of the inhabitants of the city. He goes so far as to say it becomes (allegorically) "soaked in blood" *(Arcades Project* 104) during times of absolutism and repression. Dust stands in for progress as it does for decay; it is like the double pull of the ruin, both upward toward the heavens of progress and downward toward material destruction. Dust and lint are residues, but they have an afterlife of their own.

In contrast, most of the intellectual discussions and commentaries in the Gonzaga household take place in their private library, paneled with rich woods and decorated with replicas of famous paintings. What dust is to the underclasses, artwork is for the bourgeoisie: ever-present and ubiquitous. While they discuss the country's past and its uncertain future (in their minds) in the midst of such luxury, their alienation is presented as nothing more than a tasteful subject of discussion, a topos shared by those whose daily lives appear to suffer no obvious ill effects in spite of such laments. Words cover the surfaces of the private library, not dust. The angst created by historical events among the intellectual figures in the novel, as reflected in the discussions taking place in such ritual gatherings, appears among the poor and unsophisticated as strong feelings of violence and rage leading to supposedly irrational acts. Such acts often take the form of violence against one's own, as in the murder of Evodio's brother by another member of the working class, or in the battering of women by their spouses. One particular facet of these sentiments of anger and violence on the part of the working poor is Evodio's increasing paranoia. He is haunted by the sounds of sirens, as if to signal a crisis or an emergency nearby. These noises in his head are a prelude to a series of events that will indeed be critical to the nation. His hallucinations and bouts of erotic fantasy, as well as visions and dreams of incest, play an increasingly important role in foretelling something catastrophic in both the novelistic plot and the historical schema haunting it. In the descriptions of these characters' reactions to their exclusion from the trajectory of history, and their imagination of scenarios of their own devising, it is not difficult to recognize the sense of schism that pervades modern Mexican society. While the ambulance wails inside Evodio's head, it also fills the streets of the capital in October 1968 and again in June 1971 when then-president Echevarría sent the paramilitary forces into the streets to crack down once again on protesting students and teachers.

Darkness permeates the modernity of the novel, allowing for shadows to fill the sunny tourist landscapes of progress and wealth. Julia Kristeva addresses the roots of the dilemma of a melancholic vision as the "Threshold of the Visible and the Invisible" (*Powers* 151). What she terms "a hidden Apollo" casts a light on the crucial experience of emerging from paralyzing darkness into "a sun that remains black, to be sure, but is nevertheless the sun, source of dazzling light" (*Powers* 151). The divide straddled by the melancholic would separate "appearance and disappearance, abolishment and song, nonmeaning and signs" (*Powers* 151). She offers up this allegorical reading of the struggle against darkness for the intellectual as a destructive-productive ambiguity. Taking her cue for the term "black sun" from the poem "El Desdichado" (The Disinherited) by Gérard de Nerval, Kristeva theorizes about the work's hero in terms of the darkness and the saturnine qualities of the poetic voice of this character. Writing of him as "[a] dispossessed prince, the glorious subject of a destroyed past, El Desdichado belongs to a history, but to a depreciated history. His past without future is not a historical past—it is merely a *memory* all the more present as it has no future" (Powers 150). This image echoes the paralyzing nostalgia seen by Benjamin as something to be overcome by the critic of modernity. A bleak sense of loss pervades this poem, the first-person lament of the disinherited prince who lives under the dark star of melancholia.

The prince is more than faintly reminiscent of García Ponce's character Esteban in *Crónica*. Esteban, whose voice we hear narrating numerous parts of the novel, is a similarly allegorical figure of the disinherited. As a dissident intellectual in Mexico during the 1960s, and as a representative of the younger generation of thinkers that has hopes for a bright national future, Esteban is witness to a double sense of destruction. Already critical of many of the events of the past—a history as "depreciated" as that represented by Nerval—he is exposed to a second moment of loss, a second cancellation of the future. The memory of the brutality of 1968 is overshadowed only by the official discourses that alter, deny, or glorify (through political manipulation) what transpired in October of that year. Since not even the past was glorious, but already degraded, for Esteban, the present merely compounds the blackness of the sun that envelops him. Present after present disintegrates into destruction and dispossession, a historical time cut adrift.

Owing to Esteban's overwhelming feeling of melancholy present in the novel from first page to last, we may conclude that the social body in which he must survive is inhabited by the cadavers of the Plaza de Tlatelolco. These corpses include those claimed by relatives and buried in cemeteries, those denied by the government and never recovered, and the walking dead. Mariana dies, but Esteban does not; he thus forms part of the collective abject body of society that must go on. Esteban's liminal condition, his tenuous existence on the border between life and death, signals a collapse of order and identity in Mexican society. The abject cannot be expelled from the individual or the collectivity; its presence is a constant reminder of what the social body might want to jettison from its midst but which it is incapable of making disappear. According to Kristeva, the abject "disturbs identity" (*Black Sun* 4) for the very reason that it cannot, despite all pretense, be made to go away. In Tlatelolco, the forces of government repression make an attempt to discard the abject, the dissident, the monstrous. Onto the face of youth is cast all that must disappear from view. The irony of the abject, in Kristeva's view, is that it is "in-between, . . . ambiguous, . . . composite" (*Black Sun* 9). It never ceases to exist completely; it haunts society as a melancholic ghost. The official version of events may claim that a unified, modern Mexico emerged from the Olympics at the end of 1968, but the abject social body continues to reappear when least expected. For Freud, of course, this is the return of the repressed.

Two literary antecedents of these aspects of *Crónica*, whose reflections of the narrator's excavation of the ruins of Mexican culture and their influence on the individual are components of the novel as well, can be traced to a collection of essays entitled *Desconsideraciones* [Anti-considerations] (1968) and the novel *La invitación* [The Invitation] (1972). In both the work of fiction and the volume of essays, García Ponce delves into what Goldin has defined as his "crítica social" [social criticism] which at the same time the critic refuses to categorize as "un arte comprometido" [a committed art] (9) on the order of the documentary evidence of the Onderos. The linguistic mimesis of the Onda borders more on a traditional sense of realism than on an alternative sense of aesthetic critique. *Desconsideraciones* is an anthology of essays written at different historical moments in response to particular issues and, as its title in Spanish suggests, "desconsiderar" implies a critical attitude toward social values. If "considerar" refers to the act of looking at events with a sympathetic eye, "desconsiderar" tells us that the eye of the critic in these essays is jaundiced, judgmental, and interested more in anomaly and contradiction than in the archaeology of the moment.

The positions expounded here are reminiscent of Friedrich Nietzsche's book of essays published under the title *Untimely Meditations* (written between 1873 and 1876 at Basle). In fact, *Desconsideraciones* opens with an epigraph taken from Nietzsche's text. This epigraph suggests some confluence or convolution of ideas between García Ponce and the European philosopher's radical critical position toward those who do not see, or do not care to admit, the extremely difficult and tortuous path of any nation toward modernity. If in Nietzsche's writings the "real enemies of such a culture [of intellectual and artistic life] are those who believe that the values to be striven for in the modern world are 'progress'—meaning improvements in material conditions—and the 'democratic' rule of mediocrity through the placatory politics of socialism" (Stern ix), the same holds true for García Ponce's remarks. The Mexican writer cites a fragment of Nietzsche's thoughts to preface his acerbic and melancholic commentaries on the mediocrity of the society around him and on what we might term its ruins: "trato de interpretar como un mal, una enfermedad y un vicio, algo de lo que nuestra época está orgullosa" [I try to interpret as an evil, a disease, and a vice, something of which our era is extremely proud] (8). That "something" is the facile assumption of modernity as an easy cure for social ills or as an "ossified" mural of the past. Likewise, in *Desconsideraciones*, the reality (as the space where human beings are exposed to direct experiences) created by modernity and progress is fundamentally and paradoxically hostile to humankind and, even more specifically, to that activity of humans known as art. Thus, in this scheme, art and culture might be taken as shields against the distorting powers of hegemonic reality, and perhaps as surfaces upon which are inscribed their aporias. (Realism is one of the enemies in this aesthetic battle, as we have already seen in the Onda.)

In his essays, García Ponce reveals an almost obsessive attitude toward the space of the city and its inhabitants, one reminiscent of the Benjaminian essays of "Berlin Chronicle" or "One-Way Street." As Rama reiterates throughout his essay, "[s]u mundo es el de la ciudad" [his world is that of the city] (188). After all, it is in the plazas and across the boulevards of the metropolis that Mexicans are sacrificed over and again to the goal of modernity. With the hint of a myopic gaze that zeroes in on every detail and aspect of the landscape, he is able to merge the narration of his own life (an autobiographical aspect of the narrative is implied) with the general sense of the setting he is describing. Similar to Benjamin's experience in the cities of Europe such as Berlin and Paris, García Ponce's Mexico becomes the locus of a topography to be explored to unearth its secrets. Mexico, the colonial as well as the modern, is a place brooding with mysteries that can be revealed only to the careful observer who has an unhurried quality.

Modern life requires haste, but the Benjaminian observer demands obsessive return and contemplation. Observations about topics great and small join the musings of the author regarding the curiosities of his surroundings. The subjects of García Ponce's essays vary from what seem to be the most trivial aspects of everyday life to greater philosophical issues regarding art and culture, much as Benjamin's convolutes reflect the same vast panorama. For example, García Ponce's essay whose subject is the size and shape of books ("El tamaño de los libros") appears hand in hand with an essay on the value and future of the cinema as an industry. (Benjamin's famous essay on "The Work of Art in the Age of Mechanical Reproduction" comes to mind as a corollary, as do his other pieces on the potentially liberating and awakening effects of cinema.) Another piece in García Ponce's collection, entitled "Transfiguración y muerte de la imagen" [Transfiguration and Death of the Image], turns to one of the themes most repeated in his writings. That is to say, he addresses the relationship between form and content of a work of art, and the loss of a connection between the work itself and "esa realidad que el arte suscita" [that reality provoked by art] (2001 86). His greatest preoccupation is the element of constant flux or change which, rather than opening up new manners of expression, turns a work of art inward: "no conduce, sino que se cierra sobre su propia realidad, convirtiéndose en un hecho cumplido" [[it] does not lead us outward, but instead turns back on itself, on its own reality, becoming a fait accompli] (2001 85). In the face of such a promising, as much as threatening, instability, the role of the individual observer is intensified even more.

Out of the essays in *Desconsideraciones*, the one that best depicts the fascinating (Paz) and simultaneously nightmarish aspects of Mexico City is the first. With the title "De la ausencia" [On Absence], this text paints an image of the city as a site of metamorphosis and transition where the old colonial and traditional landscapes are disappearing overnight as a result of voracious, uncontrolled development. In other words, visible testaments to modernity are encroaching on the landscape of the ruins of tradition to contribute their own debris. García Ponce ponders the process he witnesses around him as both construction and destruction: "Los edificios coloniales se transforman en amplias avenidas, las fuentes retroceden para dejar el paso a caminos periféricos" [Colonial buildings are transformed into spacious avenues; fountains give way to superhighways] (84). For the unwary inhabitants, this process leaves behind an unrecognizable space akin to a maze of cement in which, almost like magic, the streets either completely disappear or change their names and directions overnight. The same fate of the streets is shared by the buildings that are left as testimonies to a so-called glorious past, monuments to great historical moments preserved in what at the time seemed to be permanent structures. With a tone of sarcasm, García Ponce tells the story of a simple man who becomes totally disoriented because an old building, a landmark that helped him find his bus stop, has vanished in a matter of hours. The man, mesmerized by the lack of the solid structure he always counted on, is presented as having lost his sense of what is real. His reaction is an allegory of the gains and sacrifices of the processes of modernization.

> El señor que regresa a su casa, distraído, confiado en la costumbre, encuentra de pronto que su camión ha llegado a la terminal sin pasar frente al edificio que siempre le sirvió de referencia para advertir su parada. Fue derribado mientras él trabajaba metódicamente en su oficina y ahora es un nido de ratas.
>
> [The gentleman who returns home, distracted, trusting of his routines, suddenly finds that his bus has arrived at the end of the line without passing by the building that always was his landmark for getting off. It {the building} was demolished while he was working methodically in his office and where the buiding used to stand is now a nest of rats.] (9)

Thus, progress and the visible signs of modernity leave behind piles of debris that psychologically affect the city's residents and disconcert them. The effects are as violent on the human psyche as if they were blows to the body from a police baton or from a water canon. The "distraction" of routine, a favorite of Benjamin when he writes of the effects of boredom on modern culture, produces an optics that does not always perceive change until it hits home. No one notices the rubble of the demolished building until it has been passed by, until the entire route has been traversed. The street that has lost buildings looks, to García Ponce, like a grotesque mouth that has lost its teeth due to the ravages of time and decay. The sentimental value attached to parks, fountains, and monuments now becomes part of a bygone era in the subconscious of the inhabitants; they erect mental images to compensate for the missing architecture. García Ponce finds his surroundings threatening—"Decididamente, México es, también, una ciudad peligrosa" [Even Mexico is, {like other cities}, a dangerous place] (14)—but not for the crime or violence committed in it; instead, he sees the ravages of time and modernization as the enemy that leaves traces of the past in its wake even as new constructs have yet to begin. But the battles with this opposition are the dialectical encounters with the ruin that Benjamin proposes as the result of a narrator's melancholic vision.

Two specific spaces García Ponce mines as sites of ruin are his personal library and the empty museums from whose walls an exhibit has been removed. At one point of the essay "De la ausencia" [On Absence] the narrator stares fixedly at the faded paint on the wall where a work of art no longer hangs. He begins to ask himself questions about philosophical concepts of absence and presence: "¿Debe dejar de existir el cuadro una vez que nos ha revelado la pared?" [Should a painting stop existing once it reveals the wall {behind it} to us?" (13). Does the essence of the painting lie in the canvas itself, or does it leave something behind where it once was hanging? Is there a ruin to be found in the faded spot on the wall, in the dark outline left behind? The narrator finds the concept of absence to reveal as much to him as the object when it is present. The same effect occurs with demolished walls and buildings; the sites where they stood are phantasmatic monuments to the absences of what used to fill those spaces in other ways and for other reasons. The disappearance or removal of the concrete object does not imply a denial of meaning, even if hidden to the naked eye, of what remains. One is reminded in this essay of the lifeless shapes of cadavers painted by Mexican painter José Luis Cuevas as his homage to life. The absence of visible signs of life in them, lying in the morgue, only reinforces for the artist an obsession with looking at a world that has vanished and left a place for another world to emerge. In the truly problematic spaces of these encounters (those of vanishing and emergence) we find the melancholia of Benjamin and García Ponce who mourn the lost object and their own loss of connection to it (or mastery over it).

The representation of a phantasmagoric reality in *Desconsideraciones* finds its counterpart in fiction in the novel *La invitación* (1972). This work, published just four years after the violent events of 1968, dramatizes the psychological tensions and fears of different social groups caused by an undeclared state of siege that disrupts their everyday life and activities. (The idea that a state of siege might be undeclared is as contradictory a linguistic event as can be imagined.) These groups include students, professionals, businesspeople, and homemakers alike; the novel cuts across the entire strata of modern society. In a tone reminiscent of Kafka's novels—*The Trial* would serve as a good example—García Ponce's narrative depicts the streets and public spaces of a nameless city as the scenario in which an excess of power runs wild. Benjamin's absolute prince has his ruined landscape on which to play out his acts of revenge. Ordinary citizens experience this situation as a nightmare. And the official representatives of law and order, the police, instead of forming a buffer zone between the groups in conflict, take sides. The stage for this encounter is the city of the essays already mentioned, an urban landscape under the spell of modernization and change as proclaimed by the State. It becomes a site no longer recognized as human or friendly by its inhabitants. The excesses of blood and violence in the streets create an atmosphere in which the characters are no longer able to distinguish between reality and nightmare, between the material presence of others and their ghosts, between the familiar and the uncanny.

In this sense, *La invitación* may be considered a dystopian allegory. García Ponce's narrators do not acknowledge any connection between so-called real events or landmarks in the social history of Mexico and what goes on around them, but we have seen how this prying of the images from their archaeological shell has functioned in *Crónica* to create a dialogue between inside and outside. In the same sense as the allegorical setting of Ariel Dorfman's novel *Viudas* [Widows]—that is, modern Greece under dictatorships but by inference the Southern Cone during the dirty war—*La invitación* functions on several planes of aesthetic reality. As a forerunner of *Crónica*, this short novel presents a historical and political allegory of persons and events that will be developed to a greater extent in the subsequent two-volume novel. And, like *Crónica*, it slides seamlessly from internal compulsions to external repressions.

To loosen any grip on referentiality that could lead the reader to a mimetic representation of the Tlatelolco massacre, the narrative voice that tells the story, as well as the main, Kafkaesque character "R.," appear to emerge from a shadowy dream, a claustrophobic space, in which one is never certain if the story being told is part of waking or sleeping reality. Benjamin's convolutes come to mind as the figures to describe this spinning out of narratives from small, scintillating nuclei of recollections thrust out of oblivion by sparks of recognition. This effect is augmented by the protagonist, later on a victim of the repressive reality that has seemed to be a dream, who has been ill and bedridden for a long time. In the care of his family, his confinement to a space inside makes his perception of the outside cloudy at best. The fact that almost the entire first half of the novel, especially the first chapter, is told through the distorted lens of a sick person, someone removed in space and time from events, contributes to the experience of nightmare presented here. His altered state is rendered as a lack of time and sequence, as bouts of feverish narration and fevered thoughts, and as the collapse of reasoned argument. The world seems to revolve around the daily needs of a sick person, an individual self inhabiting the ruins of a healthy body, and whatever penetrates his room from the outside becomes disconnected from its original circumstances. The relationship between an internal narrative voice ("R.") and external narration produces a doubling of fragmented tales. The 'doubles' function in the sense of allegory that Benjamin finds so promising: not a symbolic stand-in but an explosion into two.

Lights, sounds, and all activity flow together in a montage of experiences on the surface of the body of the non-participant "R." The human architecture which has fallen prey to disease is incapable of mastering—or explaining, therefore—the everyday aspects of life. Even the identification of the character is reduced to a single letter of the alphabet, since he is so removed from a concrete form and from being an actor on the stage of history. His identity is as fragile as the prolonged survival of a sick body, or the preservation of an individual by means of one lone letter. The narrator reveals this fluid situation and the implied "loss of mastery and failure of control" (Krell 7) that we have seen as an opening up into the uncanny as a fruitful and perhaps even familiar narrative space. The technical (the human body) takes a turn toward not solid structure (given R.'s illness) but toward the ruin.

> R. había estado enfermo una larga temporada. Perdido en su cuerpo debilitado, sin ningún contacto con el mundo exterior, del que ese cuerpo fue alejándose, retrayéndose en su desprendida inmovilidad de todo lo que lo rodeaba . . . . haciéndolo casi inexistente, ajeno a sus propias sensaciones, dejándolo solo . . . . [E]l tiempo dejó de transcurrir durante esa época.
>
> [R. had been ill a long time. Lost in his weakened body, with no contact at all with the outside world, {a world} from which that body moved further and further away, withdrawing into its detached immobility from everything around it . . . making the body almost non-existent, alien to its own sensations, leaving it alone and isolated . . . . Time stood still during that period.] (9)

From the fragment quoted above, it is easy to conclude that a radical split has occurred between R.'s mental abilities of reasoning and the physicality of his body exposed to outside reality. Under the conditions of stress and restricted access to the world he suffers, R.'s material body becomes devoid of a wholeness of body and mind. He has been artificially transformed into a vestige of himself, a visible signature of modernity: division. While R.'s physical body loses itself amid a sea of pain and suffering, his mind exhibits a disembodiment from all physicality. This split becomes more acute if one considers that the signals and stimuli from physical reality are not processed by R.'s body/mind into a coherent whole. In other words, this split introduces another set of conditions with epistemological implications. If the voice of the narrator of historical events emanates from a sick body, the version of what happens is tinged with his painful condition and the distance suffered by that same narrator. So represented, history and its chronological sequences or structure turn into nightmarish fantasy from the dark side of human life as perceived by an outcast from it. The double sense of loss—of a healthy body, of a coherent narrator—folds back onto itself. In a visual display, this narrative would concentrate on the blackness of the chiaroscuro, and not on the activity taking place in the light. Like lint, the body seized by disease—especially paralysis—is debris from something previous. It can neither go forward or return (to wholeness).

The sense of loss in R.'s perception of reality—and his own place in it—creates an allegory for the nation that inhabits a diseased (decaying) social body. The moment of loss for R. is the instant he is taken ill; the time of crisis for others is the social confrontation in the streets of the megacity. R. is withdrawn from the events outside his window; his family fiercely desires to withdraw itself from the events which have interrrupted their banal, bourgeois existence. In both instances, this moment of rupture also reveals something about the lives they have led until then, and about the violence under the surface always ready to reach a boiling point when the conditions in society are at a critical stage. This may be seen in the displeasure of R.'s relatives when confronted with the disturbances around them.

> —¡Qué odio la policía!—dijo el cuñado de R.
> —Los estudiantes los han obligado a mostrarse—comentó la hermana.
> —Claro. Y la policía es el gobierno—dijo el cuñado y se volvió hacia R.—Será mejor que no vayamos a tomar café. Esta ciudad se ha hecho inhabitable.
>
> ["Oh what a drag, the police again!" R.'s brother-in-law remarked.
> "The students have made them come out [of hiding] again," commented R.'s sister.
> "Sure. And the police are the government," the brother-in-law retorted as he turned toward R. "Maybe it's better if we don't go for coffee. This town has become unlivable."] (105)

The student demonstrations have not only interfered with the leisure activities of the privileged family with time to spare, but they have also revealed what everyone 'knows' without saying. When the police appear in the streets to break up the demonstrators, their actions are both literal and figurative. They use violence on the bodies of the students, and they represent the power of the State in its death throes. Benjamin's princely allegory casts the isolation of the failed ruler onto the living bodies in the streets. R. is both paralyzed witness and sacrificial victim, for his impotence is both physical and social. When R.'s relative says that "the police are the government," this is a political reading of the scenario being played out (really, like the baroque theater, performed) on the streets of the city. If such confrontations did not occur, perhaps the image of the police as agents of something more ominous would take place elsewhere. The police are the actors on the stage of a social nightmare, and the protesters are their shadowy victims. The entire scenario breaks open the ruins of the metropolis as a peaceful place to dwell into the substrata of horror that underlies and consumes it.

Even R., never a political activist, is caught up in the vortex of violence. When he recovers from his illness and is able to rejoin the ranks of the 'living,' R. inexplicably becomes a member of the student brigades that paint graffiti on the walls of the city during the night. Swept up by the enthusiasm of the brigades, he is identified as one of the enemies of the State by the forces of law and order he has perceived from his sickbed but never completely understands. (We know that there is no complete understanding of any discourse in this text; everything is a constellation of discourses and experienced meanings.) He turns into an enemy just for being there, not for any explicit commitment beyond the few words he manages to utter before he is gunned down: "Soy amigo. Quiero ayudarlos" [I'm just a friend {of theirs}. I want to help them] (191). R. forms part of the historical moment by accident, by circumstance, not by his membership in any organization or adherence to any credo. History, therefore, has lost its coherence in this narrative and ends up as the fragmented images present in the mind of R. before he loses consciousness and dies.

In a kind of epiphany, in his last moments of consciousness, the character returns in his mind to the innocent days of his childhood, fragments suspended in time. Time is perceived in slow motion, as an internal flow, not as a series of logical events. R. seems to take forever to fall to the ground after being wounded. This action ends in a closed circle, a dark space which opens up to receive him: "la oscuridad, el gran círculo silencioso, azul oscuro" [the darkness, the great silent circle, dark blue] (194). Not even his friend Beatrice, the imagined or real object of his obsessive affection, can save R. from his demise. These are the death throes of the tale and its teller; this is the sacrifice demanded by the State. History and R.'s own story stop at the moment he loses consciousness. Neither can exist without the storyteller. But whether he is gunned down by the forces in control (of the narrative of history) or whether he kills himself and puts an end to his own narration is left as an ambiguous event. The last act on the last page of the novel is when a police officer puts a gun in the hand of the moribund victim, implying for future reference of those who find and identify the body that his death has been the result of a suicide. As an allegory, we are made to ask whether the nation has been a victim of assassination or whether it has put an end to its own misery.

This scene from *La invitación* will directly inform García Ponce's images of history in *Crónica*. By the time we reach his most recent novel *Pasado presente* (1993), historical phenomena again surface as debris or telluric detritus, like the ruins left after each of the earthquakes that has shaken Mexico City. Again, we find that history is measured by destruction, by what it leaves as remnant and ruin, rather than by chronological time, rational statements, or touted monuments. The spiraling structure of *Crónica* reveals the narrators' paralysis akin to the motionless body of the witness R. in *La invitación*. In *Pasado presente*, however, the narrator willfully removes himself from the currents of history, committing the intellectual suicide that was, in its first incarnation at the end of *Desconsideraciones*, a staged act. In an essay entitled "El escritor como ausente" [The Writer as an Absence], written the same year as *La invitación* but published in 1974, García Ponce remarks that his childhood was characterized by "la más absoluta indiferencia política" [the most absolute political indifference] (329), the names of politicians or the occurrence of catastrophic world events just a distant echo in the ears of children of his social class. A taste for certain colors relates to party banners and flags, but he reaffirms nothing more ideological than that in the family saga. Of course, these are the stories told by a bourgeoisie to uphold things as they are and not to offer the opportunity to others for alternate visions. As he enters adolescence, he finds both formal intellectual studies and the official rhetoric of the government causes for "náusea" (329) and abomination. A professional school degree leading to a career, and the government's use of language to justify populist projects both careen him toward the same one-way street: a loss of class distinctions in the institutionalization of the Revolution. That is to say, much like the expropriation of land by President Cárdenas, the need to earn a living and to listen to the extolling of the virtues of the lower classes goes against all that the bourgoisie traditionally upholds. With the explosion out of nowhere on October 2, 1968, García Ponce finds himself, alongside so many others, suddenly carried along by the events he had for so long had nothing to do with. In the ruins of post-1968, the evocation of "momentos maravillosos" [marvelous moments] (331) is justified in itself despite his own doubts about sustaining a political position. Pellicer sums up the resulting space for intellectuals as García Ponce sees it:

> Advirtió entonces que de nada sirvieron sus artículos, su participación en demostraciones públicas y su firma de documentos colectivos de protesta: las cosas siguieron igual o peor. Reconoció que ese vacío desde donde él se hallaba escribiendo era el espacio de la imaginación que ésta puebla con sus obras. Según él, la imaginación excluye al artista de la vida cotidiana, de la vida política, de la vida 'real.' Es el espacio de los sueños, de las manías, de las obsesiones patológicas, es el campo de la anormalidad y, finalmente, de la ficción. Pero se trata de una exclusión voluntaria pues si bien es cierto que en las modernas sociedades autoritarias se somete a los disidentes a tratamiento siquiátrico, en las permisivas se abre el vacío.
>
> [{He} came to the conclusion that his articles, his participation in public demonstrations, and his signing collective documents of protest were worthless: things stayed the same or worse. He realized that the empty space from which he found himself writing was the space of the imagination that populated his works with imaginary beings. In his view, imagination removes the artist from everyday life, from political life, from 'real' life. {The imaginary space of the artist} is that of dreams, of manias, of pathological obsessions{; it is} the territory of abnormality and, finally, of fiction. But this is a voluntary exclusion for if in modern authoritarian societies dissidents are subjected to psychiatric treatment, in permissive {open, democratic} ones an empty space opens up.] (Pellicer 47).

The "vacío" that García Ponce chooses to inhabit is not such a bad place, as he says, since it allows for what Krell has said is the opening up of interiority into the unlimited terrain of the psyche. *Crónica*'s narrative voices and scattered characters certainly populate the field of dreams and nightmares that are awakened by a reclusion from the realm of the overtly political into the realm of open spaces (either psychiatric or democratic ones). As Pellicer indicates, and we have seen, manias, obsessions, repetition compulsion, abnormality, and fiction all flourish in this supposedly empty space. And, in Benjaminian fashion, they all circle around the ruins of politics (that have purportedly been abandoned) in mournful allegories. The site from which García Ponce situates his narratives is the place of melancholic vision, the space from which competing meanings are produced and the veneer of that "nauseating" official political rhetoric can be stripped away. It does not disappear, however, but remains as a ruin inhabited by the pathological, obsessive, abnormal, fictitious characters of the literary text. Such landscapes of the imagination are populated with the corpses and cadavers of real events (those of 1968 and 1971), now the ghostly, phantasmagoric dwellers of an internal topography as contradictory as the metropolitan landscapes outside. García Ponce recalls the famous phrase of Karl Marx on the first version of historical events as tragedy and their repetition as farce (from the *Eighteeneth Brumaire*), yet he finds in the human remains left behind by the two violent decades something more than farce ("Escritor" 330). The victims cannot be left behind as debris but rather must be incorporated into the ecstatic expenditure of human bodies amid the rubble. Just as Mariana is a reanimated corpse in *Crónica*, Mexico must be resurrected from death at the hands of State ideologies so it may continue to form part of the imaginary of 'others.' The crossing and recrossing of the flesh of human bodies shifts us into the second and third panels of the triptych as we enter into the writerly space (that paradoxical emptiness) of García Ponce's next two novels, *De ánima* (1984) and *Inmaculada* (1989).

CHAPTER FIVE

De Ánima, de Corpore
The Ruins of the Bourgeois World

In his study of Austrian writer Robert Musil, Stefan Jonsson explores an essay in which the central focus is the image of the door. Seen as a portal that faces both past and present, this vestige of the house assumes great importance for the writer. As Jonsson sees it, the door "loses its function in modernity. It belongs to an earlier stage of social development . . . The door is here described as an instrument of knowledge" (*Subject* 60). Swinging in two directions, as it were, the motif of the entrance to and exit from the human dwelling is, like the Benjaminian convolute, a privileged site of revelation. One can peer into the home, and one can peek out on the social world; one can enter the stratified remains of the psyche and one can delve amid the stones of the city. Aside from the sheer architectural reference, however, something else is at work here. Jonsson writes of modern times that "new ways of building produce new bodies, new modes of perception, and new ways of relating to others" (*Subject* 61). No longer is it so facile a process to judge a house by its portal, or to define human subjectivity by the appearance of a nation's citizens; other forces lurk embedded in social institutions and in the deeper recesses of the imagination. What was once a craft—the singular fabrication of a door or, to extend the concept, the assignment of an individual to a role—becomes a process of mechanical reproduction and assembly-line construction. So the door is a ruin of a relationship between worker and craft, as well as between individual and community. And so, as Castañeda sees it, such architectural ruins become runes or visible traces of stories that reveal earlier tales and previous storytellers; they also set up, as Susan Buck-Morss says of Benjamin in the title of her masterwork on the Arcades Project, a "dialectics of seeing."

The chasm or gap between the inside and the outside, separated by the door and its frame in our trope, reflects as well the discrete categories into which modernity separates science, art, abstract thought, technology, and reason. As Krell moves from the spaces of material architecture into the realm of the human body, he points out that "[i]n Western experience these separate realities—art, science, worship—remain huddled in their separate spheres, in isolated and isolating architectures. They never cross the fluid, mucous boundary of the sexual" (169). The dissociation of technology and rapture, of science and art, of the social body and the physical body, of economics and expenditure is revoked (as Klossowski perhaps proposes in his title *The Revocation of the Edict of Nantes*) for Krell (via Georges Bataille) through a turn toward a new porosity and permeability of these constructs. In the space where the door used to be we find crossings and recrossings (Krell 170), flesh as speaking stone (Paz), openings and not closings, and "fascination" (Krell 170, but also Paz). While for Maurice Merleau-Ponty these permeable structures induce light into the picture, for Bataille they revel in darkness. For our own use of chiaroscuro, both function as the ruins of modernity's project. The building up (light) is always predicated on the horror of darkness (decay, debris, entropy) that accompanies and haunts all great dreams. The surfaces of architectural bodies and those of the architecture of the human body articulate and disarticulate possibilities, "sedimenting . . . experience" (Krell 171).

Neither the impervious door of previous times nor the membrane of modernity keeps things apart in a universe imagined by Merleau-Ponty, Bataille, or García Ponce. The ruins assembled and disassembled in the Mexican writer's texts are indeed objects of fascination rather than narratives of domination; they collide and disperse much like the convolutes that spin outward from Benjamin's narrative fragments. The fissures produced by the construction of the modern nation across the face of the capital city also appear on the skin of its inhabitants. Through such fissures erupt "mis más bajos instintos sexuales"(54) [my basest sexual instincts] as García Ponce writes in his essay "Mi primera casa en México," despite the best efforts to erect the "propicias bardas" [legal divisions of land] (54) in an effort to separate family from family and house from street. Through them also pass back and forth the political ecstasies of characters bound through their bodies into narratives of the nation. Politics enter through the portal, as do fantasies and fears. Doorways are expanded to permit the passage of cars (an emblem of the modern), and women are the portals to a "deslumbramiento" ("María Luisas" 156) that has little or nothing to do with the use of reason by the Enlightenment.

The second novel in García Ponce's trilogy of moveable panels narrates this permeability between the surfaces of social constructs and the so-called limits of the body through the medium of the diary. Writing is the new 'door' that opens the connections between subject and nation, between art and religion, and between gnosis and ecstasy. Therefore, Rama's category of an "arte intimista" no longer serves to describe the processes of experience or of poetics since what is intimate is also outside. Or, conversely, what is outside the body is there only until it permeates the surface. The same way that Octavio Paz catches a "glimpse" of the hidden stories of Indian history and its constructs, García Ponce looks for such glimmers in the recesses of the "lived body" (Krell 7), a body reduced not to technology or science but to a celebratory space. Neither monument nor prison, the human body is a hieroglyphic or ruin of writing which must be discovered and revealed by the storyteller. The body is recollection and it is forgetting; it is layers of experience (like those plumbed by the archaeologist); it is contradiction and critique. In this last case, the body is a prime instance of a constellation of evocations and holds on its surfaces and performative acts the influence of its cultural context.

Postrevolutionary Mexican society faced, among other issues and agendas, the role of women in the 'new' nation. Markers of morality and gendered hierarchies—the woman as mother, as subordinate partner, as an economically invisible subject—remain in place for certain classes while there are changes in men's behavior and social roles in others. The standards of morality after the Revolution found both the point and the break: they continued to be higher for women than for men, and they could now be used to justify (as well as be justified by) the new national project itself. As Schmidt writes, "[t]he aftermath of the Mexican revolution offered a setting in which machismo was elevated into 'a definitive and defining characteristic of what it meant to be a Mexican,' a distorting process in which the mass media, consumer society, and intellectuals all participated" (49). The embedding of critic Carlos Monsiváis's words from *Mexican Postcards* points out one of the important forces which remain showcased in the national media, yet consumer culture offers a challenge of its own besides. For workers, there are other attributes connected to job performance that relegate *machista* attitudes to the world outside the factory, for instance, if one wishes to preserve employment. Union activities would take precedence over such gendered behavior and could unite men in other ways. In addition, as Schmidt clarifies, "an analysis of post-1940 Mexico needs to employ a distinction between agency understood as cultural creativity and agency understood as resistance" (50). While he refers to the rise of popular culture as a possible alternative view to gender prescriptions, we might also turn to the idea of cultural agency as practiced by intellectuals as well. Everyday lives are one arena of practice, but a whole, complex set of other forms address this aspect of modernity's battles in other inventive ways.

Settled ideas about masculinity and femininity, especially the concept of machismo so prevalent in late-twentieth-century debates on gender, may be seen in many ways as "pure theater, a recently invented social fiction, a twentieth-century myth" (Rubenstein 226). Rather than suggesting that this exaggerated and prescribed behavior does not exist per se, Rubenstein posits it as an aspect of some sort of national modernity to be assumed by all those who wish to be included in this mythical project. On another front, anthropologist Matthew Gutmann adds a decisive element to this equation, as Rubenstein indicates: "Gutmann found recently that members of Mexico City's elite ascribe the characteristics of machismo to men of the working class, and vice versa: the word always describes somebody else" (226). Now this study was conducted at the end of the decade of the 1990s, but we might wish to extend its viability into other times. Even as State authority suffers crisis after crisis, and even as points and breaks appear with increasing rapidity, one element seemingly constant in modernity's debates is gender. Ascribing machismo to other people and other social classes means that the hyperbolic, even baroque, behavior, the violence, and the excesses attributed to this uncontrolled person occur elsewhere and not in the speaker. The mythical figures of machismo, Pancho Villa, for instance, can be picked up and sanitized as it were for State use, but those characteristics seen as mythical by Monsiváis and the rest are more difficult to clean up and rehabilitate in the guise of men and women's daily lives. After the Revolution, *patriotismo* could find a home in this larger-than-life, monumental figure, but it also met its public match in politicians such as Manuel Ávila Camacho whose persona—described by Rubenstein as "countermacho . . . , self-contained, somewhat prudish, . . . the good Catholic, the compromiser" (226)—could offer an alternative image for the national hero. Ávila Camacho's presidency (1940–46) offered the best of both worlds for public consumption: the break with the past and the end of the Revolution, alongside a legitimacy as inheritor of the energies of that period (a period, but a link). As fighters, men can be excessive and need to be; as politicians, they must learn self-control. The future of material wealth rests on the counterimage and not the violent one, at least for leadership. Moreover, the image of masculinity underwent constant and radical changes across the twentieth century, influenced by international media and by the necessity to create a modern look for the nation for export.

Any discussion of Mexican cultural politics also must include, of course, women as the flip side to masculinity's play for modernity. As a process, and not as a definitive answer to this evolving issue, gendered inequalities and negotiations surfaceed after the revolutionary period and continue to be confronted in many venues. For intellectuals, the debate has revolved around women of a certain class: the liberation of bourgeois women. Popular engagement with political forces, and popular politics of all kinds aside, it is the cultural agenda of intellectuals that has driven the image of the so-called liberated woman forward. Does this imply an immediate connection to real-life politics? Or, as Gutmann has it, perhaps instead "[t]alk about gender and democracy does not necessarily lead to a modernizing quest in which the position of women is used as a simple test of social progress" (*Romance* 166). Or might we even urge ourselves to ask whether women, politics, and modernity coexist, or could coexist, in the same breath in the characters presented by writers such as García Ponce. As inheritors of the debate, the generación de medio siglo came up with different responses to this dilemma. As sites of the reproduction of social production, the home and the family may continue the discourse of the nation being housed and promoted from within institutions and structures, but they also may explode the spaces of the private into a question mark rather than an affirmation. The diary would then reflect the character Paloma's deepest thoughts, but it could also serve as the swinging door to the alternation of the period and the break from Jameson's dialectical vision of the modern.

Having essentially required Mexicans to choose between a masculine and a feminine identity, then, the discourses of the postrevolutionary State set up for many an impossible scenario for action. If consumer society clothes those oppositional identities in specific dress, hairstyle, and media look, what of the bodies underneath it all? The political imagination could go only so far in allowing for difference, and so we may be led to search for the very skin hidden by performance and clothing to find the anomalies of modernity protected and hidden by these garments for more facile consumption. The connection between such publicized images and the formation of the modern State has been theorized by Francine Masiello as follows: "The accoutrements of gender—cosmetics, dress, and pose—are treated as commodities to be bought and sold in the image-making service of the nation. In effect, from the time of the nineteenth-century independence wars through the recent transition to democracy, patterns of dress and sexuality have formed part and parcel of the Latin American political imagination. . . . Fashion thus strengthened the projects of the modern state; it also endorsed a mode of citizenship related to sales and commerce" (220). This emphasis on the visual makes snap judgments regarding identity artificially easy, and it casts a burden on the material subject to clothe itself in something recognizable. Now that can be as much a reference to dress and makeup as it is to gender or political affiliation or age. What is revealed by such clothed bodies speaks out loud, but the voice underneath might need to articulate itself in a more literary or at least textual form. Here is where the genre of the diary or the confession might enter our discussion, where the notion of women's writing, their secrets, and an identity clothed by the nation, but not necessarily limited by, it might come to bear, and where the idea that other nations and other modernities might surface.

Laura Mulvey writes of the cinematic representation of different societies' fantasies projected onto the silver screen, but her theorizing of masculinity and femininity and her problematizing of the consumption of their visual images can serve us well in other contexts besides. After twenty-five years of reconsideration of the gendered spectatorial position of her earlier essays later collected in *Visual and Other Pleasures*, she returns to a new economics of the visual and of its fetishes in her 1996 volume entitled *Fetishism and Curiosity*. The association between the modern body and the fetish is projected across the arc—or swinging door if we return to Jonsson's image—of the media screen which calls citizens to the movie theater as it simultaneously enters the home. Over-invested images, those exaggerated and valued and codified by State institutions, displace political and economic and other types of social crises onto the bodies and figures which have historically been least able to refuse them. The role of fetish object, cast on women and on the feminine, can be sustained as long as she does not refuse it or, as Mulvey puts it, there does not occur a "psychic process of disavowal from a male point of view" (*Fetishism* xii). Readers, cinema spectators, and other participants in the consumption of media and other images must decipher things politically, refusing their ritualized abjection as Kristeva would have it, even if no political solution is found in the end. The anomalies, contradictions, excesses, and paradoxical successes can then all be addressed in such texts as "the concealed ideological narratives at work in all seemingly non-narrative concepts" (Jameson 6). *De ánima* may appeal to the curiosity of readers, but there are gendered curiosities as well as those which attract and repel. As Mulvey reflects on her theories of cinematic analysis, she concludes that "My approach to cinema is directed at its 'curious' nature, not at its 'realist' nature. Rather than its ability to reflect the world, I am interested in its ability to materialise both fantasy and the fantastic. The cinema is, therefore, phantasmagoria, illusion, and a symptom of the social unconscious" (*Fetishism* xiv). And so we return to Jameson's concept of the trope as symptom of hidden or buried narratives, of larger agendas, and even of competing ideologies. As one provisional response to those critics who find in García Ponce's text *De ánima* a singular reading of the feminine or a singular defense of masculine desire, we might want to interpose Mulvey's more complex and suggestive rereading of the fetish. While finding fetishism "one of the most semiotic of perversions, . . . not want[ing] its forms to be overlooked but to be gloried in . . ." she adds a most important other dimension to her argument. Like modernity, the fetish is not a singularity but a ruse: "to distract the eye and the mind from something that needs to be covered up. And this is also its weakness. The more the fetish exhibits itself, the more the presence of a traumatic past event is signified" (*Fetishism* xiv). As it reveals the hidden narratives of the bodies clothed for easy consumption, the fetish acknowledges its own concealment and potentially even the processes that have led to this mask.

Paloma and Gilberto perform a masquerade of sorts for readers who must be asked, as Mulvey insists, to read them politically even when politics per se do not seem to appear on the agenda. The exhibitionism of women, prevalent in García Ponce's trilogy and not denied by Mulvey as a "perversion," might then not merely "glory in" the woman as fetish but hint at its distracting function, not necessarily for Gilberto or for a male reader, but for a nation that has asked its citizens to make judgments without uncovering those stubbornly hidden narratives that Jameson and Mulvey warn us of. Instead of a defense of sexual promiscuity and display as the public "semiotics" of modernity, perhaps this suggests a demand for sifting through layers of "weaknesses," as Mulvey proposes. Fetishes would then become metaphors—dare I say allegories—for other social events and "traumas." The role of the spectator requires a change from passive voyeur (still a possibility if chosen, however) to decipherer of politics and of the fetish as a distorted symptom of the weaknesses, or the periods and breaks—of the modern. In his search to break down the opposition of the terms "masculine" and "feminine," Ignacio Corona finds in García Ponce a rich locus for such questioning. He writes: "este autor es uno de los escritores mexicanos que más ha profundizado en la representación literaria del origen, búsqueda y manifestación diversa del deseo sexual . . . Su obra ejemplifica . . . el impacto del pensamiento europeo sobre la narrativa mexicana con respecto a la exploración del comportamiento humano" [this author is one of the Mexican writers who has most delved into the literary representation of the origins, search for, and diverse manifestations of sexual desire . . . His works exemplify . . . the impact that European thought has had on Mexican narrative as far as an exploration of human conduct is concerned] (136). With Mulvey, one might wish to use the plural of "desires," as Jameson has done with the term modernity, and add the narrative of hidden ideologies to the narrative of visible textual writing on the surface. If we start here as our point of departure, though, Corona opens the door to an examination of sexuality itself as fetish and the exploration of "eros [como] la experiencia última de la libertad humana" [eros {as} the ultimate experience of human freedom] (141) and not as a prescribed set of actions or appearances set up to bolster the projects of the State. In this scenario, the voyeur and/or the active participants Gilberto and Paloma would all contribute to exposing the situations on which other constructions of sexuality are built. The added attribute of the visual upon which voyeurism is based, needless to say, creates a counterpoint to the unseen and the masked lurking beneath the surface of dress codes, conduct, and the look identified as the 'new.' The "distractions" of prescribed pleasures—"'[v]er' se traduce como revelación y como gozo" ['seeing' is translated as revelation and as pleasure, enjoyment] (Corona 143)—can be turned as well into the attractions of looking at oneself as a consumer in the economy of pleasure. If we keep sight of Jameson's hypothesis that modernity contains the seeds of its own destruction, its own internal period and break dialectic, then the revelation of the fetishizing and empowerment of sight could and should lead to something 'other.' Let us consider, therefore, the primacy of sight as part of the trope of the modern which García Ponce will have turn its eye on itself.

If we return to Habermas's notion of modernity as "the consciousness of an epoch . . . as the result of a transition from the old to the new" (3), as an exaltation of the present, as the cultural concomitant to social modernization, then its ruins lie both in the structures and in the bodies that build them. Cultural norms and ideals intervene, of course, in the construction of monuments; so when things fall apart, the relics they leave in their wake are fragments of the stories told that have reached some aporia. The bodies disciplined to carry out the projects of modernity have visible scars (as Benjamin sees them on the city) from the processes of containing ideals in some material shape. As Habermas writes of the incomplete project of modernity (in Europe), aesthetic experimentation alone, such as in the case of the Surrealists, does not carry with it an emancipatory effect. Instead, with the ruination of the cultural containers, "the contents get dispersed" (11). So in the particular case of García Ponce, the debris of European culture and the ruins of Mexican national culture come together to form a swirling collection of fragments from which one might be forced to recollect the antithetical aspects of modernity as seen in twentieth-century Mexico. The emancipation of the expression of sexuality, for instance, is more a ritualized element of modernization than a structural change. It is one molecule of the "cultural dispersal" that Habermas finds in the Surrealist project. Like emigration to the city, like the adoration of the media, the body becomes part of the national economy that is evoked for public needs. For García Ponce's characters, like Bataille's and Klossowski's characters before them, the body is the site of struggle between finding a home in the economy of the State and enjoying the liberating experiences of expenditure. There is no working out of the paradoxes between the two; rather, there is a constant play among the remnants of one (the State) and the ideals of the other (the libido). In the end, the container (modernity) loses its coherence and the dispersal of debris leaves behind a constellation of fragments and residues.

The resulting text is a palimpsest whose layers are constantly showing through without memorializing any aspect, privileging one or another, or finding a coherent relationship among them. The third Benjaminian proposition for the development of an urban critique, once again, is a momentary flash of recognition and not a permanent integration. There is no erasure of previous cultural writings, but a constant superimposition of narratives and a problematizing of the link between present and past. Between the presence of the physical bodies with which these narratives are constructed, and the grafting on of 'foreign bodies' from other discourses, body and soul (spirit), *corpore* and *anima*, flow across the spaces of the narrative. García Ponce's works are ecstatically palimpsestic and "totally plural, in the sense that [they refuse] to imprison [their readers] within conventions or compel any particular interpretation" (Fowler 181). This plurality is articulated in *De ánima* (1984) through its plot and structure, and through its recreation of obsessions and fascinations culled from previous texts by García Ponce and by other writers.

As the reader is drawn into the narrative structure of diary writings, and into the shifting perspectives of the narrative voices, especially in their ritual reenactment of bodily experiences, the aforementioned struggles come to the surface. At first glance the archetypal encounter between mastery and innocence, between master and dominated, between loss and obsession occurs when Gilberto and Paloma meet, but there is more than a facile dichotomy created. Many critics of García Ponce's works—among them Salvador Elizondo, José Emilio Pacheco, Ethel Krauze, Octavio Paz, and Angel Rama—agree that the word innocence appears with great frequency in nearly all of his novels. The concept takes on a different guise in these contexts, however, no longer fitting into the connotations more commonly associated with the word. In *De ánima* and other novels, innocence refers more often, and perhaps predictably so, to situations of expenditure and *plaisir* disguised as innocence, or to innocence used to reach the object of desire, than to a literally innocent site of interpretation. All sense of purity is removed from the so-called innocent character and instead she (for they are always women) is made the locus of revelation for the male character and, in the end, for herself. As Octavio Paz indicates regarding such a reconsideration of this traditional idea of incorruption in the works of García Ponce, and in the concomitant control or mastery over experience, "innocence . . . is invariably allied to those passions that we call evil or perverse: cruelty, rage, lust, the deliriums of the exasperated imagination, and finally the entire range of pleasures that we condemn severely and yet at the same time find fascinating" (*Introduction* xv). This brings us full circle to the remnants of the pre-Columbian past that Paz finds both fascinating and horrifying, for they ignite a spark of recollection yet blur the boundaries set up by modernity between moral categories. In addition, the sublimation of political passion—especially after 1968—can resurface as erotic passion.

If we take into consideration that, as Matthew C. Gutmann concludes, "a large number of people in Mexico lost their political innocence" (*Meanings* 61) after October 2, 1968, then an enchantment with the notion of innocence itself has been ruptured. As the "fiesta desarrollista" [celebratory development] (Monsiváis, qtd. in Sefchovich 184) of the decade of the sixties comes to a close with the violent events of 1968, and the *sexenio* of Luis Echevarría looks to bring the alienated bourgeoisie back into the fold of State projects, the political and moral lines in the body politic become increasingly blurred. Sefchovich calls the bleak moments following the so-called glories of the 1960s "la hora de la pesadumbre" [the hour of sorrow and mourning] (183). A time of chiaroscuro on the public stage as much as it is behind closed doors, García Ponce's "arte intimista" of this era carries in it the seeds of political contradiction even as it explores the expenditure of the body. The ingenuous, the guiltless, and the blameless in politics turn into a rhetorical stance of political parties, much as the childlike, guileless, and unblemished Paloma is only the reflection of a discourse about her. The two sets of diary entries, one by Gilberto and one by Paloma, address this structurally in the novel for they visit and revisit the same scenarios just to find themselves reconstructing their own stories among the ruins of their relationship. Two years together produces evidence of a relationship built up and then left to decay. This is true in particular for Gilberto for he turns to the fragments of his diary to attempt to reconstruct a life about to end. Diagnosed with a terminal illness, the only vestiges left to him are the written words about his previous life, the bits and pieces of experiences as retold by the storyteller himself, but at a distance in his own texts.

The double-edged sword of the simultaneous condemnation of and fascination with *plaisir* cuts across the entire range of García Ponce's 'innocently' constructed texts. While presented with the raptures of innocence, the reader is also conscious of the shadow of what has been termed the perverse (taboo pleasures) that haunts all acts of the bourgeois characters. The dual axes of innocence/perversion continually intersect in *De ánima* without the moral sanction that traditional society would encode on them. They are, then, freed from categorization to coexist as driving forces underlying bodily experiences even as the social community struggles to assimilate new (modern) codes of conduct and behavior. Even the title's presumed 'innocent' look—its suggestion of the soul or the *animus*—is contradicted by the immediate predominance of what is *de corpore*, things of the body rather than of the disconnected spirit. In fact, the *ánima*, as Ann and Barry Ulanov write, "can be read as the breath of life or the creature endowed with it" (9). So *De ánima* is a textual, corporeal edifice, a body of words, whose every aspect takes on life thanks to the density and insistence of the voyeur's gaze, whose indiscretion or attraction puts into motion the mechanisms of repeated ceremonies focused on the human body. This voyeur might be the reader, the narrator, or the participants themselves in the textual/sexual ceremonies. *De ánima* is a text in which transgression and glory, satisfaction and death, are entwined in the dialogues between and among the bodies. The dialogic aspect of Benjamin's critique of urban culture comes to life through them from the ruins of the political and the personal structures embodied in the narrative. This novel, akin to the description of the character Paloma's sensuous body, is like skin "that is impossible *not* to touch, visible at all moments in that perpetual contradiction and affirmation of itself" (*De ánima* 187). Just as Paloma is the sum of her past and present experiences, just as she is a collection and recollection of herself with others, so the novel is a palimpsest of narratives on the body. *De ánima* displays a strong emphasis on the visual, establishing a link between film and prose, and between voyeur and reader of the layers of this sexual/textual surface or 'skin.' Like the *subsuelo* [geographic subsoil] on which the foundations of the modern metropolis are laid and anchored, human flesh is a layered set of remains. Among the scars on its surface, as well as amid the mental images retained, one might find vestiges of social ideals and prohibitions. Human bodies are, like the Ángel de la Independencia, monuments to successes and to failures that may remain aloft, or fall with the natural disasters that beset the city.

In terms of what Patrizia Calefato terms the body as "a mobile edifice . . . [that] registers the ambiguities of desire" (223) we move away from the icon of the feminine as permanence and immobility to the allegory of the body as the shifting terrain of ruined desires and nascent fantasies. The 'innocent' gaze is deployed to penetrate the dense and disconcerting spaces of fascination that the secret dialogues between bodies and subterranean currents of fantasy proffer. Of course, desires and fascinations are fed from external sources and then become internalized into fragments and images that often seem uncanny until they find a space to inhabit from which they no longer disturb the discoverer. I orient my study in particular toward the crossovers among *De ánima*, Pierre Klossowski's *The Revocation of the Edict of Nantes* (1959), and Jun'ichiro Tanizaki's *The Key* (1960), the last two providing García Ponce with pre-texts for his novel. While Klossowski's work lends him the structure of the diary, the remains of Tanizaki's novel fill García Ponce's prose with a charged erotic language that is the key to the subterranean fantasies embedded in the characters' psyches. All three texts, in addition, are tales spun around multiple visions of a central core, the format of the diary or day-to-day record of individual experience, interpretation, and remembrance (akin to Benjamin's recollections). Each text should not be read as a guidebook to García Ponce's narrative but instead as part of the field of cultural debris from which characters, relationships, and social ideals have been recovered. Like the pyramids and the Christian churches, the structures underlie one another but are actually recycled bits that are patched together to form new structures. We should not conclude, therefore, that García Ponce merely wishes to reconstruct an era or a society for that would respond only to some nostalgic impulse. What he takes are the fragments of stories that are removed from their contexts and placed in what he calls the "free" spaces of literary creation.

Like *De ánima*, *The Key* is composed of two alternating fictional diaries.[1] One belongs to a middle-aged university professor who, in order to explore his own sexuality, provokes situations in which his wife of many years will (possibly) act on her own repressed desires toward another, younger, man. Kimura, a friend of the couple's daughter, is a student at the university as well as her possible future husband. He is charged with escorting the two women around the city, at the request of the professor. To document their activities in his absence, Kimura is given a Polaroid camera. At first, the game appears (paradoxically) innocent enough and the pictures taken represent enjoyable scenes of the three in public. But we have already adjudicated neither moral superiority nor condemnation to acts of innocence or guilt. Rather, they assume a guise of ambiguity much as the political culture of the Mexican nation does after the close of the 1960s. They are also a possible projection of the professor's own crisis at midlife. The afterlife of the image of innocence taken from *The Key* is complicated further by the multiple voices and the loss of faith in the purity of language in *De ánima*. As everything else, the power of linguistic signs to represent categories such as innocence becomes a function relative to the power of the speaker/writer or to the problematic relationship between that source and the words set in new contexts.

It is not long before the photographs in Tanizaki's novel begin to reflect a more intimate relationship between Kimura and Ikuko (the mother/wife). The catalyst of this intimacy, as we read in his diary, is the professor. Yet the relationship between the older woman and younger man progresses, perhaps even beyond the original intentions of the provocateur.

While he has induced them to experiment desire, he has also presented it within certain limits from the outset. In the first entry of his diary, written on New Year's Day, the professor expresses both his interest in keeping a personal record of their own relationship as well as his pursuit—at the level of fantasy and imagination in the beginning—of challenging what he calls Ikuko's "old-fashioned Kyoto upbringing . . . with a good deal of antiquated morality" (3). It is this attitude of tradition which forms the target of his experiment, although where it might lead could even be the destruction of the social mores out to the test. And the twist is that he is unaware, or at least unsure, of her knowledge about the whole scheme. Morality is the social monument whose shadow haunts both texts.

The title of the story, *The Key*, is an icon of the furtive relationship between the couple regarding what they reveal to themselves in their diaries. Each supposes these records to be both secret *and* accessible to the other. "The key" is what locks the diaries away from prying eyes; yet it is also the object left out in the open on purpose to provoke the desires of the other into investigating what is contained therein. The key is literally an instrument to open the diaries, but it figuratively gives access to erotic spaces besides. What is traditionally considered private writing is paradoxically made the object of shared interest; like Musil's door, the key gives entrance to secret realms. It is not merely a key but an allegorical figure that might suggest decipherment by multiple readers. As they write their thoughts down on paper, both characters seem to be aware that they are manipulating the reader with the very lines they are composing. The role of the imagination becomes increasingly important in the representation of reality; the same holds true for the pictures recorded by the lens of the camera. Both words and photos are read by the individual in different ways according to predispositions, expectations, desires, and perhaps even unexpected recollections.

The professor's and his wife's recorded versions of events, similar to those of Paloma and Gilberto, anticipate actual or imagined physical pleasures. After retrieving his intoxicated wife from Kimura's home one evening, the professor writes, for example, "I came up to my study, and have quickly jotted down all of the night's events—all that has happened so far, that is. In the midst of writing, I have savored the thought of the pleasures which are to follow" (79). The anticipatory aspect of desire is what functions most clearly here, as it does with García Ponce's Paloma and Gilberto. But in both instances, it is also the tale retold that stimulates fantasy even more: Paloma's remembrances of her relationship with her uncle, and Ikuko's often feeble or foggy memories of her encounters with Kimura. Imagination is the 'key' to both stories, what García Ponce touts as the terrain of "freedom" when faced with the so-called immovable monuments of social norms. The last entries of both diaries, Ikuko's and her husband's, contradict the appearance of innocence given at the outset on New Year's Day. By June, when the professor has recently died of a stroke following his acting on his own desire for Ikuko, the reader discovers that each of them has been leading the other on. Each has known all along that the other has had access to his or her private thoughts. Yet this in itself is ironic, since each has also revealed the temptations of the voyeur in the writings. Both the professor and Ikuko have made the private format of the diary a public spectacle instead; the privacy is merely a masquerade. While the Olympic Games as spectacle are the relics of the modern project in *Crónica*, *De ánima* provides us with another 'fascinating' spectacle in the performances of the characters built from *The Key*. What is conjured up by their two-faced game of innocence and experience is reminiscent of the debris piling up at the feet of the Angel of History who is its witness. Words pile up in the diaries of *The Key* and of *De ánima*, yet actions cannot be contained by them in some complete and finished form. The ruins of modernity pile up as well, the remnants of intellectual projects and dreams, yet to hold them back and restrain them is impossible. At the end of each novel, the instigator of the experiment dies and the couple is no longer. All of the characters are pushed inexorably toward the future. The collision of two forces, tradition and modernity (the so-called freedom of the subject), reduces the experiment to rubble, yet it presents the possibility of a melancholic reading to force the contradictions on which it is predicated to spring forth.

The second characteristic shared by the narratives of García Ponce and Tanizaki is the consciousness of time embodied in the relationships between these women and their lovers. The concept of an irrevocable time, one objectively measured by all sorts of technological instruments, appears to be of little importance here yet it forms a haunting strata of culture ticking away in the distance. Anderson writes of a community imagined through the print media, one in which a reader of the daily newspaper can find a sense of correspondence by imagining all those reading at the same moment. Perhaps the same simultaneity draws together characters belonging to a political community (which they are forced to suppress in favor of another type of experience of individuality) in communion through the literary imaginations. This is far from their grounding in the "primordial, timeless cultures" (Gutmann, *Meanings* 221) often associated with archaeological tourist sites, but rather is the imagining of Paloma and Gilberto and the professor and Ikuko within a shifting terrain of literary and cultural influences that are not directly political. Roger Bartra ponders the question "Is there an age-old continuity in Latin

American culture?" He is led to respond, "No! . . . All signs of life in pre-Hispanic societies were eradicated. Today Latin America is irrevocably an extension of the West" (qtd. in Gutmann, *Meanings* 221). While it is impossible to conclude that Tanizaki is a model from the West, despite his adoption and adaptation of Western narrative models to Eastern uses, we need to embed García Ponce's narratives within both Eastern and Western traditions of literary monuments to cultural moments. Being "part of the West" would then indicate a greater imagined community of modernity and a greater set of contradictions on which to draw. Mexico and Japan might share some of these crossovers from tradition to modernization alongside astonishing contradictions and survivals.

The temporal advancement from an initial impetus (otherwise called progress) inevitably brings disillusionment in this narrative, as it did in *Crónica* with the erosion of dreams into nightmarish scenarios. What matters to the characters of Tanizaki and García Ponce is a cyclical time, one of renewal and regeneration, repetition and obsession, that competes with linear time. This sense of time is not passage and wearing down, but ritual invocation through the erotic exercises that plunge characters into situations previously redemptive and now in a 'ruined' state. Ikuko, Paloma, and others all serve the male characters as 'keys' to perpetually renewable energy that is posited in that allegorical sense we have cited from Benjamin. Pulling in two directions, both as destroyer of systematic thought and as moment of redemption, women as allegory are, without a doubt, the perfect embodiment of the baroque excesses to which Benjamin also makes reference. Never contained simply within their skin, they take over, provoke, and otherwise exemplify the excesses of signification that our model has proffered as challenging rather than limiting. This situation becomes, as David Pollack has written, "a quandary of self" (67) in the male character's obsession with the woman, yet his dependence on her for these rituals. Indeed, one of the paradoxes of the tales is that many of the male characters, Gilberto and the professor included, die before their stories have been told to completion. Then it is left up to Paloma and Ikuko to reflect on the entire narrative up to that point, at least as far as some vague and incomplete totality is concerned. The women have the last word, and they assume the storyteller's role. Tanizaki's "fetishization and demonization" (Pollack 69) extend to *De ánima* as well. Paloma as the embodiment of the sublime and the infernal is both innocent and perverse, both the source of sexual power and the explosive site of the unattainable. In spite of all their discussions about "possession," Gilberto and the uncle will never, in the words of Paloma herself, "possess" her. Ikuko and Paloma are undeniably complex; their erotic rituals are maintained beyond the irrevocable time of the lives and deaths of Gilberto and the professor, and they function as more than a literal voice of the feminine.

The novel *De ánima* represents the confluence of two diaries, two bodies of writing, belonging to Paloma and her most recent lover, Gilberto. Together, the diaries as recordings of past physical and mental experiences first converge and then diverge in order to offer the reader (who is challenged with trying to 'make sense') a constellation of images or representations of the same events. Seen from two very different and distinct perspectives—the intellectual, quasi-philosophical eye of Gilberto, who is obsessed with transforming erotic feelings into aesthetic categories and, in diametric opposition, the supposedly uncontaminated eye of Paloma—the contents of the diaries cover a time span of almost two years. Both diaries and characters are interrupted only by the sudden death of Gilberto as the result of the rupture of an aneurysm. Both texts construct a space of writing and intimacy in which the characters invent and fantasize about themselves in the open time of the present while remembering (making and remaking, reliving one more time, reinterpreting in different contexts, 're-calling' in the spark of the Benjaminian moment) the diverse sexual encounters they have experienced.

The reader of *De ánima* adds to the pleasures of the text by casting yet a third perspective on the episodes and by picking a path amid the recovery of the ruins of the narrations of Paloma and Gilberto. Octavio Paz puts this crucial role into perspective when he insists that

> the reader [is] turned into an onlooker [who] contemplates, or more exactly *watches* the action. In certain cases, . . . one does not have the impression that one is present at a performance in a theater but, rather, that one is peeping through a keyhole: the 'tableaux vivants' of pornography transformed into a ritual of signs that come together and separate to form, literally, figures of a language irreducible to words. Bodies link together like signs, form sentences, and *say* (*Introduction* xvi-xvii)

Paz's remarks are quite appropriate to our discussion since they underscore the action of the indiscreet eye granted access through the peephole, behind the artfully closed doors of narratives and the closed, exclusionary categories of the modern. Obviously, the indiscretion of the eye watching through the framed space of the peephole is not unseemly in the context of this narrative. Rather, it recalls the previous sense of an innocence that implies otherness and that imbues the imagination with innumerable possibilities and not merely static dichotomies of good and evil, past and present. The expansion of the Janus-faced Angel of History or the two-voiced diary into a multiplicity of readers rummaging around the fragments of stories allows for allegory to play out into hitherto unexplored, but maybe strangely familiar, spaces. How could one imagine that Paloma might participate willingly in such ceremonies? By assuming that she is guileless and naive, we cast her into the stricture of traditional limits. But by finding clues to other stories within her, perhaps as limitless as the number of readers, or the number of experiences she faces, she is given the chance to piece together remnants long forgotten and "bewitch" us—and Gilberto—not just with the expected but with the sublime (Paz). The notion of splendors rarely includes surprises, one imagines, but rather expected glories, repeated rituals, and reinforced celebrations. Here, nevertheless, the splendors of Paloma are her ability to evoke fascination and horror, to encounter in all of the dilemmas of modern life not dead ruins but living relics. This includes her willful acceptance of the human body as an edifice with movable surfaces and, like the skyline of the metropolis in which she lives, a constant building up and tearing down of walls and boundaries. The *bardas* that García Ponce recalls in his essays of *Personas, lugares y anexas* are what Paloma finds to be shifting panels of a living retablo.

Perhaps without Pierre Klossowski's novels *Roberte Ce Soir* (1954) and *The Revocation of the Edict of Nantes* (1959) it would not be possible to think about the layered composition of *De ánima*, a novel which reconstructs and then dismantles the characters and structures of Klossowski's texts. García Ponce has both acknowledged his spiritual debt to Klossowski's thought—as seen in the extensive list of his works dedicated to the ever-present subject of crossovers among what are so often the discreet units of theology, pornography, and the concept of the sign that also coexist in Klossowski's literary volumes—and deliberately pursues Klossowski's ideas as represented by the two novels cited above. Klossowski's writings form part of that "dialogical process of reflective intercalation" (*Museum* 17) Castañeda discusses as he describes the "oscillation" between the 'real' world of objects and relations and the imagined world of the text. Even as García Ponce reinforces his refusal of the overtly political, Castañeda suggests once again that cultural discourse is forever open to all of its components because "all cultures are imaginary machines: real representations of identities, communities, and belongings forged in contestations of power" (*Museum* 17). The power of discourse, as an antidote to political impotence or disinterest, is the "machinery" that allegorizes social relations into imaginary worlds. As his characters find their bourgeois, patriarchal, provincial universes on the verge of collapse and unrecognizability, they reproduce ceremonies of mourning and loss over and over, even as they cannot find *plaisir* amid the glories of the modern.

It would be as mistaken to take the works of Pierre Klossowski as the representative of a 'real' France during his lifetime, as it would be to consider García Ponce as a univocal image of 'the real' Mexico. Each one's imagined understanding of experience is embedded in his characters and their compulsive returns to issues and images, such as relations of power and functions of community. In pondering cultural and philosophical issues from within a general Latin American context, Mexican philosopher Leopoldo Zea emphasizes the urgent need for internal dialogue within and among the "contestations of power" of social as well as psychological structures and their constructs. Zea writes that "Latin America is the daughter of European culture; it is the product of one of its major crises. . . . whether we want it or not, we are the children of European culture. From Europe we have received our cultural framework, what could be called our structure: language, religion, customs, in a word, our conception of life and world is European. To become disengaged from it would be to become disengaged from the heart of our personality" (361, 363). The profiles of García Ponce's characters, then, would have some similar roots and stories as those of Klossowski, Musil, and von Doderer for their commonly shared palimpsestic surfaces on which stories are superimposed. If the sagas of empires and their demise create "men without qualities" (to paraphrase Musil's title) the first time around, then the characters of García Ponce are traces of an erasure long in the making.

Topographies of the mind form the interconnections of cultures between Klossowski and García Ponce. Although approximately twenty-five years and two very different contexts (Europe, Mexico) separate their works, they share a desire to create and recreate allegorical characters, ones imbued with almost divine characteristics, who function as the axis of each of their erotic universes. In the case of both writers, this allegory explodes outward from the material (textual, of course) body of a woman: for Klossowski, it is Roberte; for García Ponce, Paloma. As he has written of the architectural constructs of his childhood and adolescence before, García Ponce finds in enclosures a strange and inviting openness he seems to see reflected in the human body. If as a child he is lured to look over the *barda* and salivate over the games in progress on the other side, ones from which he laments his exclusion, then now in *De ánima* characters are tantalized by fascinations with other exclusions and other secret games. Among these are challenges of knowledge and innocence provoked by the appearance of a body close at hand yet fundamentally inaccessible.

Klossowski, like Tanizaki, provides the key to what this allure of the woman might hide. Benjamin writes of the dialectical images provoked by, for instance, the parting glance at a railway station before vehicles and passengers disappear into the distance. For García Ponce, before Gilberto disappears (he dies) and before Paloma becomes a movie star (essentially disappearing as a 'real' person to become an actress playing many roles), parting glances in allegorical form appear on the pages of the diaries. Thus writing holds special privilege as an object of "awe and wonder" (Gilloch, *Myth* 130), revealing characters and situations only to leave them unresolved. Opening the cover of the diary is like opening the door in Musil's novel; these spaces are both sacred and profane, both private and public, the sites of the ruins of cultural discourses and composed of remnants themselves. García Ponce is specific about Klossowski's Roberte as such a "holy site" (Gilloch, *Myth* 130) amid the facades of so many texts produced in modern times.

> Para mí, unas de las preguntas capitales de las obras de Klossowski es una pregunta sobre la identidad personal y sobre la necesidad de un signo único. En su caso ese signo, que vale por todos los significados y ocupa el centro del mundo, es un nombre arbitrariamente elegido, se llama Roberte. Y Roberte es un personaje, o sea una imagen, que el arte hace aparecer.
>
> [For me, one of the most fundamental questions in the works of Klossowski is one of personal identity and of the need for a single, unique sign. In his case, that sign, which stands for all signifieds {meanings} and which holds a place at the center of the world, is named Roberte. And Roberte is a character, that is to say an image, which art makes appear.] (García Ponce qtd. in Ruffinelli 29)

His reference to a singular and "unique" sign to hold all of the explosive energy of Roberte (or, for that matter, Paloma) is a fundamental paradox in García Ponce's theorizing. In his search for some sort of personal identity impervious to the ravages of time and the destruction of signs, he reads a "center" on the allegory that cannot hold. The excess of allegory, its spilling beyond its artificial container (language, sign), its combining of sacred and secular attributes such as the redemption of other characters through communion with the flesh (à la Bataille) might well create sites of "expectation" (Gilloch, *Myth* 131) but not, as a necessity, "centers." The mourning over such a loss can only find its expression, then, in "what art makes appear." If we wish to consider Roberte, Ikuko, Paloma, and others as obsessively repeated "monuments" (Gilloch, *Myth* 131) to unreal and by now uncanny expectations, then we may begin to find their fascination and their horror. His narrators repeatedly and insistently conjure up figures and spaces that are akin to Benjamin's "dream architecture" (Gilloch, *Myth*

131), housing a phantasmagoria of possibilities not unlike modernity's own promises and perhaps comparable to Krell's movable and disjointed "archeticture." The melancholic gaze of Gilberto or of other narrators is bound up in this, and even overwhelmed by it as he focuses incessantly on Paloma. He does not survive to reach the final, mournful conclusion (that the desire for the center lives on in art alone) but he also needs Paloma to close the door behind him by filling in the final pages in his place. Gilberto's persistent return to "borrow" the body of Paloma for the exteriorizing projection of his own ghosts, to the "contradicción inherente a mi deseo" [contradiction inherent in my desire] (175–6), makes her into the sign of what is impossible since she can never contain all that he can imagine. While he ponders such a situation, and even as he continues writing about it, Gilberto waits in expectation for something about himself to be revealed through her: "Repito a Paloma, vuelvo a Paloma, encuentro y transformo a Paloma" [I repeat {keep reproducing} Paloma, I go back to Paloma, I run into and transform Paloma] (176). She is not a monument like those made of stone or bronze, then; she, like the characters of *Crónica* and *Inmaculada*, performs the function that Laura U. Marks attributes to "fossils or fetishes" (224). She is a material medium in which originary experiences (ones charged with special meaning) are condensed into cryptic histories that can be conjured up in melancholic and obsessive readings. Marks refers to primordial landscapes; Paloma is imbued with the same sense of enchantment and spark of redemption for Gilberto who finds her too much to contain in one singular episode and too little for what he imagines he can do through her compliance to his wishes.

Klossowski's figure-sign of Roberte fosters a double reading throughout her diaries: Roberte is the embodiment of Octave's fantasies and, at the same time, the source of his frustrations. The character Octave, a well-known professor of Scholasticism, wants to discover the other side of Roberte, the dark side, and the secret dimensions of this other Roberte that might call up his own unrecognized and repressed desires. These secret, intimate dimensions can be made to interface with the 'known:' "obligan a Roberte a ceder a sus propios deseos y actualizar a la *otra* Roberte" [force Roberte to give in to her own sexual impulses {desires} and actualize the *other* Roberte] (García Ponce, *Teología* 27). In other words, Octave is calling upon that allegorical doorway between inside and outside, between cultural vestige and 'real' society, between imagined and lived experience, to bridge the distance that separates or divides his wife from the other side of herself. The dimension of privacy or secrecy in modern life, those fantasies kept out of circulation from the economies of goods, surfaces here to take its place among the products of culture.

Roberte's husband Octave conceives of a ritualistic erotic game that allows every male guest of the family to become Roberte's lover for one particular night. "Rules of the game, referred to in the text as the "Rules of Hospitality," are simple and easy to follow for the participants.[2] Each guest room has a list of regulations posted conveniently and accessibly just above the bed. They indicate that during the time frame allotted to the game, in which the guest has agreed to take part voluntarily, neither emotional sentiment nor moral values should be invoked in this temporary relationship. But the contrary is true, in fact: these rules open up a new dimension, for the reader as well as the participant, and must be kept apart from surrounding circumstances and codes of morality. Such games "enable the prostituted spouse to provide the husband with a multiplication of views and references, thus deepening the experience and knowledge of the wife seen through the eyes and caressed with the hands of many others" (Weiss, *Aesthetics* 33). At the same time, self-knowledge, arising from new chains of associations and recollections, is produced. Feelings of fidelity, infidelity, betrayal, jealousy, and so on are banned from the text as vestiges of the world outside the ritual, even though we know that this outside is always lurking at the surface of the inside, ready to cross over and back. The sexual relations between Roberte and her guests are solely for the purpose of Octave's plans; yet they are a vehicle through which she might render visible her own ghosts, phantoms, thoughts, and repressed desires. This might be called a freeing of her secret self, or even a contamination of innocence by knowledge.

The game, however, presents another dimension not noticed by Octave at first. Through ritualistic acts and simulacra or performances, Roberte manages to discover to her own satisfaction another set of experiences belonging to herself alone. While staged at the service of Octave, the game is instrumental in establishing Roberte's own knowledge as well. This outcome is not the one posited by Octave, and it does not appear to be of fundamental interest to him. Yet the reader may be encouraged by such counternarratives. Once again in her room, after an intense day of hard work in the Censorship Council headquarters where she has the task of editing her husband's writings, Roberte is able to explore herself in different ways. Exposing her nude body to the mirror on the wall, she proceeds through a series of narcissistic poses, all the while enjoying the spectacle of her own appearance. She delights in finding a multitude of angles from which to spy on the reactions of her own body as it changes and adapts to every move she commands it to make. Once divested of the tailored suit that acts as a straitjacket to any expression of personal feelings or emotion, while simultaneously laboring at the censorship of the feelings and language of others, Roberte is freed to explore new surfaces and dimensions of herself. Overcoming the gap between social readings of the body and interiorized judgments, Roberte produces a reconnection between inner and outer life that Octave himself cannot make. Despite his apparent power over her—and his rhetorics of power over all situations in which she participates—he is, in the end, uncertain. He must satisfy himself that he has not lost anything by constantly reiterating her obedience to his will in a sort of repetition compulsion of unresolved struggles.

We as readers and observers are witness to Roberte as she leaves one set of circumstances behind and delves into her own fantasies: "Roberte da libre salida al deseo a través de sus pensamientos, al tiempo que se deja fascinar en el espejo por su cuerpo" [Roberte gives free reign to desire through the vehicle of her thoughts, at the same time that she gives herself over to a fascination with her own body in the mirror] (García Ponce, *Teología* 26). Recalling that fascination is something overwhelming and at the same time charged with the horror of the unknown (the flip side of what Paz calls the "sublime"), these scenes can be read as remnants of previous sensations resuscitated through a visual encounter with the surfaces on which they have been played out. Several of the possibilities of who Roberte might be are dredged up, and Roberte, the severe aunt of nephew Antoine, gives life to the other Roberte, who is the embodiment of a free spirit. Her room becomes the site for rich imaginings in which her erotic fantasies are stirred and possessed by the characters she has read about during her workday. While Octave requires Roberte to respond to his imagined scenarios, Roberte incarnates what she reads on her own flesh. This inspiration comes from an internal response to that "cultural machinery" Castañeda finds in all textual representations of culture. For Roberte, there is an excess to be played out on her own skin, a circularity of erotics in which "la imaginación sale del cuerpo y se encuentra en el cuerpo al poseerlo, obligándolo a ceder ante ella" [the imagination leaves the body and finds itself in that body upon possessing it, obliging the body to cede to the desires of the imagination] (García Ponce, *Teología* 26). We must not lose sight of the fact that Roberte is incited to fantasy by the act of reading, by the very signs of language that our diary writers will leave behind in *De ánima*, as Inmaculada is incited by the books in her employer's library (and as García Ponce finds in his grandmother's library in Mérida).

What appears to be a displacement of Roberte is instead the acquisition or revelation of other dimensions whose residues form the sediment of who Roberte is at the moment and who she might turn out to be at any time. Octave and his prohibitions (the "Rules of Hospitality") are strangely unidimensional, therefore, since he is reduced to a voyeur of his own creation and condemned to keep offering Roberte to his guests. Appearances to the contrary, the tables are turned and the character Roberte as allegory is enriched by the experiences that look as though only Octave will benefit from. Roberte has become the embodiment of a monomania for her husband; Octave yearns to capture a totality of the fragments of his own identity by means of joining together the moments perceived through his acts of voyeurism. Roberte represents the search for the utopia of a unified subject for Octave, yet in the ritualized process she learns about herself much more than he ever will. What the reader is left with at the end of the story of Roberte and Octave is a thick, heavy, disarticulated, and fragmented diary whose confessions originate in the depths of obsession but spiral outward into unexpected dimensions. As a ruin, the diary lives up to Fuentes's image of the half-completed, half-dreamed allegorical artifice to be inhabited in the future by some unnamed and imagined guests. It is never a finished project and, as such, never ceases to produce new imagined scenarios and dramas. The architecture cannot speak once and for all; only the act of storytelling remains to revive the mourning of unfulfilled expectations.

Like Klossowski's novels, the text of *De ánima* is also the product of an obsession with knowledge. Like the cityscape which Benjamin ardently hopes will reveal its secrets from behind the attractive facades of modernity, Paloma both resists and promises. She is a labyrinth to be plumbed yet simultaneously an impossible collection of fragments that form an antidote to systematic thought. Both she and her diary are mere pieces of stories, aggregates of experiences, which cannot be transmitted in the traditional economy of everyday language. Instead, she is constructed and reconstructed from gestures, silences, and glances which offer the melancholic Gilberto a series of entryways into her psyche. Paloma becomes a palimpsest on which she and others can inscribe an intensity lost amid what Benjamin calls the "atrophied experience of modernity" (Gilloch, *Myth* 173). The fleeting glance, the chance word, might evoke a recollection of something hidden away from the drive for progress and innovation. The allegory of ritual, the appeal to a timeless time, allows for a site of rupture in the forward-looking discourses of politics and economics that rule in the 'real' world. Can any tradition survive intact, uncontaminated by these forces?

Each of the erotic games in *De ánima* is sutured onto the body of the text as a building block of the narrative, but the tenor of each diary changes dramatically in response to its author's perception. All is contingent on that momentary spark of relationship between individual and experience. This is due to different reasons or hidden motivations on the part of each character, but also on the intensity of the "tictonic" (Krell 7) or openness to the entrance of the uncanny into the territory of reason.

For Gilberto, as a professional writer, writing represents a ritualistic act of reinscribing the female body into a recognizable discourse. He affirms that the constantly renewed contact between the "pura superficie" [pure surfaces] of their bodies creates both constant discovery and everlasting insatiability: "no hay saciedad posible" [there is no absolute satisfaction possible] (46). He finds this to be true "por lo que descubro en su cuerpo, en la capacidad de ese cuerpo que parece encontrar su placer en el que da" [because of what I discover in her body, in the capacity of that body that seems to find its {own} pleasure in the pleasure it gives {others}] (46). The paradox of a lack, the inability to conclude the search for "saciedad," drives the ceremony into an unresolvable obsession.

Whatever is uncovered is never enough, but the hint of a redemption still lying amid the debris keeps them coming back in expectation and frustration (as a strangely positive motivating force). In Gilberto's diaries one can find the reenactment of the Klossowskian principle of the full communicability of the body expressed in opposition to the constraints imposed on it by any linguistic system; the spaces of their encounters are filled with the ruins we can mine for traces of those promising confrontations. The allegory of the body is again the site of antisystematic thought. As Weiss points out in his discussion of the repetition and codification of world, body, and language, "one is taught to express oneself in stereotypes, and then belie and obfuscate the multiplicity of the libido, of the body" (*Aesthetics* 36). To put this another way, Gilberto's writings are desperate attempts to recover that "multiplicity" as if it had disappeared naturally and not by ideological imposition of morality and virtue. At a loss, Gilberto turns to the reinvention of a language of desire which he feels he has lost but which Paloma has yet to acquire. (Let us recall the distinction between *Onda* and *Escritura* here in the satisfaction with linguistic communication for the first and the need for something indescribable and evocative in the second). This is put into concrete form when he speaks (or writes) of Paloma and the act of writing itself: "Desnudándola es siempre encontrarla de nuevo por primera vez" [Undressing her is always finding her once again for the first time] (52); the elements of discovery and innocence are always there in both instances—in the physical encounter and in the linguistic representation of it. The erotic encounter with the observed body is echoed in the writer's engagement with the evocative powers of language; both create a spark but both fail to live up to what he wishes them to be. Instead of the narrative and corporal completion of a story, the reader finds a montage of silences and voices, of dreams and desires, of Gilberto's absences and Paloma's presence. Gilberto's privileged gaze sparks a moment of personal epiphany: "sólo por Paloma puedo decir que conozco, al fin, el sentido de la contemplación dentro de la vida y en la realidad contingente" [only through Paloma can I say that I have come to know, at long last, the meaning of contemplation in life and in contingent reality] (182). The accidental or aleatory interpretation of experiences—the "contingency" of the quote—indicates that this is not a static model but one that will possibly never be repeated despite an obsessive urge to do so. He cannot guarantee what will happen in any circumstance, despite his desire to "know" why. Elsewhere in the novel, Gilberto believes he has reached the secret passage connecting the erotic with the power of artistic creation, all by means of Paloma once again: "En Paloma puedo contemplar lo que durante tanto tiempo he buscado . . . Yo conozco esa mirada. Se ve así cuando se quiere hacer una obra. Pero ella no va a permitir esa reducción. Su propia persona *es* la obra" [In Paloma I can contemplate what I have sought for such a long time . . . . I know that look. One gets that look when one wants to begin the creation of a work. But she isn't going to permit a reduction to that aspect alone. She herself *is* the work of art] (183–184; emphasis added). Paloma is the repository of both sensuality and innocence, of all of the dichotomies rolled into one. The work of art is a mirror, then, of a process and not a finished product. The "look" that appears on the face of the artist is merely the externalization of an uncommunicable experience equal to the enigmatic representation of Paloma.

The gaze, what García Ponce refers to as "la mirada profunda," does not stop with the mere act of looking per se. Throughout the story of Paloma and Gilberto, the woman's body is infinitely recreated in the eyes of others. From the novel that Gilberto has just published, a work inspired by Paloma's sexual experiences, a series of illustrations are created by a friend of the couple, images strikingly similar to those depicted in Klossowski's works. This friend is a man who has incidentally also had erotic encounters with Paloma, and who makes the claim that only through the physical possession of Paloma's body can he capture the essence of his subject in pictorial form. (We are already aware that she is less essence than allegory.) From the illustrated novel, the next step is a movie version of her story, a concept planned and plotted by Gilberto but discovered by Paloma only when as she reads his diary after his death. Unbeknownst to her, he has taken on the role of storyteller in her place. There she finds the script-in-progress, one written without her knowledge or direct input, but rather culled from his perceptions and impressions of her. As an homage to the memory of Gilberto, Paloma toys with the idea of playing herself in such a screen version of their lives; as such, she would come close to becoming a simulacrum of herself through the visions of another. It is not far-fetched to think of a script for modernity in similar terms. Whose version of the modern plays out on the stages of any community is a question of the

State's understanding of the project, or need for it. There are no absolute tales here but implicit questions of autochthony and authenticity.

In the end, Paloma's body is reproduced in a variety of media, from narrative to illustration to screenplay, each of which reflects an intimate vision of her but also one of its creator. But the use of the concept of simulacra in this text confronts what Klossowski proposes as ritual with what Baudrillard presents in his discussion of the same. In Klossowski's philosophy simulacra refer to a repetition of shadowy figures behind which there is always an ontological representation: "the simulacrum in its *imitative* sense is the actualization of something in itself incommunicable and unrepresentable: properly speaking, it is the phantasm in its obsessional constraint" (Klossowski qtd. in Weiss, *Perverse Desire* 122). However, for Baudrillard simulacra imply surface alone. One is an empty sign, the other is filled (albeit with secrecy and mystery). Baudrillard writes: "the euphoria of simulation [is] free from the anguish of the referential" (qtd. in Weiss, *Perverse Desire* 124). Any future repetitions of Paloma's photographs and films may be perceived as a phantasmagoric ceremony of attempting to represent the unrepresentable, of a desperate search to connect the phantasmagoric with some referent (for instance, patriarchy's control over the feminine, now convoluted and contaminated with Paloma's own desires). The "anguish of the referential" is what García Ponce has supposedly exiled from the reign of the aesthetic even as it haunts its surfaces and depths.

As a text anchored solidly in both verbal and visual schemas of representation, *De ánima* confronts the reader with that give-and-take of power and powerlessness adjudicated to the female form by many of the members of the Surrealist movement, and by the photographer Man Ray in particular. Both container of emancipatory myths and agent of their dispersal, women's bodies are sites of ruinous encounters that reproduce aporias for those who hold them in their gaze. In what the Surrealists see as the marvelous realm of the infinite reproducibility of the female form, the Surrealist aesthetic strives for the glorious depiction of an image of the ego and libido released from the hold of the subconscious. In the case of García Ponce, however, the duplication and reduplication of Paloma's body represents two facets of the same concept. First, the allegorical dispersal of images in García Ponce's text serves and fulfills Paloma's own narcissistic desire to be seen: "si Gilberto quiere exhibirme, lo ha logrado; pero si lo ha logrado es porque hay algo que me hace olvidar el hecho de que me estoy exhibiendo" [if Gilberto wants to put me on display, he has indeed achieved that; but if he has achieved that it is because there is something that makes me forget the fact that I am displaying myself] (222). Paloma assumes an innocence that is pure simulacra. She has been made to confront her own image in its appropriation by others, much as Zea finds Latin America has had to do in the eyes of Europe and, subsequently, the United States. As the "daughter" of Europe, as the almost-Surreal image of a dreamed promised land of utopian proportions, Latin American culture is exhibited and visualized by all but herself until she takes stock of this. Can she—America or Paloma—come to find herself amid what everyone else sees in her? These are the questions posed through the allegorical exhibition of her material form. (This is not the first time that the continent has been imagined as woman, of course.) Can Mexico become modern without being reduced to a simulacrum of something else (whether "shadowy ontology" or merely surface)? Perhaps modernity can only appear as ruin.

Secondly, this scenario is not just the locus for the representation of "women possessed by the demons [of the flesh], but also (and perhaps above all) of men possessed by the phantoms and images of the women they love, desire, or imagine. The Surrealist image [and, in this case, Paloma's] is not simply that of the body deformed by desire; it is also the sign of desire *informed* by the body" (Weiss, *Aesthetics* 94). In this more optimistic vein, imagination (desire) is therefore fueled by what it has before it, but it also projects images back on real (material) bodies of experience and on what has come before. Imagined and imaginary fulfillment, on the part of Mexican society as well as Gilberto, play out across the topographies on display. Animated by their observers, and those who believe they are in control of placing them in public view, Paloma (and, through her form, Latin American cultures) magnifies the cracks in the strata of cultural inheritance and national identity. Of the greatest myths underlying the State's vision of culture, as we have seen, is that of linearity and continuity. When Zea writes of Latin America acknowledging her autochthonous cultures, he uses a concept that we might apply to Paloma as well. Becoming conscious of one's own objectification, one can demand (or at least imply) some sort of reciprocal contribution even as one is still under scrutiny. Zea refers to being a "collaborator" (363) as Paloma comes of age (that is to say, realizes from her encounters with Gilberto that she has been part of something that he has orchestrated). It seems impossible to require of Paloma some linear narrative voice under these circumstances; it would also be a paradox when the only way to tell her story is through a montage of fragmentary experiences.

What García Ponce constructs, then, is a house of mirrors in which Paloma's desire, wrapped in the erotic edifice of her flesh, is provoked and reproduced incessantly from differing angles and perspectives. It is possible that the mechanical reproduction of desire—in the written text, in the photographs of her, on movie posters—hinges on the idea that the act of creation is a spectacle that is public in nature, or at least in the best of all possible worlds should be so, and that, as he writes in the introductory notes to Klossowski's *The Baphomet*, "language [whether written, photographic, or cinematic] allows the creation of a series of images that can be achieved by listening to that language . . . Anything can happen if language is capable of making it visible and, indeed, anything will happen until a new gnosis is created, a new form of knowledge that is in fact spectacle and as such offers itself to us" (García Ponce, Introduction xvii). Language and text, Paloma and her body: both are sources of potential knowledge. Paloma as such a spectacle, and therefore possibly new gnosis, is celebrated insistently in the novel through specularity. Her image is multiplied on a variety of different surfaces, for the consumption of those whose gaze is trained on them and for her own recognition. She is also problematized as a mysterious conduit through which we might get access to privileged "knowledge" that may not even be formulated into words. Beyond language, the power of erotics brings lost human traces back to the surface.

The gnosis pursued by García Ponce's characters, by Gilberto in particular, leads them to metaphysical inquiries about the nature of the work of art and its relation to everyday life situations, with special emphasis on the written artifact subsequently produced. But this metaphysical search distances itself from traditional speculations proposed by the idealist thinkers of Western philosophy.[3] Instead, it converges with Bataille's philosophy of the erotic universe of the *écriture corporelle* at the critical point where the obsessions that affect the human mind become forces to be embraced as life-affirming. Rather than repress them into hidden and mysterious sources of the creative process or scars on the psyche, García Ponce writes them visibly on the surfaces of Paloma, Inmaculada, and other characters. When discussing Bataille's concept of the "Pineal Eye" as a hidden organ through which to perceive traces of an "erotic universe," Stoekl observes that "the answer here is that at the *end* of reason, at the *end* of the Cartesian pineal gland (the supposed seat of consciousness) there is only orgasm and a simultaneous fall, a simultaneous death. Death and perversion do not take place in splendid isolation; instead, they are at the endpoint of the human" (xii). Modernity would keep these categories of rationality and excess discrete, yet they intersect in *De ánima* and *Inmaculada* in an attempt to reanimate a social vision of limits rather than ecstasies. If modernity demands separation (Habermas), then the rise and fall of "orgasm and death" as allegories of anti-modernity pervade García Ponce's texts.

In *De ánima* one can witness the transcription into language of what are often termed perverse actions such as sodomy, homosexuality, sadomasochistic rituals, and exhibitionism. But it is not just any language.

Rather, it is a type of signs endowed with a powerful force that Bataille defines as the power of transgression, even if, as the transgressive visual language of the Surrealists, it ends up being contained within aesthetics. The dispersal of erotics into the greater cultural discourse implies both integration (into the structures of power) and a confrontational display of difference which might continue to play out against and in the face of the permitted or the sacrosanct. Neither wins out in the texts of García Ponce but instead coexist on the cultural ruins of discourses of modern sexuality. Within the transgressive act, the process of writing "is a consecration undone: a transubstantiation ritualized in reverse where real presence [Paloma's physical body] becomes again a recumbent body [Paloma's frozen image] and finds itself led back to silence in an act of vomiting" (Foucault xxxvi). Transgression, it must be remembered, is composed of both a challenging of limits and the shadow of the presence of those limits; it is an act of freezing the image or representation in a ritual that is a constant reminder (or echo) of the real material body which, as Calefato reiterates, is always a movable edifice. A recovery of the materiality of the human body defies its reduction to social norms, economics, or as an object (victim) of repression and elimination by the State.

The characteristics which signal and identify Paloma's behavior ever since her early youth, when an effusion of sexual acts leads her to become the lover of her uncle, not only "engage" her with social norms but "disengage" her from being a passive object. Zea's language of engagement and disengagement may contribute to our understanding of her relationship both to her surroundings and to herself. As he writes, "We can no more deny that [European] culture than we can deny our parents. And just as we have a personality that makes us distinct from our parents without having to deny them, we should also be able to have a cultural personality without having to deny the culture of which we are children" (363). As part of an imagined community, of a social family, Paloma is on display for so many eyes and subject to so many discourses, yet she reveals more about them and about herself in the process of watching them watch her than one might find in a more directly analytical text. Discourses of the erotic carry within them, like America bears the seeds of Europe, an articulation of pleasurable expenditure and taboo. A moment first judged negatively by Paloma, her incestuous encounter with her uncle turns into something more when reencountered in the text of the diary. First a material act, then a written story, the incest winds up as tale retold out loud to Gilberto and somehow redeemed once it has become linguistic representation. Rereading the event and its participants, she emphasizes her complicity in this erotic pact with her unnamed uncle (94) and comes to a more positive, if not downright ecstatic, conclusion. This is not mere performance, however. Even before her initial recounting of this story to Gilberto, she concludes that it represents an act that she strongly *desires* to retell him, just as she speculated earlier that, likewise, "no hubiera sido difícil confesarle [al tío mismo] lo que pasó cuando, en su casa ya, le conté [a Gilberto] que mi tío había sido mi primer amante" [it would not have been difficult to confess to him {the uncle} what happened when, in Gilberto's house now, I told him {Gilberto} that my uncle had been my first lover] (95). The language of confession is, then, the language of desire; it reflects a personal need to recall an act of passion through the imagination, and a need to permit Gilberto to imagine his own version of events taken from hearing her story. The twice-told tale, the first time to Gilberto and later in her imagination to her uncle, is continually retold throughout her diary. The first transgression of her incestuous relationship breaks the rules of a generally recognized social taboo across Western society that forbids the sexual relations among close members of the same family or group, a phenomenon discussed by both Freud in *Totem and Taboo* and Bataille in *Erotism*. The subsequent recreations (simulacra) of transgression with close friends and acquaintances reinforce an emancipatory act of revelation through language, both a simulacrum that reveals an originary story and one that (with Baudrillard) recreates the surface image.

What might be read as so-called perversion in Paloma points toward other realms of erotic experience (the exploration of what earlier was referred to as her innocence). For this character, the intimate physical contact with her uncle appears to be devoid of any guilt or frustration, much as the "Rules of Hospitality" forbid such vestiges of traditional morality. On the contrary, Paloma understands this potentially problematic action not as a sexual act aimed at human reproduction, nor as proper social behavior, but instead within the general category of ubiquitous erotic activity that confirms her presence. This activity, explains Bataille, "unlike simple sexual activity, is a psychological quest independent of the natural goal: reproduction and the desire for children" (*Erotism* 11). Throughout her life, Paloma's body becomes the necessary referent (and domicile) for her discovery of that fundamental quest delineated by Bataille. The search turns inward as the constraints of the social norm close in on the door to her corporeal edifice. In one of the earliest entries in her diary, we observe Paloma's awareness of this tempting encounter.

> Siento mi cuerpo igual que lo sentía cuando después repasaba una y otra vez con mi tío cómo había empezado todo entre nosotros. No puedo reprocharle nada porque sólo le agradezco que me hiciera descubrirlo *fuera de cualquier regla*.

> [I feel my body just as I did when I went over again and again with my uncle how everything between us had begun. I can't reproach him for anything because I can only be grateful to him for making me discover it {my body} *outside any rules*.] (29)

It is questionable whether there is a space "outside any rules" of society, of course, but Paloma is enticed to think so perhaps as any citizen might be tempted to imagine a world beyond the 'real' one surrounding us. She seems to be under the spell of societal norms—by thanking her uncle for his 'gift' to her—even as she formulates the idea that this relationship will somehow free her. Perhaps this is the "fascination and horror" to which Paz refers, the enticement of experiencing what may end up provoking moral censure. The same paradox of the Surrealists—that aesthetic experimentation frees the social body—is written on Paloma and her story for she uses the language of taboo to express her liberation. (Her liberation to become the erotic partner of her uncle might conjure up other notions, nevertheless.) But she turns the issue of any possible guilt into a rhetorical question for her own subsequent consideration: "¿Culpable de tener diecisiete años y ser tan bella, de conocer mi desnudez y saber buscar mi propio placer?" [Guilty of being seventeen and being so beautiful, of knowing my own nudity and being able to seek my own pleasure?] (29). The implied answers are evident—that adolescents have no guilt, that she is just playing her role, that women are disposed and predisposed to find themselves through the guidance of an older man.

The story is not new for we find it in Klossowski, in Tanizaki, and in so many other places across modern cultures. But its reiteration by García Ponce's characters is evidence of its relegation to ruin by the time we reach the 1980s. The sexual relations with her uncle do not fade into memory or even the bliss of forgetfulness but instead reappear in Paloma's life in two forms. The first is as a primal memory that reignites the feelings of pleasure once again each time she reads her own diary (the language rekindles the experience in the flesh even as the wick of the storyteller burns down with the passing years of her life). Then, there are the infrequent but persistent encounters with her uncle, episodes that survive intact despite her marriage (and later divorce) and a long series of occasional lovers, including Gilberto in the present. If Paloma is the vehicle for men to reach out for redemption, they are no less for her. The double helix of this structure creates a constant reengagement with the contradictions that keep the taboo alive in the collective cultural memory. Perhaps in one of the instances or another the uncanny tale will finally burst into pieces and fly off into so many directions that there will never be enough to rearticulate again. In the meantime, Paloma will turn into Inmaculada in the third panel of the triptych in yet another twist on the allegories of (cultural) repression, desire, emulation, and the anguish of time lost.

For Paloma, a return to her native place, to her parents' home in the Mexican provinces, is a willful return to an original place and time in which some spark might incite a revelation. It is a full circle back to the source or sacred place where sexual energy purportedly runs freely, unrestricted by social taboos, and where she consequently renews her incestuous relationship with her uncle. Following the Sadeian philosophy in which incest and prostitution form the two fundamental pillars of transgression, García Ponce presents her acts of incest as a pure form of human activity, one still uncontaminated by cultural taboos and therefore of the greatest innocence. But the reader is aware that innocence carries within it the opposite: knowledge (not perversion nor taboo but consciousness), and that "immaculate" purity is already a social construction.

> La tentación al incesto es considerada así como una inclinación natural originalmente, producto de la sexualidad pura, indiferenciada, que no reconoce limitaciones hasta que éstas le son impuestas al hombre por una fuerza exterior y con la ayuda de la violencia, para que empiece a gozar, gracias a ellas, de los beneficios de la civilización y el progreso, y de la maldición de la moral.
>
> [The temptation of incest is considered something like a natural inclination originally, a product of pure, undifferentiated sexuality, one which recognizes no limits until they are imposed on man(kind) by an exterior force and with the help of violence, so that he may begin to enjoy, thanks to these limits, the benefits of civilization and progress, and the curse of morality.] (García Ponce, 151)

Freud's notion of unrestricted sexuality is evident in the first part of this statement, but there is more of a connection back to our discussion of modernity explicit in the last part. "Differentiation" of what is permitted and what is not comes into being with the moral categories of the modern. The "exterior force" of violence noted in the last lines sounds much like the echoes of the State in the background of *Crónica* as the immigrants to the capital make their way through the labyrinth of the city's streets. Coming from the provinces, one must move into the spaces of both domestic and cultural structures if one wishes to belong to what the myth of the city promises. The "progress" and "civilized" society of Mexico City demand morality. The door to the city is, like Pandora's box, a portal to good and evil which are, one is told, easily distinguished. Paloma is placed in the position of seeing this evidence but finding that it recalls, in a Benjaminian sense, something long suppressed in her and in a society that is emerging. We might find, of course, that the need for the uncle to bring it out is perplexing and troublesome rather than natural. If the family epic is being replaced by the story of the nation, then those vestiges (or ruins) of the past must be embodied in lost and unrecoverable family relations as a transgression of modernity.

Paloma's family home becomes a reservoir for her anxieties and mixed feelings about pleasure and about herself. But in the end, each time she sets foot in the family's hacienda she reenacts the so-called ancient ritual, one apparently forgotten (or repressed) but nevertheless still present deep inside her psyche. Her journey back is a return to bodily pleasure and that alone, the joy of the physical body. Her inner feelings and experiences remain separated, far away from the physical act being consummated. She writes in her diary that

> lo que es seguro mientras hacíamos el amor y en todo momento *yo fui yo misma. Era yo la que gozaba* . . . Después, en la cama, a mi lado, mi tío volvió a ser el intruso que había sido cuando lo vi entrar al cuarto. "¿Qué ganaste?" le pregunté. "*Te he tenido como antes*. Lo sabes tan bien como yo. No necesitamos ni siquiera hablar de eso. Lo hemos sentido los dos," contestó. "*No niego que lo he sentido; pero no me has tenido en ningún momento*" le dije.
>
> [what is certain is that while we were making love and at every moment *I was myself. It was I who enjoyed the pleasure* . . . Later, in bed, at my side, my uncle once again became the intruder he had been when I saw him enter the room. "What did you get out of this?" I asked him. "*I have possessed you like before*. You know as well as I do. We don't even have to talk about that. Both of us felt it," he answered. "*I don't deny that I felt it; but you never possessed me, not even for a moment*," I told him.] (92; emphasis added)

The lack of the need to put things into words—"We don't even have to talk about that"—or perhaps the fear of doing so since that would transcend the singular time of the event, signals a crucial element in the retelling of this story. Whose words are they? The uncle tells her what she does not need to say, but he cannot feel or tell what she finds in this experience. As a strange (uncanny?) possession alongside her own body, this language belongs to her alone. She constantly stresses the fact that "yo fui yo misma," [I was always myself] and not the object of the other (the uncle) in her recounting of those moments. From adolescence through the last entries in her diary when she has become a movie star, a woman representing *herself* in a variety of versions on stage and screen, Paloma's behavior regarding her frustrated marriage and subsequent lovers shows an unmistakable tendency toward what Bataille calls a festive praise of baseness, eroticism, and perversion.[4] Although it might appear contradictory, this is a celebration of innocence. Paloma reaffirms this quest for knowledge in one of her entries in the diary:

> Sola conmigo misma, prefiero repasar una y otra vez mis sensaciones, siempre las mismas y siempre diferentes. *Saber que puedo sentir que estoy enamorada como suponía que lo estaba de mi tío*, porque alguien—cualquiera—me lleva al reconocimiento de este cuerpo que ahora solamente espera. *Las mujeres no somos más que nuestro cuerpo*. En él empezamos y en él terminamos, él provoca y guarda nuestros sentimientos.
>
> [Alone with myself, I prefer to examine my sensations over and over, always the same and always different. *To know that I can feel that I am in love, as I supposed I was with my uncle*, because someone—anyone—helps me reach an understanding {acknowledgment} of this body that now only waits. *We women are nothing more than our body*. In it {the body} we begin and end, it stimulates and stores our sentiments.] (30–31; emphasis added)

The recollection of sentiment supercedes the actions themselves, according language greater potential power over the representation of an event that is "always the same and always different." Appearing among the pages of a diary that then forms part of a novel, this recognition empowers both writers. The same thing holds true for the empowerment of the woman, for even if it sounds like she is reduced to "nothing more than" physicality, we already are aware that this physical site is not, as some might have it, just a "house of the soul" (Krell 4) but a shifting architecture of mastery and loss. Studied more closely, this crossing over of boundaries shows signs of the Dionysiac frenzy expounded by Nietzsche in *The Will to Power*. His description of the intensity of this eroticism coincides with Paloma's reaffirmation of her acts as intensely frenzied moments.

> The states in which we infuse a transfiguration and fullness into things and poetize about them until they reflect back our fullness and joy in life: sexuality; intoxication; feasting; spring; victory over an enemy; mockery; bravado; cruelty; the ecstasy of religious feeling. *Three elements principally: sexuality, intoxication, cruelty*—all belonging to the oldest festal joys of mankind, all also preponderate in the early 'artist.' (Nietzsche 421)

Nietzsche pulls into the mix the very two same ingredients we have established as the significant layers of engagement for character and for writer: language and representation ("poetizing" about events), and the admixture of sexuality, violence, and joy in the psyche. Paloma's joyous free spirit amid the ruins of Mexico's bourgeoisie, with an unrestricted expenditure of libidinal energy, appears repeatedly in the entries in her diary. Her sexual encounters with various lovers are almost like a frenetic struggle between two planets as their orbits intersect. In these encounters, a release of energy is created by two bodies, provoking an eclipse that, in the words of Bataille, is the point of impact or "blind moment [a black spot in the erotic universe] when eroticism attains its ultimate intensity" (*Erotism* 40). Such a confrontation occurs, for instance, when the bodies of Paloma and film director Mario Guerra rejoice in the "absoluta alegría" [absolute pleasure] (189) of their act of self-definition and absolution. They become figures of innocence imbued with knowledge through erotic intensity (thereby creating an intersection of gnosis and eros). Just maybe the real innocent, however, is the narrator who imagines such a delirious and ecstatic moment free from all bonds and ties.

In the dyad established between Paloma and each of her lovers-in-turn—the uncle, the husband Armando, Gilberto, for instance—the triad of elements which composes the "festal joy" proposed by Nietzsche resurfaces incessantly. This creates a convoluted territory in open defiance of a society conditioned by the arresting and harnessing of both libidinal expenditure and economic consumption for the benefit of society. Both production and reproduction serve the ends of the State. In the words of Roland Barthes, expenditure is a force or strength which cohabits with economics in the nucleus of modern society and which presents two simultaneous tendencies. Barthes clarifies the duality as follows: "On the one hand, a bourgeois economy of repletion; on the other, [the transgressive force of passion in] a perverse economy of dispersion, of waste, of frenzy" (Barthes 84–86). If all energy is not placed at the service of the project of modernity, then these characters perform a spectacular display of the ruins on which the modern is built (the sacrifices of personal joy, and of "festive" display.)

Like Klossowski's and Bataille's heroines Roberte and Madame Edwarda,[5] Paloma is engaged in an exaltation of the libido along the lines of their intoxicated and obsessive quest to combat the stultifying world of reason and bourgeois social order. The satiation and abundance of bourgeois society is counteracted by the obsession with what Bataille calls "the notion of expenditure" (116). About halfway through the text, Paloma states "Si hay alguna institución especialmente ridícula, esa es el matrimonio. Hay que ser siempre amantes y vivir en la irregularidad" [If there is one especially ridicuous institution it is that of marriage. You must always be lovers and live outside the norm] (139). Her so-called perverse gestures and actions already described obey a situational logic. These are the physical signs of a struggle, a refusal to be appropriated by the universal domain of the bourgeois world and its morality, that instead substitutes in its place the decision to assert the self: "Cuando pienso en cualquiera de los amantes que tuve al llegar de San Luis, no estoy pensando en verdad en ellos sino en lo que fueron para mí y no los busco a ellos, sino a mí misma" [When I think about any one of the lovers that I had after I arrived from San Luis, I am not really thinking about them but about what they were for me, and I am not looking for them but for myself] (72). The figures of these lovers do not exist in and of themselves, but only in her perception of them as vehicles for her own self-realization. Only under these circumstances can one attempt to understand and contextualize Paloma's behavior, since it otherwise might be read as degenerating into facile prostitution if viewed according to traditional rules of bourgeois conduct. Paloma thus represents, for the storyteller, a contradiction at the heart of the tale he wishes to tell. She is not quite the embodiment of what he wishes to retain despite so many social changes, but he has found no alternative.

Seen from this perspective, Gilberto's monomania regarding Paloma's body can be taken as an allegory. For him, the textual geography of her desires can be comprehended only through the act of Bataillean expenditure.[6] But this dispersion, when "continuously affirmed, without limit, . . . [gives rise to] . . . that brilliant and rare thing which is called exuberance and which is equal to Beauty . . . , the exuberance of the child whose narcissistic scope and multiple pleasure nothing (as yet) constrains" (Barthes, *A Lover's Discourse* 85). This opens up social restraints and limits, thereby allowing some internal force to run free in opposition to the constraints of modern culture. The "exuberant beauty" of Paloma assumes a new form in Gilberto's writing. Exuberance—the amorous exuberance of Barthes; the festal and intoxicating joy of Nietzsche; the uninhibited expenditure of Bataille—in *De ánima* is the affirmation of life within death, the positive act stemming from a melancholia of vision that resuscitates a fear of extinction, blindness, and cosmic absence. It is a material reaffirmation of the individual subject. As Zea sees it, this does not resolve issues posed by the contradictions of culture but rather recalls the inescapable problems of expressing them. Like Paloma's material human body, and Bataille's and Nietzsche's celebration of such, experience and its articulation do not have to be at odds. When Zea considers the task of the philosopher in Latin America, he concludes that "[he] does not have to give up being a philosopher to face the many problems of a reality different from theory" (370). What modernity might wish to inscribe on Paloma, or Europe desires to erect in the Americas, are part of the monuments that a writer must evoke around the edifices of real, lived bodies. Certainly, Paloma is only a character. But she herself represents a ruined form of such an encounter. She is neither "pathological" (Bataille, *Visions* 116) nor relegated to social "violence" as a result of erotic pleasure; her survival more or less intact goes against the expected consequences of her actions.

When everything in the diaries has been written, when all imaginable physical and erotic experiences have been performed, there survives the idea that the act of writing itself provides an amorous feeling and that writing is an act of construction and destruction. At the end of the novel, the reader discovers that all of the erotic games, all the simulacra and performances, all the acts of voyeurism, are powerful efforts to defeat death and disembodiment, while at the same time reaffirming life through ecstatic pain and aesthetic creation. Like Octave in Klossowski's tale, Gilberto is dying. In his attempt to stave off that menacing specter and continue on, Gilberto finds that he actually assumes the persona of pain for at least through it the body feels something other than paralysis or anesthesia. The two become fused into one living, suffering body: "Son [los dolores] una constante compañía que llega a pertenecerme. Cuando descubro su alejamiento, de pronto, en cualquier momento, siento como si me hubiera abandonado una parte de mi propia persona. . . . La enfermedad. No tiene lugar en la memoria. Es una pura sensación. Llega hasta nosotros y de inmediato se convierte en parte de nosotros" [They {the pains} are constant companions that end up belonging to me. When I discover they have gone away, suddenly, at any given time, I feel as if a part of my own being had abandoned me. . . . Illness. It has no place in memory. It is pure sensation. It comes to us and suddenly becomes part of us] (224). Pain and passion inhabit the same physical space of the human body; they are not rationalized away as modern science might have it, nor are they intellectualized through language, but are experienced and narrated as facets of material life in modern times.

At the end of García Ponce's novel, Paloma as the excessive spirit of experience is the one who performs an act of closure on Gilberto's diary. The three texts, the two diaries, and the entire novel end with her last entry after his death. She concludes the narrative by stating that "ahora yo escribo en tu cuaderno la que también será la última anotación del mío" [now I write in your notebook the last entry, which is also the last entry of my own diary] (232). With this act, with these words of finality and closure, the final copula beyond death has been achieved in the written body of the text. Yet reading and rereading live on, potentially ecstatic experiences provoked by the ruins (death) of the diarists themselves.

Through his textual confrontation of cultural remnants, whether from the erotic narratives of Tanizaki or the transgressions of so-called civilized sexuality by the incestuous relationships taken from Klossowski, García Ponce has created in *De ánima* a clear example of what Fuentes has described as an attempt to "fill in" the cultural voids of his own tradition (MacAdam 14), given up as sacrifices to the discourse of the modern nation. Or, better still, we might take them as floors of that building-in-progress on the promissory horizon of modernity. The hidden or dark eros of Paloma's psyche fills in what the light areas of the cultural chiaroscuro omit or repress; they also recall an unfamiliar Europe slighted by nationalist tradition. García Ponce's characters and their tales are not copies of originals, either lost or on display in cultural museums, but innovative and evocative works in their own right, not to be measured against the aesthetics of Asian or European cultures, but instead as monuments to the sacrificial acts required by modern times. To reduce his novels to pornography, as some critics have done, is to relegate them to a realm of unidimensional reading. Beyond marginality or titillation, appropriate for the most popular of cultural artifacts, they would have no "afterlife." In fact, they would fulfill the most perfunctory of roles in an economy of consumption which his characters constantly and consistently reject.

CHAPTER SIX

Modernity, Contingency, Compensation

In *Consequences of Enlightenment* Anthony Cascardi reexamines the relationship of the work of art to the society that produces it under the aegis of contemporary theory's indebtedness to notions inherited from the Enlightenment. In particular, he addresses the difficulties and challenges of modernity understood "in the manner of Baudelaire, as having a fundamentally aesthetic and non-transcendent basis. Modernity names the epoch of the 'transitory' and the 'fugitive' (Baudelaire), of 'revolutions, contestations, assassinations, explosions, and impatiences' (Barthes). It is the space of the politics of antagonism, of the unsuturable whole, of a fundamental contingency" (220). He goes on to clarify that, in this sense, "the 'modern' does not stand opposed to 'ancient'" (220), but instead signals a rupture in the perception of the temporal, what we have seen in Habermas as an "exaltation of the present" and a consciousness of nothing beyond or behind the surface (including any measure of the historical). One is tempted to conjure up Benjamin's Angel of History as our witness to the pile of rubble gathering at that point where the debris of the transitory and the fugitive accumulates: the "unsuturable" present. This image of "unsuturability" and rupture has pervaded our discussion so far, be it in the aesthetics of the textual body (Benjamin's convolutions and fragments) or in the echoes of voices and stories intermingling among sirens, noises, and other disembodied sounds of alarm. In addition, when we find no "oppositional" configuration between ancient and modern, we articulate yet another juxtaposition of remnants, neither break nor new beginning but an overwhelming consciousness of time (as Habermas has stated). The lengthy nature of his works of fiction attests to García Ponce's measure of time as 'accumulation,' not a coherent narrative reflective of, say, a national story on the order of the traditional nineteenth-century novel.

By focusing on his later essays in *Camera Lucida*, Cascardi places Roland Barthes in line with Baudelaire through a consideration of the photographic image as an emblematic site of the modern. For Barthes the photo is both object and loss, a piece of paper that ages and fades as does the scene it reproduces; neither original nor copy remain but as remnants if at all. Not a transcendent "communion with the dead" (Cascardi 220), Barthes finds in photography the ruin as Benjamin encounters it in the mineral images of Marseilles and the stones of the city streets and alleys of the French capital. The seemingly fixed image, for Barthes, becomes enigmatic for it encompasses both moving and static notions of time.

> It flourishes a moment, then ages. . . . Attacked by light, by humidity, it fades, weakens, vanishes; there is nothing left to do but throw it away. Earlier societies managed so that memory, the substitute for life, was eternal and that at least the thing which spoke Death should be itself immortal: this was the Monument. But by making the (mortal) photograph into the general and somehow natural witness of 'what has been,' modern society has renounced the Monument. A paradox: the same century invented History and Photography. But History is a memory fabricated according to positive formulas, a pure intellectual discourse which abolishes mythic Time; and the photograph is a certain but fugitive testimony; so that everything, today, prepares our race for this impotence: to be no longer able to conceive *duration*, affectively or symbolically. (Camera 93–94)

Barthes's investment of the photograph with the loss of permanence, the absence of the past, the image to be discarded as it fades and decays, imbues it with all of the attributes of the ruin. If what has been officially proclaimed as "History" or the official story (of a person, of a nation, of a community) becomes in modernity "revolutions, contestations, assassinations, explosions" (Barthes, *Camera* 94), then can the Monument exist? How might a State, proclaiming itself modern at all costs, erect Monuments to its own contingency?

The gap between the perception of continuity (of History, of the nation) and sheer singularity or particularity evokes the space in which García Ponce and his generation found themselves after 1968 and into the difficult political climate of the 1970s and 1980s. Theirs is the point of intersection of two losses: the original object and the one that has kept it alive (even though now materially ceased and deceased) for a fleeting moment. When both the portrayed and the portrayal—the event or scene or personage, and the photo itself (that is the "fugitive testimony," the aesthetic representation)—fade away, modernity has drawn its finest dilemma. Contemplation of the ruins of this double 'disaster' can only lead to nostalgia (aesthetically pointless, as Benjamin has shown) or mourning. This sense of mourning is doubly dark: it elicits a melancholic vision of the individual's loss of the past and of a preservation of the images of that past through any means. So both story and teller converge in a space of absence. Immutability and eternity are things now lost as well, disappeared along with some sort of permanent rules that art need follow. In modern times, art is instead "performance and practice" (Cascardi 247), not codification into theory. One could hardly create a Monument from "performance," given its emphasis on the moment, but one might truly mourn it by ritually reproducing an allegorical encounter with absence. That absence, that black hole as it were, is the storyteller's monument to the ruin. In philosophical terms, Cascardi finds that Nietzsche and Kant "are equally drawn to a romantic hope in the power of human passion to fill the world with a purposiveness it has lost and to the modernist awareness that the world is ultimately no more determinate than our passionate investments in it" (265). Modernity turns our focus from an innate meaning of things to total contingency based on human intervention.

This innocent hope, joined with the irony of a desperate desire for awareness, is where we encounter García Ponce's engagement with modernity and its darkest effects. He sets up this confrontation in the very title of the novel *Inmaculada o los placeres de la inocencia* [Inmaculada or the Pleasures of Innocence] wherein absoluteness (immaculateness, innocence) meets pleasures (affect, the body) on the grounds of the cultural and aesthetic ruin. In his characters' "salvific relation with an object irrevocably lost" (Avelar 3), the writer posits two immediate scenarios of mourning: the return of a woman to a relationship long broken asunder to find few if any traces of herself in it (except in the reiterative and ceremonial sense of a recovery of the dead), and the return to a place that can no longer be reclaimed. Inmaculada has lost both a material place (her ancestral home) to fugitive time and a notion of herself as part of a "whole" schema into which she might "suture" her life and experiences. Each has gone the way of the Barthesian photographic image. The compensation or substitution for such a loss is, for Inmaculada, something that (like the fragmented sense of History) is neverending and never settled. The debt with her lost past is, as Idelber Avelar writes, "never simply completed. It is in this sense, then, that one speaks of the interminability of mourning work: mourning necessarily poses itself an unrealizable task. Unlike the replacement of old by new commodities, the substitution proper to the work of mourning always includes the persistence of an unmourned, unresolved, remainder" (5). The temporal measure of mourning is, thus, immeasurable and stagnant, but monumental is its overwhelming observance of rites that conjure up what cannot really appear or be resolved. The "remainder" of the provincial bourgeoisie is evident in the traces left in Inmaculada's name and in her impossible task of returning to the lost past. The same holds true for the act of telling her story and finding a resolution.

In his groundbreaking study of postdictatorial Latin American cultures, Avelar calls upon Benjamin's concepts of allegory and mourning to elucidate the relationship between before (State dictatorships) and after (market dictatorships), but also between the just-before and the ruins that come after the fall. He recounts that, for Benjamin, "[i]n much Baroque drama the final condensation of meaning around a corpse imposes upon the audience a pressing consciousness of its own transitoriness and mortality" (Avelar 3). The "corpse" might be an allegorical figure for society, for its cultural products in decay, or for the human body without history. Avelar continues his argument with the assertion that "[t]he mournful subject who confronts the loss of a loved being displays a special sensibility toward objects, articles of clothing, former possessions, anything that might trigger the memory of the one who died" (3–4). Yet, as Cascardi finds in Baudelaire and Barthes, when those same objects afford no end to mourning, such a rescue cannot occur. Affect is left without object; melancholy condenses into the eyes of one who has lost even the object of his gaze in the yellowed, crumbling photographic paper. The corpse is our allegory of the ruin we have been exploring; it is the leftovers of life or the afterlife of the human body. And, as Habermas proposes and Avelar emphasizes, allegory is imbued with an extremely acute sense of time: time that fades, is discarded, comes back to haunt. Avelar writes that "the allegorical temporality of mourning clings to the past in order to save it, even as it attempts ultimately to produce an active forgetting of it" (4). Caught between the salvation of the past (left only in the problematic remnants of darkened and shadowy memory) and a contradictory desire for modernity, narrators reiterate, obsess, return in circularity, but do not resolve. So García Ponce's narratives wind around stories and ghostly images, but they are circular, spiraling around but never reaching an ending or an answer (either by absolute recovery or by permanent loss). Thus it is that the triptych's panels can be repositioned time and again, but their images never quite satisfy the redemptive searcher.

García Ponce revisits the times of his grandparents in an essay entitled "Otras voces, otros ámbitos" [Other Voices, other Environments] and enumerates all of the lacks characterizing them. 'Time,' as he obliquely refers to it, appears as if it were suspended, neither retrievable nor absolutely disappeared. It rushes toward him, the paralyzed observer of a scene, only to rush away into nothingness.[1] While he cites sunrise and sunset as the natural beginnings and endings of days, he cannot measure time in other ways except in terms of a cycle of life and death. There are befores and afters but, like Barthes's photographs, all fades away to haunt the 'now' time and again. The corpse of the past never dies; it lingers on for the melancholic, enticing but elusive.

> Cuando nació la abuela no había luz eléctrica; cuando nació mi padre no había automóviles; cuando nací yo no había bomba atómica ni televisión; cuando nació mi hija el hombre no había salido al espacio; cuando nació mi nieta ya había ocurrido la catástrofe de Chernobyl. Uno no puede dejar de interrogarse: ¿se puede o se debe estar contra el progreso? Yo estoy contra el progreso emotivamente; sin embargo nuestra impaciencia cuando se va la luz, cosa que ocurre con mucha frecuencia en el Coyoacán donde vivo, es angustiosa.
>
> [When my grandmother was born, there were no electric lights; when my father was born there were no automobiles; when I was born there was no atomic bomb or television; when my daughter was born humans had not gone into space; when my granddaughter was born, the castastrophe of Chernobyl had occurred. One cannot help but ask: can or should one be against progress? I am against progress on an emotional level; but our impatience when the lights go out, something that happens frequently in the part of Coyoacán where I live, is distressing.] (25)

Modernity's myth of progress is reduced to the "explosions and impatiences" of Barthes's assessment. Do electric lights, cars, television, or outer space have meaning or are they just a string of events and accomplishments that hold no connection among themselves? Are they Monuments to some project or just "explosions" of science, technology, or futile human endeavor? And even more pertinent to our discussion, how does García Ponce's "emotional" reaction to these occurrences translate into the work of art? Public monuments are erected with every *sexenio*, as we have seen. But those "explosions and impatiences," those "revolutions and assassinations" that do not get memorialized fade as do the photographs. Chernobyl is a time-marking event, but so are 1968, rises and falls in political fortunes, the fading away of familial lineages, or the waning of a human body wasted by disease. How can one mark such catastrophes except "emotivamente"? Perhaps this term conveys some sense of such a melancholic vision in its reference to "distress" and disorientation. Perhaps the sporadic eruptions of progress produce the aporias of their demise (in the case of Chernobyl, for instance). One answer seems to lie in Benjamin's "memory-as-theater" cited by Avelar and not "memory-as-instrument" (10). Trapped in the artwork amid a loss (if also potential recollection) and a spectacle, allegory comes alive to perform the mourning rites. And, once again, for García Ponce the allegorical comes alive in human form, in particular in the shape of the woman.

Barthes begins his "Reflections on Photography" with a short passage on his reaction to studying a 1852 photograph of Napoleon's youngest brother, Jerome. His noted "amazement" (perhaps like Paz's "bewitchment") is not that of meeting the eyes of the young man in the image, but the fact that "I am looking at eyes that looked at the Emperor" (3). What he sees is an absence, a body not there except in the implication of a gaze captured on photographic paper. The eyes are the vehicle, not the end of the amazement; they perform a connection with the past but do not lead back to it literally. (In other words, they mark a desire but also mark its inaccessibility.) The "desire" that Barthes finds kindled, that "particular, irreducible, pleasure and pain that the object may call forth" (Cascardi 219), unleashes not just a momentary encounter but the beginning of an evocatory ritual. As Barthes writes, "What the Photograph reproduces to infinity has occurred only once: the Photograph mechanically repeats what could never be repeated existentially. In the Photograph, the event is never transcended for the sake of something else: the Photograph always leads the corpus I need back to the body I see, . . . in short, what Lacan calls the *Tuché*, the Occasion, the Encounter, the Real, in its indefatigable expression" (4). One is reminded of Benjamin's well-known essay on "The Work of Art in the Age of Mechanical Reproduction" with its discussion of the aura that might be resuscitated in the moving image of cinema if not in the static one of the photograph. As Barthes returns to revisit the image of the Emperor's brother and the faded likeness of his own mother, so García Ponce produces reiterated ceremonies using Inmaculada, ones which embody "the tireless repetition of contingency" (Barthes, *Camera* 5) as desired compensation for what whirls by "at the very heart of the moving world" (Barthes, *Camera* 6). Both Inmaculada and those who gaze at her create the contingency of a momentary reprieve from the irremediable pull of History and 'progress' into the unknowable future.

Cascardi notes that the photographed image of Barthes's dead mother never finds its way to the pages of the text of the essay. It is encountered in words, in affect, but not in material presence. At the heart of Barthes's essays, then, is something evoked through mourning but something we cannot see with our own eyes. As the author rummages through his mother's desk, hoping without hope to "find" her (*Camera* 63) among her belongings, little meets his expectations (which are unclear to him anyway) except that "neither as a photographic performance nor as a living resurrection of the beloved face" (*Camera* 64) does any image work for him.

"History," he concludes, separates him from that recovery, from that life. Cascardi indicates that these photos serve as "triggers" (219) for Barthes, as sparks of contingency that provoke some form of affect beyond mere recognition. All disappoints him, but he continues to leaf through the objects in his search for a relationship now lost to the image (as ruin).

Curiously, and of importance to our act of storytelling, the third-person omniscient narrative voice that opens *Inmaculada* presents the reader with a circumstance similar to that of Barthes. As a young girl, the character Inmaculada visits her maternal grandmother and, in the course of eavesdropping on a conversation, discovers that the person Inmaculada has always thought to be her mother is, in fact, a stepmother. The reader is already acquainted with the 'true' version of events, that she is "la última de siete hermanos . . . cuya madre murió pocos días después de que naciera ella, tal vez por su culpa" [the last of seven children . . . whose mother died a few days after she was born, {and} perhaps she is to blame] (8). Growing up under an illusion, surrounded by an absence compensated for by her family with an alternative story and a performance by her older sister Rosario who steps in to care for her, she now has to confront a different History. Always dressed in white, always singled out as the youngest and the one named by her grandmother (and visibly marked by her name), Inmaculada is suddenly faced with what her sister suggests by the words "mal" and "malo" (13–14): an innocent child, spotlessly whitened by her given name, meets up with the potential personification of good and evil. Can her father be a 'bad' person? Can her (dead) mother be substituted by a stand-in? Rosario affirms that the lie is not an evil deed, that her father is not bad, and that the woman who is not their mother is not a wicked person. Each has been cast in a role in the family drama that plays out the performance noted above by Barthes in the case of his mother. Although sporadic episodes show conduct from her father that might be less than fatherly, Inmaculada dwells less on these fragments than on her absent mother. She is driven to convert this overheard story into what she calls "conocimiento" [{firsthand} knowledge] (14), and accompanies her grandmother and sisters to the cemetery to find something material to link to her. In *De ánima*, Gilberto seeks knowledge through Paloma, as Inmaculada is motivated to 'find out' about herself through her dead mother. Like Barthes's rummaging through the ruins of his mother's desk, Inmaculada enters the family crypt to fill in what is missing. She will base her storytelling on the ruins she finds there.

After that short visit to the burial site, Inmaculada returns to the family home to study a photograph of her mother. This is a gift from her grandmother, a monument to her act of "conocimiento," but at the same time a sign of unknowing because the person in the image is unrecoverable. Inmaculada cannot even find the will to pronounce the word "mother," and she does not know what to experience each time she looks at the photo: "debía significar todo pero no lograba sentir qué era eso" [it should mean everything {to her} but she just couldn't feel what that might be] (15). She has no word to represent the emotion, as she has no way to know what the feeling of meeting up with her mother should be. Rather than a definitive retrieval of something lost, the photo opens up a new curiosity (15), a new sense of suspicion, and new secrets. Life can no longer be "immaculate" and orderly but becomes a jumble of things to forget, to cover over, to bury in the sediment of storytelling. Inmaculada is herself a vestige of those tales, of that past, of someone no longer there. She finds herself only a remote part of the family from now on; she acknowledges that she finds little in common with her younger siblings, but at the same time has nowhere to turn for "authentication" (Barthes, *Camera* 107).

Opening a parenthesis at the start of the story, Inmaculada leaves the provinces for Mexico City, a place to both lose and find herself. There she spends a number of years working, only to return home to seek out a former fiancé with the intent to marry him even after so long an absence. After the intervening years of physical excess and emotional relationships, Inmaculada makes the journey back to her own mythical place of innocence, goodness, and platonic love. The novel circles back to the family homestead, the grown siblings, and the grandmother's house in which she is put in her old room for the duration of her visit. As she opens the wooden door to the clothes closet, she finds the photo she left behind long before. Her stepmother places it in her hand as if she signals that she can take it with her to remember her filiation with a place, a time, and a family. But Inmaculada returns the image to a drawer, never to remove it again from its original existence in the house. Inmaculada is drawn to the cemetery before she leaves, but here the similarities with Chapter 1 end.

In her absence, the cemetery has been engulfed by the provincial city and she hardly recognizes the family crypt. Cities have grown, but so have the weeds around this monument. Time has obviously passed, yet Inmaculada is witness only to the results, the ruins; she has missed the intervening process. She confronts the deterioration and "abandono" [abandonment] (325) of the paths, of the vegetation, of the tombs; standing before the crypt "[r]esultaba inverosímil" [seemed uncanny] (325). Yet there is little difference between the time she has spent in the capital and the time she revisits in the provinces; they conflate into one. Since she has returned to recover a lost love, little could make that relationship less uncanny than the recovery of a lost parent. One she has suffered for reasons outside her control; the other (her marriage) she chooses to provoke but under similarly questionable conditions and motivations. Each scenario is as mysterious as the other. In the time she has been gone, her grandmother has joined her mother in the family crypt and absence accumulates on absence. This time around, she refuses to ask the details of her grandmother's death, but makes herself a promise never to return to the cemetery. Strangely, however, she does not abandon the town itself. She and her sisters share tales of the family's comings and goings, but the story beyond her own ends there. The past, an object of mourning embodied in structures and their architectural vestiges, is buried but not buried, for it is visible among the weeds. It is both there and not there, visible and unreachable.

The reader cannot see the photo of a fictional woman, of course, but both mother and grandmother play the same role for the character as the photograph does for Barthes. Like the stones of India that contain hidden stories for Paz, like the ruins that tourist guidebooks give voice to, the photo that lies at the center of this tale is made to "speak" (Barthes, *Camera* 64) for Inmaculada by her own encounter(s) with it. When it no longer says anything to her, she leaves it behind materially but carries it with her as "an animation" (Barthes, *Camera* 20) within herself. As "contingency, singularity, risk" (Barthes, *Camera* 20), the photograph within her conjures up the melancholia of confronting death-in-life or, allegorically, past-in-present. When this moment of confrontation is resuscitated, what might have been "immaculate" can no longer be so. It has been darkened by the photographic remembrance of loss. She cannot recognize herself in her mother's photo, but she does find traces of her sisters (the known) in the face of the unknown. In her return, Inmaculada sets up the relationship between allegory and mourning that Avelar calls "the end of the magical" (68). No longer are the small towns of youth the province of a romantic return or the realm of magic realism; nature contains instead, in this vision, "an immanent process of putrefaction" (69), which allows her to inhabit the spaces of decay and allow us to consider the text as ruin. So Inmaculada's own story is part of that strata of phantasmagoric relations in which the uncanny—death on paper, death within life—does not seem so unfamiliar after all, for everything around the character is as ruinous as the tomb she stands before. Through allegory, the reader can be brought to evoke death in so many other forms as well: the deaths of 1968, the corpse of the city that has a shiny new veneer of modernity, the underbrush that shares the space of planned expansion and construction. What might have seemed unfamiliar in the juxtaposition of so many elements of the old and the new is now part and parcel of the everyday, the snapshot that citizens carry with them each time they leave home for work and return. The photograph of Inmaculada's dead mother can remain hidden in the closed drawer for it is not the only object that reminds of what is all around and it is no longer needed to bring forth the feeling of loss. It is one fragment among so much debris.

Barthes's anguish over his own appearance as a photographic image destined to be seen by eyes unknown to him, and destined to survive as a trace of a momentary experience, introduces a concept of "posing" (*Camera* 10) that carries us into the text of *Inmaculada*. The focus on the body as the essence of the photograph, what is left as an image after the physical body has moved on, connects Inmaculada's posing for her many lovers to Barthes's "transformation" before the lens of the camera. He writes that the process, the performance, of the act of being photographed "creates my body or mortifies it" (*Camera* 11). While he stops short of considering this a political act (one he does encounter in the Communards posing on the barricades), Barthes finds at the center of the photo "a delicate moral texture and not a mimicry, . . . my (mobile) image, buffeted among a thousand shifting photographs, altering with situation and age, should always coincide with my (profound) 'self;' but it is the contrary that must be said: 'myself' never coincides with my image" (*Camera* 11–12). The confrontation between the heavy, static 'self' on the piece of photographic paper and the movable body is the dilemma presented through Inmaculada for all of the narrative voices. As they attempt to keep her image from moving on, she cannot be fixed to a still pose. The ceremonies that desperately (and melancholically) try to stop time from dragging life toward decay only reiterate the idea that they are monumental acts of "mortification" (Gilloch, *Myth* 137). Inmaculada, outside of any historical context, is on display as are the commodities of the urban marketplace for Benjamin. She is an allegorical figure of the impulse of modernity to configure a socially redemptive story while producing debris that might be gathered up and reused time and again by all those who meet her. Her time frame, however, is reduced to a constant present. Gilloch summarizes this as two contrary impulses: "Ruination and redemption—these are the Janus-faces of allegory" (*Myth* 138). All takes place in the now which conjures up both darkness (ruin) and light (salvation, redemption) in a chiaroscuro of its own.

Attracted to Inmaculada like provincial residents are drawn to the metropolis, male characters impose their fantasy worlds on her only to find that they will become witnesses to catastrophe. Along with the Angel of History, we are all caught up in the storm (of progress) that confronts Inmaculada at home and in the city. The challenge is to make sense, if possible, of the fractured pieces that pile up at our collective feet. Faithful to her name, Inmaculada is like a bright white light—not a black sun—blazing in the center of the narrative universe. For those around her, she lives in a perpetual present, outside the realm of value judgments and of chronological time. Her features do not age, and her acts do not progress from innocence to guilt; she is solely the accumulation of her experiences. When characters draw closer to her, what they find is an "unsuturable whole" as we have read in the essay of Barthes on photography, a performance portrait. Inmaculada is what Barthes terms "the figure of sovereign *innocence* (if you will take this word according to its etymology, which is 'I do no harm')" (*Camera* 69). Neither good nor evil, as the language of her sisters invokes when faced with the secrets of their parents, Inmaculada is just herself.

As in his other novels, in *Inmaculada* García Ponce focuses on "the embodied character of human existence" (Gill xii) found through the ambiguous consciousness of a just-as-ambiguous knowledge that Inmaculada desperately but unsuccessfully seeks. Not an abstract body but a lived one challenged by the 'real' world (of the text, of course), Inmaculada lives space and time in all of their contingencies as she tries to acquire knowledge of surroundings and of herself through her senses. As a repository of experience, the body remembers, but only with difficulty and only through connections with new experiences which explode outward into many directions. According to Maurice Merleau-Ponty, such an elicited "memory is, not the constituting consciousness of the past, but an effort to reopen time on the basis of the implications contained in the present" (qtd. in Carbone 2). In other words, if we return to Habermas, this signals an increased perception of time itself. As Benjamin's *flâneur* animates the city to come alive with sparks of recognition long hidden among the stones, so Inmaculada's body is awakened in a "succession of instances of *now*" (Merleau-Ponty qtd. in Carbone 2) by her encounters with others. Like the photographs awakened by Barthes through his gaze on their images, each takes from this instant of involuntary recollection a unification with the world that, paradoxically perhaps, he or she seems overtly to reject. That is, for example, the "atmosphere of 68" that Martré uncovers in *La invitación* and that we have found in *Crónica*, here it is the perception of province and city, of a collection of sexual relations, all in "a single movement, the different moments of which flow into each other" (Carbone 3).

In her discussion of García Ponce's fictional works, Duncan emphasizes this temporal notion as central to the development of all of his narratives. Although she refers specifically to his story "El gato" [The Cat], the same could be said of the novels, including *Inmaculada*. Duncan reviews their structures to find that "[t]he series of scenes that compose the text have no irrevocable order, since each novel is primarily an account of the gradual involvement with others and acquisition of a sense of identity on the part of initially isolated beings" (27–28). Not referred to as chapters, the sections that compose the novel *Inmaculada* appear as fragments of ongoing activity. Each narrative piece is listed in the Table of Contents solely by its first few words, much as lines of poetry are listed in anthologies. Therefore, we do not find a progression of Inmaculada's life from childhood to maturity, as one might encounter in a traditional *Bildungsroman*. Instead we read a narrator's account of an action: "Pero con ella no hice nada" [But with her I didn't do anything], "Álvaro dejó a Inmaculada" [Álvaro left Inmaculada], or "Inmaculada, con su falda negra" [Inmaculada, with her black skirt], suggesting a series of experiences of equal importance and without any particular order. In addition, the constellation of narrative voices around these lived experiences are foregrounded by references in the third person. Inmaculada has, like Barthes's photograph, an afterlife in these stories.

Any initial sense of the character's isolation, or of a rupture between inside and outside, between body and world, is broken through the interrelated relationship between mind and body posited by Merleau-Ponty. It is his sense of an optics of corporeality, the centrality of the human body in the fabric of the social world, which infuses the essays and narratives of García Ponce with a presumption of the human body—both interiority and exteriority—as an integral part of the world, not as a subject separate from it able to stand back and take it all in at a glance. Among his organic metaphors for this relationship, we find the use of tissues, membranes, and threads (Gill 4), images we might use to tie together Inmaculada and her pleasures (much as Paloma exhibits in *De ánima)*. If we have deployed architectural images for edifices, social constructs, and even for the human body, we might now add these tropes to refer to the vestiges and remains of the corporal edifice and its experiences. Elizabeth Grosz reminds us:

> Merleau-Ponty begins with the negative claim that the body is not an object. It is the condition and context through which I am able to have a relation to objects. . . . For Merleau-Ponty, although the body is both object (for others) and a lived reality (for the subject), it is never simply object nor simply subject. . . . The body is my being-to-the-world and as such is the instrument by which all information and knowledge is received and meaning is generated." (86–87)

Relationships between subjects and objects are based on the actions and meanings negotiated between them, on the space-time opened by their encounters, like Benjamin's finds amid the cobblestone streets of Paris and Marseilles. The location of the body, the alteration of geographical space, and the continual change of perspective all contribute to the sense of Inmaculada as a character who moves through the world in the chiasm of object time and subject time. Between lived temporality and the "coagulation of time" (Carbone 4) into a storytelling subject, Merleau Ponty clarifies that "we must understand time as the subject and the subject as time." Temporality, then, is not outside perception but perception itself: "time *is* someone, . . . temporal dimensions, in so far as they perpetually overlap, bear each other out and ever confine themselves to making explicit what was implied in each, being collectively expressive of that one single explosion or thrust which is subjectivity itself" (qtd. in Carbone 4). The circularity and redundancy of *Inmaculada* responds to this concept of lived time or life-in-time. So it becomes obvious that the only way to enter into the world as seen in this manner is through the flesh that experiences it.

The bodily situation is understood by characters at different times in different ways, according to what Merleau-Ponty terms the "corporeal schema" (Grosz 91) or body image as an access to relationships with other objects. The body schema is a field of possible actions in which a subject's identity as and in a particular body takes place. So it is not just the (male) observer who is incarnated in the flesh in García Ponce's novel, as some have posited, but Inmaculada herself in a variety of lived and shared experiences. The relationship between the seer and the seen, the woman and the voyeur, is not singularly and permanently established but, in Grosz's words, a "palpitation of being" (96), a continual movement and shifting in the space of possible or unforeseen actions and encounters. That they may all fade into nothingness as does the image in Barthes's photo means less than that they have taken place at all.

Through a recounting of the life story of Inmaculada, we join in an exploration of the inner world of a woman, from childhood to the eve of her impending marriage. Yet the construction of this inner identity is not disconnected from the outside, but shaped by the experiences of the body. Innocence—not doing harm but acquiring knowledge—offers a variety of pleasures contingent on situations, not just some abstract notion of what the title refers to as "pleasures." The narration of her activities is slow and deliberate in its details, as if the eye of the reader were witness to the delicate movement of light and shadow over the course of time as they ebb and flow over the subtle changes in the body and personality of Inmaculada. Space and time become concepts relative to her orientation in them. The different angles from which the narrative focuses on Inmaculada's story create a totality of fragmentary visions all evolving around her momentary perception of her relationship to those around her. An eroticized nature is constantly present as a backdrop, at times as a pleasure for the senses and other times as a terrible enigma that needs to be deciphered to make sense of the world. But the counterpoint between coherence and mystery changes at every turn. What lurks behind the forms surrounding her? Is there something to be perceived at one moment and not the next? And the 'making sense of the world,' that quest for knowledge we have witnessed in Paloma and others, remains as a vestige, a remnant, a ruin of an Enlightenment ideal that is slowly fading into the past.

The manner in which the story is told creates a deception of sorts, for although it begins with a more traditional third-person narration, it later shifts to confront the reader with a disembodied voice that has been conversing with Inmaculada off and on throughout the text. The reader discovers that this voice belongs to one of her lovers who is also a psychiatrist and her boss. Her tale is a confession—whether meant for self or others—which penetrates the depths of her psyche and gives the reader an impression of a character in front of a multifaceted mirror. As she scrutinizes the images before her, in her thoughts and imagination or on the surface of the glass, Inmaculada recalls episodes from the past as well as she anticipates moments in the future. After all is said and done, at the end of the narrative it is unclear if she continues her erotic quest for self, or if she abandons it to join the ranks of the bourgeois society she claims to detest. The ritual of marriage looms over her, although it is not the only ritual practiced in the novel. The final choice in this story is not made by the narrator, but is left for the reader to imagine (or fantasize) into the story playing out, thereby joining forces in the telling of the tale.

Like the nation that reveals fissures and cracks filled with ruinous images of the past, the narrative self in this novel is composed of layers that do not coexist seamlessly. Rather than conform to conceptions of selfhood in which the subject appears as the repository of truth, knowledge, or eternal values (although her lovers might seek this in and through her), Inmaculada's search for "conocimiento" immerses her in a palimpsest of evocative experiences. Merleau-Ponty envisions this as the superposing of layers which metamorphose and cross over between the silences of the "mute world" and the "flesh" of language (qtd. in Carbone 40). Past and present are therefore enveloping one another, shifting and changing as they encounter each other once again. Sedimentary evidence of previous time is part of both "the invisible and the visible" for Merleau-Ponty, so the human body contains secrets that might be revealed by new experiences that bring to light unexpected images and reactions. Inmaculada is the surface on which this palimpsest becomes visible, if only for a brief moment. She functions like the photographic plate which fascinates us as the outlines of an image come into focus mysteriously from out of nowhere.

Inmaculada's work in a psychiatric institution in the Mexican capital is far from an accidental choice of venue, and it hints at the underlying current of illness in society. An obsessive return to the labyrinths of the human mind, specifically the clinical conditions referred to as psychosis, paranoia, and schizophrenia, constitutes one of the sites of engagement for reopening a window on the ruins of the past for Inmaculada and the other characters. (One might recall Fuentes's construction once again as a figure similar to this since it haunts the skyline with former promises as it also embodies present decay and future rebirth.) A precursor of the characters in *Inmaculada* is found in García Ponce's short story entitled "Enigma" in which the protagonist—a renowned psychiatrist and director of a mental institution, who also narrates the story—becomes just another patient among many. The cause? The narrator's state of paranoia has been provoked by a case of "mad love" (*l'amour fou*) and sexual excess à la Bataille. The character Inmaculada is represented as a conjunction of two privileged elements that open up time toward past and future: the imagination and sensual excess. While the surface of the skin is the locus of the second, the psyche as part of the human body and its lived experience completes the picture.

Since this novel, the third of our visual panels of storytelling, is constructed on an economy of excess, it seems only logical that Inmaculada is represented as spending all of her time immersed in bodily experiences. Her physical body is the vehicle which allows her to access sensations of the sublime, or states of madness, depending on the interpretation of the reader. Inmaculada intuits that only in the space of alterity—here, the ward of the psychiatric hospital—will she be able to give voice to those sensations elicited by events, images, and provocations (those interventions and antagonisms described by Barthes as interruptions into the progress of history). In one scene of the novel, for instance, her quest leads her to perform sexual acts with mental patients to test the limits of social acceptability and to see how she will react. As Alphonso Lingis states of this eros, "Eroticism is not satisfied with contentment; it is the ecstasy of our passions. It is the breakthrough, out of one's body contained within the embraces of another, toward the beyond" (31). The limits of Inmaculada and her world constantly shift, as do the artificial social and cultural borders between innocence and experience, or good and evil, or passivity and cognizance, as she strives to go beyond charted social territories into the so-called realm of the abyss. Pleasures are drawn from this very act of redrawing the cartographies of taboo experiences into maps of the unknown, the innocent, the discontinuous, the random, the repetitious, the ritualized and, perhaps, even the pleasurable. The vestiges of these acts are the scars and marks on the surface of the flesh, on the social body, on the psyche. As such, these are the focal points to explore what has vanished but left its traces.

Rather than use colloquial language, or what has been considered popular vulgarity, to portray these characters and their actions, García Ponce instead turns to *écriture* once again. It is the power of suggestion, the lengthy panoramic description or suggestive and detached observation, and not overt depiction that reigns on these pages. If Susan Sontag is right, as I believe she is, eroticism and pornography are not really about sex; they have more to do with matters of life and death ("Pornographic Imagination" 224). In this confluence of forces, of death-in-life, we return to the images resuscitated by Barthes through photography. Inmaculada and her bodily activities confirm such a vision of eros and its affirmation of the lived experience of excess, coming as close as possible to the brink of death. García Ponce, as Klossowski and Bataille before him, plunges into the "dark continent" of sexuality (as Freud sees it), the dark side of eros, to reach beyond the binarisms of good and evil, positive and negative, sanity and madness, the same way Merleau-Ponty has posited a breaking down of the binarism of mind-body. Eroticism is the instrument for breaking through the limits of consciousness and knowledge, it is a consideration of the flesh as "a raw, formless, bodily materiality, the mythical 'primary material', . . . capable of acting in distinctive ways, performing specific tasks in socially specified ways, marked, branded by a social seal" (Grosz 118). Inmaculada knows, not rationally but through her corporeal senses, that her recognition of self lies behind the world of appearances and connects them to her. To reach them, to pass through the veil of the surface and the visible, she must cling to experience. In this sense, then, "los placeres de la inocencia" [the pleasures of innocence] reflected in the novel's title, are in actuality the joy and necessity of experience.

For Barthes, the framed photograph is in itself an image haunted by the ghost of painting. He writes that "it [photography] has made Painting, through its copies and contestations, into the absolute, paternal Reference, as if it were born from the Canvas" (*Camera* 30–31). At this moment, Barthes comes closer to Benjamin than at any other time. His conclusion that the early link between the cult of the dead and theatrical production (in China and Japan, for example) is evoked in the play of light and shadow of photography as well. So while the "Paternal Referent" of the painterly continues to be part of the strata of the artwork, a chiaroscuro layer shining through, that facade created by actors to portray the dead on stage sounds much like Benjamin's baroque mourning play. The fight between "the primacy of interiority and the self" (Avelar 23) and the cultural and intellectual ruins of the nation comes into play on the stage where Inmaculada and her cohorts perform their acts. That "condensation of meaning around a corpse" (Avelar 3) that Benjamin finds as an allegory of social death is what Inmaculada and the others obviate in their recreation of life among the psychiatric patients. From the photograph of her mother, she moves on to mourning a lost love, then participates in the simulacra of the hospital world, to return once again to the rejected photo as souvenir. After her departure for Mexico City, Inmaculada is fascinated by Diego, a young man whom she is forbidden by her relatives to see. His death in a motorcycle accident removes him from the picture, and she can only resuscitate him through gazing at a photo he has left behind. In a second ceremonial act, Inmaculada finds that time has wiped out their relationship and that Diego "es cada vez más, por encima de todo, una fotografía. A veces me parece que tampoco lo conocí, que todo lo que recuerdo de él es inventado, igual que me pasa, siendo verdad, cuando veo la fotografía de mi mamá . . . Los dos son sólo una fotografía-. . . . Inmaculada siguió—Diego fue mi novio sin ser mi novio y mi mamá lo fue sin que yo supiera que lo era, tengo que ver su fotografía para conocerla" [is increasingly, more than anything, a photograph. Sometimes it seems that I didn't know him either, that all I remember of him is invented, the same like it happens, truthfully, when I see the photograph of my mother . . . Both of them are just a photograph. . . . Inmaculada went on—Diego was my boyfriend without being my boyfriend and my mother was just that without me knowing she was; I have to see her photograph to get to know her] (94). Each of the paper images fixes death, not life, on the page. But each is singularly capable of linking Inmaculada, and therefore the narrative, to the past through an evocatory image in danger of disappearing. What each brings forth, additionally, is the power of "invención" or storytelling.

The turn from photography to spectacle and ritual takes place in the hospital and in each of the sexual relationships Inmaculada has with its residents. But here the paternal frame of reference returns in a dialogue between narrative and painting, blending the two into one interwoven series of interconnected images. Many of the narrator's descriptions of Inmaculada suggest the production or reproduction of a painting. Scenes, events, and actions are framed in blocks of space, creating the illusion that the reader is contemplating a sequence of slowly swirling, mobile images. In reality, they exhibit subtle changes from frame to frame, as if the light cast on them were slowly changing its angle or as if a camera were tracking across the room during the time it takes for the sun to rise and set. The connection between the seer and the seen, the visible and the invisible (to paraphrase a title of one of Merleau Ponty's last works, dated 1968), is not by any means accidental. The intermingling of the subject and the object, the inside and the outside, the toucher and the touched, is described here as taking place across flesh, a notion of the tissues of experience uniting and disuniting bodies in the field of experience across time. All of this he sees as taking place in terms of the visual, and in this aspect it is a concept taken up by García Ponce as well. For both, vision appears to be the sense most capable of capturing the idea of the "palpitation" of being-in-the-world. Sight is privileged as the sense best able to encompass a web of relations between one's body and another's, and between the social world (the visible?) and an assimilation of its experiences (the invisible?).

It follows that the figure of the painted (the seen, the young woman, the model) and that of the painter (the seer, the male gaze) come together in the space of the narrative to evince an encounter of opposing forces. As Merleau Ponty affirms in his essay "Eye and Mind" ["L'Oeil et l'esprit"], "by lending his body to the world, [the artist] changes the world into paintings" (162). So it is that the various perspectives of the artist, the world, and the image (Inmaculada) are all interrelated since they produce an embodied vision of the moment and the space in which they all come together. This mobile relationship is at work at the heart of *Inmaculada* and it evokes what Merleau-Ponty calls "an emerging organism" (Gill 28), the mediation of the world through the vision of the artist. Like Paloma in *De ánima*, Inmaculada is also given her moment of mediation wherein she recounts actions from her own perspective. Since the senses link the world and the mind through the body, they are the site of a two-way interaction: "we see with the whole body, not just with the eye, in the same way as we think with our body" (Gill 31). The eye (of the painter, of the seer, of the storyteller) focuses on the visible in order to unlock the invisible, that hidden and even uncanny 'recollection' sought by Benjamin as well. This privilege turns from outside to inside and back again as the fragments of the narrative spin around the ceremonies set up by Inmaculada and her lovers. As allegories of access and denial, these activities conjure up celebration as well as mourning, or perhaps we might even consider a celebration of mourning in their midst.

The body as an assemblage of perceptions and self-perceptions is the cornerstone of Merleau-Ponty's discussion of French painter Cézanne's optics. It is also that of Octavio Paz's vision of artist Manuel Felguérez's fundamental change to the optics of the muralists of the Mexican Revolution. Felguérez (and Cuevas, among others) turn the eye of the seer on the world as they also see themselves as part of the process of producing meaning from that world at the same time. Such a double gaze (or meta-vision) is instrumental to the narratives of García Ponce, suggesting a more complex relationship between subject and object, between masculine and feminine, between the long-view of time and historical interruption. For Paz, the mirror is the "philosophical instrument par excellence" ("Will for Form" 26), both transmitter of images and simultaneous critic of them. It occupies a space of privilege in the artworks of Felguérez as a reproducer of spaces, engendering and enforcing the reproduction of reproductions. But it also reproduces the enigma of the body simultaneously seeing and being seen: "It [my body] sees itself seeing; it touches itself touching. . . . It is not a self through transparence . . . . It is a self through confusion, narcissism" (Merleau-Ponty 162–63). García Ponce picks up on this same image when he describes Inmaculada in terms of a vision in a mirror, an image of a young woman seemingly unaware of being observed but suggestively mirroring the gaze of the viewer at the same time. For the narrative voice in this work, as it is for Inmaculada when she dictates her story to her lover-boss-psychiatrist Miguel Ballester, the linguistic medium appropriates the role of the artistic (visual) one. In her confession, story, or fantastic tale Inmaculada is charged with performing the work of mourning—the past, the lost, the unexplained, the mysterious—on herself and of simultaneously turning it into a narrative. Their episodic encounters serve to recall a longer time that strings together her fragments of experience into some sort of whole, even if tape-recorded by her psychiatrist and therefore artificial. This desire apart, her excesses become a spectacle of a life headed toward death, a spiral of ecstasy that culminates in a lack of words and an absence of people: her mother is gone; Diego is gone; she cannot return home. The fact that she pretends to recover a previous lover back home lights a spark of melancholia since the dramatic irony of the situation is evident: the reader is aware that she cannot return to an innocent past without consequence.

As Avelar concludes of postdictatorial Southern Cone literature, and we might surmise could be applied to post-1968 and postdevaluation and post-NAFTA Mexican culture, "the distinction between mourning and melancholia has to do with the locus of the loss, either situated outside the subject, having a profound impact on him/her but being ultimately comprehensible as one's loss of something else (mourning), or yet ubiquitous to the point of engulfing the mourner him/herself in the loss, so the very separation between subject and object of loss disappears (melancholia)" (232). The loss of writing, seen by Avelar as a keen signal of the inability to use language except to express that loss and a concomitant enclosure of the writer within it (232), does not envelope all of García Ponce's characters and narrators. Scenes of storytelling, albeit amid the "murky gray area where mourning borders with melancholia" (Avelar 232), emerge with Inmaculada as fragments of other tales (of nation, of community, of historical past) only to dissolve into shards picked up during the next therapy session (and, with it, a formalized repetition compulsion). Her words may be preserved on tape, and the meetings between the two may occur again, but all hope of explanation, of definitive knowledge, of understanding vanish into empty ritual. Nevertheless, their ceremonies go on; they never relinquish the reenactment of this storytelling desire.

In García Ponce's essay entitled "La pintura y lo otro" [Painting and otherness], we find a continuation of the interplay between the optics of art and narrative. He writes of the action of painting as an encounter in the space between the bodies of subject and object(s), which offers a latent field of possibilities of knowledge and of breaking through the isolation and offering a chance for the exploration of self and other (or the self among others). The privileged position of vision—for Merleau-Ponty, Paz, and García Ponce—results from its access to what are seen as "raw events." Of the sense of sight Hans Jonas tells us that "a view comprehends many things juxtaposed, as co-existent parts of one field of vision. It does so in an instant: as in a flash, one glance, an opening of the eyes, discloses a world of co-present qualities spread out in space, ranged in depth, continuing into indefinite distance" (Jonas 313). Sight therefore unifies various objects in both time and space, placing the subject's encounter with such an original or raw series of artifacts into the field of vision of the artist, who, as García Ponce writes, "aporta su cuerpo a la acción concreta de pintar" [brings his body to the very concrete act of painting itself] ("Pintura" 393). One is reminded once again of Benjamin's engagement with the cinema and the photographic image and with their potential to break into the everyday life of the audience with images that awaken citizens from their stupor. He writes that "[t]hc radio broadcast, like the photograph and the sound recording, meets the beholder halfway" (qtd. in Gilloch, *Myth* 169).

To uncover the purportedly hidden, invisible, or secret mechanisms through which the self can be perceived or constructed, *Inmaculada* problematizes the phenomenon of seeing much as it does that of being seen. Both subject and object of the gaze are under scrutiny in these recorded dialogues with self and other as experiments in the phenomenology of perception à la Merleau-Ponty. Although it is true that many of the male characters engage in the act of scopophilia, that is to say they revel in the pleasures of looking, and that this behavior might be construed as another example of the male objectification of the female, there is more to *Inmaculada* than meets the eye. The subjection of a woman to a controlling and curious gaze ("Visual" 16) is not the only coordinate on the shifting axis of this narrative tale; it is one of many remnants of social discourse that mark the surface of the narrative. Inmaculada herself is frequently caught looking at her lovers, male or female, reversing the roles of so-called active subject and passive object. She also delights in the pleasures of observing herself acting in and on the world around her, even as she intuits it as fleeting. The transitory nature of event in modern times, as we have stated earlier, meets up with the ritualized repetition of story, yet the recovery of narrative continuity (linked points of time) eludes Inmaculada and her listeners.

One of the aesthetic 'ruins' on which Inmaculada is built may be found in the work of Balthus, painter and brother of writer Pierre Klossowski. Balthus's representation of women, in particular adolescent girls, creates the impression that they are the constant object of the gaze of the (male) painter; yet, at the same time, they return that steady gaze in ever more subtle and discreet ways (see figure 6.1). The world does not just belong to the artist; it also acts upon and through him. His painted figures seem to know they are being looked at, and they catch the eye of the spectator in a complicity of innocent pleasure and, as Inmaculada herself seeks, knowledge. One is again reminded of Tanizaki's *The Key*, with its hint that the private diary is also the secret public ritual exhibition of which both writer and reader are aware. As Lingis writes of the experience of ecstasy, "The body that sleeps [or feigns doing so] is not inert, it is incandescent with the delicious aurora borealis that streams in its blood, sweat, and discharges. The erotic rapture sweeps the flotsam and jetsam of the impassioned flesh unto the tropical and arctic regions where tempestuous sirens and demons chant and howl" (32). The invisible—mind, physiology, the rush of feeling—melds with the visible body to form the half-closed eyes in the portraits of adolescents peeping out from the canvases of Balthus. We might start with the howling of the demons on the surface of the flesh as remains of the "explosions and contestations" that both Baudelaire and Barthes find in the experience of modernity.

Those seemingly innocent of the world, cognizant only perhaps of social impositions and taboos, are in both Balthus and García Ponce the erotic subjects par excellence. In what Lingis terms a "transitional state" (43) between childhood and adulthood, these adolescent creatures are poised at the threshold of multiple possibilities. As such figures of promise and fleeting appearance, as modernity incarnate, Inmaculada and the Balthus girls are facades of promise, enticing the onlooker to seek beyond only to frustrate any true access to knowledge. Inmaculada is poised to marry and, according to convention, lose this quality of innocence; the Balthus portraits reflect a moment in time and perception captured by the artist before all of the elements in the frail equation of innocence change. Each embodies what Barthes seeks in the photograph: some sense of the person represented and some intrusion into the time-space frozen in the portrait.

To further pursue the analogy between painting and writing, and the problematic relationship between the male gaze and the female figure, we might focus on the narrator's depictions of Inmaculada's body. She is described in pictorial terms as if she were being placed in the focus of a magnifying lens to scrutinize her inch by inch. The terms used evoke in the reader the feeling of standing in front of Manet's *Olympia* or Titian's *Venus of Urbino*. Like Olympia or Venus, Inmaculada is aware of the fact that she is being observed, and that her body is a source of inspiration for the projection of another's erotic desires onto the canvas. However, even though these three female figures are depicted from the privileged position of the male eye, they refuse to be reduced to static objects. They consistently return the gaze in a challenge to the empire of the male. Inmaculada is represented then as being made aware of the possibility of her body being circulated as a token in the erotic economy of the male (which she rejects), but at the same time she takes pleasure in the recuperation of the gaze to promote her own version of the story.

The text of *Inmaculada* reflects a circular structure reminiscent of *Crónica*, except for the fact that in the earlier novel the characters' voices that return to haunt the narrative come from beyond the grave. Within the confines of his room, Esteban 'hears' the voices of Mariana and the others who have been dead since the beginning of the chronicle. But they are now only a product of his memories; they are disembodied. In *Inmaculada*, early childhood experiences appear in the first chapter of the novel and reappear at the end. The same holds true for the adolescent lover who participates in Inmaculada's initiation into erotic experiences early in the narrative; then he reappears as he is scheduled to marry her as the text comes to a close. In between these two moments, less of a progression than a collection of experiences, rituals, and ceremonies mark the life of Inmaculada. The condensed experience of time brings historical narrative into modernity with its emphasis on the contingency of perception.

Called by Moreno-Durán a "crónica de una iniciación" [chronicle of initiation] (45), *Inmaculada* is based on a deliberate suspension of judgment regarding any of the acts committed within its pages. Unlike *De ánima*, whose characters remain in a constant (and paradoxical) state of alert regarding the morality of their actions in the eyes of the public (perhaps this is the reason for the *Laws* of Hospitality), Inmaculada has already cast out conscience from experience. She inhabits an Eden-like space, playing the role of a truly innocent Eve before the Fall. From her youth in the provincial family home, to the ward of a psychiatric hospital, and back, this pristine time-space is preserved. Her paradise is predicated on the code of no codes, "la ausencia de juicio moral" [the absence of moral judgment] (Moreno-Durán 45).

In a conscious submission to pleasures alone in any and all of their possible or imagined varieties, Inmaculada is the element that structures the ritualized events of the entire novel. As a willing initiate in the excesses of eros, this character participates in ceremonies that expose her to multiple possibilities of physical experience. An innocent horseback ride becomes the chance to fantasize about a more intimate contact between the body of the horse and her own. A chance encounter as a child at the door of her parents' bedroom while they are in the act of making love—the classic Freudian primal scene—is processed by Inmaculada throughout the rest of her life as an erotic memory that repeats each time she confronts a closed door. Once again, the doorway explodes as an allegory of so many openings and closings, so many evocations almost forgotten.

Her early erotic encounters with her playmate Joaquina, and their experimentation with dolls as phallic objects, echo in the last pages of the novel where it is suggested that Joaquina will remain Inmaculada's lover in spite of her impending marriage to Eugenio. Joaquina is charged with initiating Inmaculada into the realm of the autoerotic, interestingly enough behind the walls of the life-size dollhouse they share. This edifice is a reproduction in miniature of the domain of the traditional family and, through their transgressive acts, the erotic makes its entry into the familial domain. Yet they never pause to examine what they are transgressing, nor are the two young girls presented with any sense of guilt. Their fetishized children, the dolls, take on a role that does not seem—in this context, at least—to contradict their innocence as playthings. Just like the character Inmaculada herself, the dolls can be both innocent and erotic. Instead of losing one identity to become something else entirely, they accumulate meaning: "Ellas las cambiaban, no podían evitarlo, las muñecas nunca volverían a ser las muñecas como lo fueran antes, ahora las dos sabían que eran otra cosa *además*" [The girls {Joaquina and Inmaculada} changed them, they couldn't avoid it. The dolls would never go back to being what they were before. Now they both knew that they were something else *besides*] (26; emphasis added). Just as Inmaculada's identity is a sum of her experiences, the dolls constantly acquire meanings in new circumstances, without sacrificing their former value.

As an adult, Inmaculada wanders through life—literally as well as figuratively in search of herself—gathering together a collection of experiential moments. Much as the characters in *Crónica* traverse class divisions and social groups, from the countryside to the sprawling urban centers, Inmaculada becomes acquainted with a variety of persons and pleasures. In each case, what looks like an innocent situation on the surface reveals her own reading of it as something more ritualistic, another step in her acquisition of knowledge. Inmaculada is offered a job as the secretary of the director of a hospital yet, for her, this position opens up new opportunities for breaking her isolation (as Duncan has pointed out). To her employment in such a problematic space is added the possibility of reaching beyond the limits of herself, by means of her body, into the unknown realms of those who are considered 'sick' or somehow outcast from normal society. It is not just a hospital where she works; it is a mental hospital and therefore a privileged space of access to what society has repressed, excluded, or made abject. Here resides the debris of modernity's project.

Behind the walls of the psychiatric ward, sex therapy sessions are presented as rituals of erotic experience that strikingly parallel all the other moments of her life. Sex as pleasure and sex as therapy are one and the same. The prescribed rituals with patients—what are called treatment sessions—are curiously similar to the ceremonial sadomasochistic sessions that Inmaculada shares with coworker Arnulfo. A former patient himself, Arnulfo now functions as an assistant to the director of the hospital. It is he who is in charge of keeping daily routines running smoothly, making sure that patients are restrained, that they are in their cells, that they eat at appropriate times. It is he who maintains order within this space of liminality for those who are being 'cured.' It is he who holds the key to open all doors. No one is safe from his supervision or observation. But it is also Arnulfo who offers Inmaculada an encounter with the more violent side of eros, a shadowy realm suggestive of the bondage rituals described by the narrators of the Marquis de Sade or, more recently, in Réage's *Story of O*.

More than once, Arnulfo leads Inmaculada—who follows his lead willingly—down a long corridor, past room after room of drugged patients, to a dark, secluded space, supposedly far from any witnesses. Looking like all of the other rooms on the ward, this one is different in that it functions as a place of pleasure and restraint at the same time. There are no drugs present, but there are manacles and belts. Yet these are endowed with meanings for Inmaculada that go beyond their obvious use. Like the dolls in the domestic scenarios acted out with Joaquina, the shackles and ties take on additional significations in the erotic rituals. At the point of beginning the ceremony, Arnulfo abolishes all distinctions between Inmaculada and the rest of the occupants of that wing of the hospital. He warns her: "Si gritas pidiendo auxilio nadie se extrañaría. Hay muchos que gritan aquí dentro" [If you scream for help no one will pay any attention. There are lots of people who scream inside these walls] (293). While she assures him that she has no intention of doing so, going along with the ceremony of the scene he is setting up, Inmaculada is placed in a role that is no longer distinguishable from anyone else there. She voluntarily submits to his rules, leaving behind her job as

Figure 6.1 Balthus (Klossowski de Rola B.) (1908–2000) "The Living Room (Le Salon)," 1942. Oil on canvas. Estate of John Hay Whitney. The Museum of Modern Art, New York, NY, U.S.A. Digital Image © The Museum of Modern Art/Licensed by SCALA/Art Resource, NY © 2006 Artists Rights Society (ARS), ADAGP, Paris

Figure 6.2 Balthus (Klossowski de Rola B.)(1908–2000) "The Street," 1933. Oil on canvas. James Thrall Soby Bequest. The Museum of Modern Art, New York, NY, U.S.A. Digital Image © The Museum of Modern Art/Licensed by SCALA/Art Resource, NY © 2006 Artists Rights Society (ARS), ADAGP, Paris

secretary of the (absent) director, and places herself in the hands of someone who offers her a new experience. What she does not expect, at least judging from her surprised comments, is that some of the other *enfermos* [sick people] are part of the ritual as well. These witnesses—and participants, through the presence of the voyeur—have access to the spectacle through a window that opens onto their hall. Arnulfo makes clear their planned role in this scenario, one which the reader is told also has a positive effect on Inmaculada: "Inmaculada no pudo olvidar la mirada detrás de la ventana porque el recuerdo de que la habían visto aumentaba su placer" [Inmaculada couldn't forget the gaze behind the windowpane because the very thought that they had watched her increased her sense of pleasure] (295). Such a scopophilic event is repeated in several versions within the walls of the same room. But it also appears in other episodes of the novel, including an instance when Inmaculada poses in the nude for a painting in which all of the other models are clothed. Set up by the artist as a visual spectacle for the delight of those who look on, the painting of Inmaculada exposes her to the traditional role of model in the gaze of the artist.

Like Manet's *Olympia*, Inmaculada returns the gaze of the voyeur. Feal and Feal remark that the model for *Olympia* is said to have been a prostitute (165), adding an additional twist to possible similarities with Inmaculada, yet this convergence sells her short. We may conclude that Inmaculada is a woman aware of her own body and is not willing to feel shame or avert her gaze. She is not about to forfeit her experience for the sake of propriety or tradition; the moral vestiges of the past have been subsumed into alternative narratives by Inmaculada in the frame of the 1980s. In their defiant attitude toward the male onlooker, both Olympia and Inmaculada challenge him to admit his own role in public, to confess (as Inmaculada does on tape) his complicity in the setup. As Friedrich writes of Manet's painted subject, "[t]he public nakedness of a beautiful woman sometimes becomes a question of politics" (1) since her image summons forth unspoken rules and relations. The gaze is therefore politicized in both painting and text. The problematizing of the representation of the feminine continues here, as we have seen in *De ánima* with Paloma, through the evocation of a controlling gaze along with a contestatory one. The female body appears objectified—Paloma is made into a film and a painting; Inmaculada's image is found in a photograph and a portrait—but there is an attempt to create space for a storytelling subject as well. Both Paloma and Inmaculada—their names evocative of the white dove and the pure angel—are commodities to be consumed by the eyes of the spectator and consumers in their own right. So the palimpsest of the story of Inmaculada is not reduced to others' versions alone but several narratives woven together in a time frame of the always-now. Critic Rafael Moreno-Durán can thus make the claim that Inmaculada "se instala en un calendario inmóvil" [takes up residence in the pages of an immobile calendar] (45), never aging and marking the passage of time only through the stimulus of external sensations, owing to the fact that she is a "body with organs" who is in the constant process of creating herself.

The ambiguities of Inmaculada and her redefining of pleasurable innocence carry through in the use of the color white as a sign or marker of these contradictions. Named by the matriarch of the family, Inmaculada wears white at all times. The metonymic relationship between moral or physical purity and spotless whiteness is transgressed by the erotic activities of the woman so clothed, revealing the artificial surface on which the story of innocence has been written. During all three epochs of her life Inmaculada is dressed in white: as a young girl, as a nurse, and as a bride-to-be. On the occasion of her First Communion, a ceremony observed with all rigor and devotion by traditional Catholic families, Inmaculada feels she is part of a masquerade, but she is a willing participant. "Era como ir disfrazada" [It was like being in a costume] (17). She enjoys the idea of looking different, of standing out and being watched, of playing a role. More important than listening to the words of the priest, or responding at the correct time, Inmaculada imagines herself in the eyes of others: "Había sido más importante caminar, sentarse, arrodillarse con su nuevo traje, saberse observada por su abuela, su papá, su tía y todos sus hermanos" [It had been more important to walk, sit down, kneel with her new dress, know that she was observed by her grandmother, her father, her aunt, and all of her brothers and sisters] (18). Not only is the day of her First Communion a rite of passage into the community of the church and adult society, but it also is her initiation into eroticism by Joaquina. Coincidence or not, the two friends share the sacrament of Communion on the same day. But they also take part in erotic rites of the body that very afternoon when they proceed to their dollhouse.

The medical uniform that Inmaculada wears for her job at the hospital separates her from outside society in that it represents a person who is dedicated to health and to restoring the functions of the bodies and minds of the sick. The cleanliness of the white dress marks her as an employee, but it also indicates her entry into the world of Arnulfo and the escapades they share. As he divests her of the symbol of her profession at the start of each rite, Arnulfo opens the door for Inmaculada into the world of sexual experimentation.

In the last chapter, as her adventures come to a close, Inmaculada returns home to marry Eugenio and, evidently, to become part of the bourgeosie she has claimed to detest all along. Divesting herself of the trappings of her previous roles, she dons the visible sign of purity, the traditional white gown. Her gown represents tradition in that it has been handed down from grandmother to mother, and from mother to daughter. As Inmaculada stands before the mirror in the symbolic attire of her new identity, she is pure contradiction. The dress is symbolic of that which is untouchable and chaste; by covering the body it marks an absence, a promise of pleasure yet to be fulfilled. At the same time, it is the garment of a bride, a woman about to give herself over to pleasure and, one is told, to the unknown. The reader is also aware of her complete story, so the happy ending functions as an allegory of the inventions of the bourgeoise storyteller. As Miguel, the director of the hospital, reveals to his son Sebastián, on the last page, Inmaculada already has a "history." The narrator tells us: "Miguel le contó [a Sebastián] la verdad" [Miguel told {Sebastian} the truth] (332). Whether on Miguel's tapes that contain Inmaculada's confessions, in his own words at the close of the text, or by means of the narrative voice that has related her story in the third person throughout this narrative, the reader already has access to more than meets the eye. There is no innocent reading of Inmaculada possible, that is to say, reader and character share knowledge of what has transpired. While the reader is privileged to all of her story, Miguel's confession to his son opens up the hidden aspects of Inmaculada to society for the first time; it has been unaware of anything but her public persona up until now. Knowing that Eugenio is the official *novio* or betrothed and, having met him on the pages of the text when they are still adolescent sweethearts, the reader can use this information to piece together the fragments of the story of Inmaculada, leaving nothing out. Therefore, when we read that one of Eugenio's sisters makes the following remark during the rehearsal dinner—"es maravilloso que los dos se hayan esperado durante tanto tiempo" [isn't it wonderful that they both waited for each other for so long] (331)—we are privy to information that makes this nothing short of the lie on which a socially acceptable story must be based.

Returning to Merleau-Ponty's ideas on the body not as an object but as a "condition" through which one relates to other bodies and to the world of objects (Grosz 86–87), it might be fruitful to point out Inmaculada's embodiment of his concept of the contingent. Finn discusses the corporal structure that inhabits the social one:

> Merleau-Ponty's phenomenology is sometimes described as a philosophy of contingency, that is, a philosophy that takes contingency as both its point of departure and its intentional end—its value . . . [For

> him,] contingency refers to the fundamental materiality of every human being and every act of consciousness: the situatedness, the 'anchorage,' of both being and thought (of both what is and what is known) in concrete, particular, local, and historical conditions in a world that surrounds us and is never still" (qtd. in Grosz 94, note 19).

Inmaculada's knowledge of the world around her is generated from her relationships with, for example, Joaquina, Eugenio, Miguel, Sebastián, and all of her former classmates from Catholic school. Given this framework, it would be inappropriate to conclude that Inmaculada's marriage and her continuing affair with Joaquina somehow contradict one another. Like Fuentes's skyscraper, Inmaculada is always a construction in progress which we see rise and fall before our eyes. She is incomplete, as is the project of modernity.

The figure of Miguel, the director of the psychiatric hospital and one of the many lovers of Inmaculada, functions as a narrative bridge among her identities. The 'truth' that he recounts to his son Sebastián on the eve of Inmaculada's nuptials is one of the narratives told, and shown, regarding his perception of her. When Miguel receives a personal invitation to Inmaculada's wedding to Eugenio, he is enticed to turn into a story what he has experienced with her. As an art connoisseur and collector of paintings, he possesses works that show in a different medium some hidden aspects of Inmaculada's life. In his collection are at least three portraits of her (332). The first shows Inmaculada in an ivory dress that immediately suggests to the reader a connection to the wedding gown she is about to wear for her formal ceremony. The second painting shows Inmaculada in stockings, garter belt, and high heels. In the third she is dressed in a sequined gown, with one of her female lovers, Rosenda, between her legs. After listening to Miguel's narration, Sebastián requests as a final souvenir the formal portrait of Inmaculada in white. At this point we have already seen the ambiguity of the white gown, and his preference for this version of her identity does not necessarily indicate a preservation of some type of perfect, unblemished image. Miguel chooses to hang the other two paintings in the living room of his home, a place intriguingly located in one wing of the hospital where he works. By placing the less acceptable images of Inmaculada in such a public arena, he is in actuality making the same type of statement that Sebastián has. Neither type of portrait is superior to the other; they are all representations of her as seen by the artist. And it is to the artist that García Ponce turns for the difficult task of portraying Inmaculada and her paradoxes.

Inmaculada, in a rare visit to the privileged space of Miguel's library in the clinic, opens a book, seemingly at random, and thumbs through the pages. What she finds there is, in reality, not a casual discovery. Reproductions of paintings fill the text, among them what is described as "una reproducción a color donde el hombre vestido de blanco con la viga al hombro atravesaba la arbitraria calle poblada por tantos seres y acciones extravagantes" [a color reproduction where the man dressed in white with a beam on his shoulder crosses the arbitrary street filled with so many extravagant people and activities] (286). Inmaculada immediately personalizes what she sees and compares the man in white with Miguel (the center of focus), making all others the inhabitants of a strange world akin to that of the hospital. She finds the painted street scene as uncanny or alienating as she does the corridors of the clinic. What makes this random choice of pages in the book more significant is that the painting signals in fairly concrete terms a direct reference to one of the strongest aesthetic influences on the writings of García Ponce.

As described in *Inmaculada*, the painting bears an uncanny resemblance to a work by Balthus entitled *The Street* (1933) (see figure 6.2). Moreover, García Ponce has analyzed this painting in the context of the rest of the artist's production in his book *Una lectura pseudognóstica de la pintura de Balthus* [A Pseudo-Gnostic Reading of Balthus's Paintings]. Of this particular painting, he writes in detail that

> todo ocurre, en efecto, como en un sueño; pero los sueños diurnos que habitan la imaginación de Balthus en ese cuadro o que alimentan con su presencia esa imaginación parecen querer borrar, querer destruir todo espacio en el que exista alguna posibilidad de inocencia. La creación es la obra de un deficiente demiurgo menor y malvado.
>
> [everything occurs, as it were, as if in a dream; but the daydreams that inhabit Balthus's imagination in that painting or that with their presence nourish that imagination seem to wish to erase, or destroy, all possible space in which any type of innocence might be able to exist. This creation is the work of a deficient demigod, a minor and evil one at that.] (17)

His reading of the painting, and the inclusion of it in a novel as the property of the director of a psychiatric ward, indicates a rereading of a supposedly inconspicuous scene of everyday life (17). Such an interruption of superficial harmony is done with what García Ponce calls "una intolerable naturalidad" [an intolerable naturalness] (17), indicating a transformation in perception and a chance for that "fleeting, fortuitous Proustian *mémoire involontaire*" (Gilloch, *Myth* 207) evoked through a reencounter with the crowds of the streets (now on canvas).

When the painting is scrutinized, it reveals an even greater parallel with Inmaculada and her world of the hospital. What García Ponce describes as the confluence of monstrous children, artificially painted women, and a ventriloquist's dummy is rounded out by the appearance of "un hombre de aspecto mongoloide [que] ataca sexualmente por la espalda a una niña" [a man with the face of a mongoloid {who} sexually molests a girl from behind] (17–18). What seem at first glance to be casual passersby along a street turn out to be interpreted, by Inmaculada and García Ponce, as witnesses to a secret ceremony on a unique corner. Inmaculada identifies with the young girl, the innocent object of the monstrous desires of the 'abnormal' adult, whom she compares to Arnulfo. But the crossovers between Balthus and García Ponce do not end here, nor do questions related to aesthetics.

As Inmaculada continues her perusal of Miguel's art book, she lingers over reproductions of paintings of young girls in a variety of poses. "[H]aciendo comentarios sobre el aspecto de las niñas sobre todo" [Commenting especially on the faces of these adolescents] (286), Inmaculada directs her words to a male acquaintance, René, who listens to nothing she has to say. Instead of looking toward representation, he starts with her arm, but slowly moves along her body to caress its entirety. Sitting close to her, with the book on his lap, and his arms touching her, René duplicates in his actions and his physical disposition the painting she describes to him in words. García Ponce's page frames a reproduction of a painting that appears on the page of a book at which his characters are looking. Life imitates art but, as we have already examined, García Ponce rejects such crossovers in favor of a declared (artificial) separation between the two. Mimesis aside, Inmaculada is, then, a fantasy construct of the writer. As such, she herself becomes a ruin of his own relationship to society's laws and she performs on the page as in the baroque drama of Benjamin's interest. She is pure excess, in body, in spirit, in space, and in time. Feal and Feal write of Merleau-Ponty's philosophy

> By rooting thought in perception, or, in other words, by ascribing to perception an intellectual energy of its own, . . . he erases the traditional borderline between two activities that are considered to be distinct and hierarchically subordinated (with thought holding primacy over sensorial perceptions in Plato and philosophical idealism). Thus Merleau-Ponty succeeds in introducing a temporal dimension into the domain of the visual arts . . . Accordingly, each painting, like each perception, does not end with the initial effect of surprise that it is likely to produce; rather, it constitutes a departure point for future explorations into the reality that was initially observed. (13)

In *Inmaculada* thoughts occur in direct relationship to the senses; reason does not obliterate the body. Paloma and Inmaculada, like the dreamy-eyed girls in Balthus's drawing rooms, evoke a temporal dimension rather than a spatial one for their liminality, their agelessness, their capacity to evoke effect upon effect in the spectator. Youth, for Balthus, is an ageless, limitless, and perpetualized dimension of the subject. Similar to the "immobile calendar" of Inmaculada, the adolescent girls portrayed in his paintings never change; they only accumulate moments of time, endlessly repeating scenes in which light and shadows (evoking some vague notion of day and night) vary, but only slightly. Adolescence is an eternal moment, one to be preserved and constantly evoked for its promise of innocence before the contamination of knowledge. García Ponce comments on these paintings that, in them, "[l]a presencia de lo visible es inmutable y en su indiferencia le da la espalda a la historia" [the presence of the visible is unchanging and in its indifference it turns its back on history] ("Balthus" 26). Merleau-Ponty's contingency persists; one is the sum of one's relationships with the world of immediacy. History, and therefore the domain of reason and knowledge one assumes, is cast out unless it becomes a factor in the personal perception of the world.

In Balthus's paintings, innocence and experience perform in manners akin to García Ponce's Eden-like universe created in and for Inmaculada. Whatever protest that might arise against the so-called sexual obsessions of the artist must be considered in the light of Merleau-Ponty's thoughts on perception once again. The "initial observation" of the painter is available for the "future explorations" of spectator after spectator; there is no essence of pornography or pedophilia to a scene or a character. They must be viewed, instead, as experiences brought to the text by the perceiver. It is within this frame of thought that Davenport describes Balthus's subjects as "sexy, charming French adolescents painted with humor, with wit, with clarity, and with an innocence that we can locate in adolescent idealism itself rather than in an obsession" (59). It is as if García Ponce were holding a simultaneous conversation with Balthus and Davenport when he concludes, at the end of his essay on this painter, that "[d]e [una] suma de ambigüedades y contradicciones está hecha una obra. Es el triunfo de su propia desnudez [la del cuerpo] que por el camino del crimen nos hace cómplices y nos lleva a la inocencia" [a work {of art} consists of a sum of its ambiguities and contradictions. It is the triumph of its {the human body's} own nakedness that makes us accomplices on the road of crime and leads us to innocence] ("Balthus" 33). Inmaculada observes her own body in the mirror (as Paloma has done before in *De ánima*); her erotic companions are spectators of her own discoveries; the writer experiences their encounters;

and the reader is the last voyeur. In Balthus's paintings, the same multiplicity of contingent observations holds true. And, like Paloma and Inmaculada, Balthus's adolescents are endowed with a gaze that they turn back on the viewer. When the holder of the gaze pretends to extricate innocence from an object, there is no longer a passive relationship between the two. The presumption of innocence—whether political, social, or moral—is cast amid the discourses of knowledge.

Apparently abandoned to passive repose or indifference, the girls and adolescents depicted by Balthus seem to correspond to the objectification of Inmaculada noted by some critics. With open bodices, bare legs, and heads thrown back in abandon they are ripe for the predatory eyes of the consumer. García Ponce describes these figures in paintings such as "The White Skirt," "Girl with a Cat," "Thérèse Dreaming," and "Katia Reading" in terms of the ambiguity represented in their eyes: "tienen, con mucha frecuencia, los ojos cerrados. Sin embargo, tal vez no duermen exactamente. Sus párpados parecen haber caído pesadamente sobre esos ojos, como si una fuerza invencible los guiara obligándolas a tender un velo que permita suponer la existencia de un olvido tras el que se ocultan cuando toda su figura se abre a la revelación" [with great frequency, they {the female figures} have closed eyes. Nevertheless, maybe they aren't dreaming exactly. Their eyelids seem to have fallen heavily over those orbs, as if an invincible force were guiding them down, forcing a veil to be lowered, a veil that allows one to suppose the existence of a forgetfulness behind which they {the eyes} take refuge at the moment when the {entire} naked body is revealed on display for others] ("Balthus" 25). Referring to them as catlike, García Ponce notes in the representation of these eyes the possibility of the object becoming a subject, the hint of the viewer being looked at, even if through narrowed slits. The hint of an ambiguity in the eyes as images of innocent sleep, half-closed reverie, passivity and an open invitation to the spectators gaze, but also as a hidden observation of one who has been given such a scenario in which to choose how to participate, has much in common with Inmaculada's figure. She not only allows herself to be watched—on the playground, in the hospital, in the artist's studio—but she learns from this act, even as it "contaminates her" ("Balthus" 32). Like the sleeping nation which appears in order to be observed by outsiders in search of evidentiary traces of modernity but turns its gaze back on the onlooker, these women look like 'innocents' only because that is projected onto them. They are the center of a universe that extends into the distance, but they are isolated and alone in their closed, interior spaces. Figures of women such as García Ponce's Inmaculada, and Balthus's Katia and Thérèse inhabit worlds that are, as García Ponce puts it, crumbling around them ("[e]l mundo se ha desmoronado") ("Balthus" 32). In their solitary postures at the center of the painting or of the triptych, the woman "se contempla a sí misma y rompe la separación entre apariencia y conciencia" [contemplates herself and breaks through the separation between appearance and consciousness] ("Balthus" 33). Inmaculada and her painterly cohorts bring together reason and the senses into a single act of perception.

Citizens of the modern inhabit "unsuturable" spaces, those of limbo and incompletion, entering and withdrawing from them, as Barthes reminds us, and constantly accumulating experiences. If a collective move toward a common future, that dream of modernity for all of its citizens, is not rendered visible in *Inmaculada*, then the character herself must provide for a destiny of her own. As the urban world is left behind, and as she 'innocently' attempts to interpellate herself into provincial life once again, Inmaculada is readable less as embodying the celebratory triumph of the modern than as the dancer amid the ruins of the social corpse (Avelar).

CHAPTER SEVEN

A Brief Return to the Ruin

In his recent work on traumatic experiences of three world-class cities (as they are called nowadays by promoters) Andreas Huyssen opens the discussion with an essay on "the crisis of history." His comments are pertinent to the texts and contexts we have been examining over the past six chapters. As he notes changes in the discourse of history after the fall of the Berlin Wall, after the dictatorships in Argentina, and after 9-11 in New York, Huyssen concludes that "[h]istorical memory is not what it used to be. It used to mark the relation of a community or nation to its past, but the boundary between past and present used to be stronger and more stable than it appears to be today" (1). With the advent of modern technologies such as photography and the cinema, the past has not disappeared but has remained as trace evidence of something that haunts the present. This phantasmatic ghost is contained in discourse, but also in the constructs of what Paul Julian Smith calls a "fragile modernity" (116). So we have come to call this problematic relationship, for Benjamin promissory, between historical times and the space of the ruin. Whatever faith in modernization is promoted by official sources such as the State's organizations is inevitably tinged by the daily experience of the collective members of the social body. Smith's vision of a "divorce between the conception and the experience of urban life" (117) in modern Spain becomes not a rupture but a shadowy double vision in the texts of García Ponce. Mexico City's detritus is also its "incompleteness" (Woodward 15); the "narrow one-way street of time" (Smith 113) is Inmaculada's timelessness; geometry and monumentality are both grandiose ambitions and catastrophic labyrinths. Even though Huyssen finds that "memory fatigue has set in" (3), García Ponce joins Benjamin in rooting out the potentials of the Proustian *mémoire involontaire*.

The physical bodies of García Ponce's characters inhabit an implicit and shadowy historical world, whether they choose to face it squarely or experience it through crisis. Inmaculada wanders through society's liminal spaces and outcast citizens; Evodio has to be dragged into the world through the maddening wail of the ambulance sirens. External geographies permeate internal ones; both are provisional and contingent in what Bammer calls a "shifting social and psychological geography" (ix). Huyssen examines German, Argentinean, and United States cultures after a series of traumatic events as palimpsestic surfaces on which the seepage of the past into the present grows ever more convoluted. I propose that García Ponce wrote in a similarly posttraumatic time after 1968, a watershed year around the world and one which indicated more than ever a difficult and "fragile" encounter with modernity.

In 1993 García Ponce added a coda to the trilogy of novels that we have envisioned as the shifting narrative panels of the triptych. Even as Huyssen titled his study of urban reconstruction *Present Pasts*, García Ponce found in the same phrase an allegorical reference to the politics of the ruin. His novel *Pasado presente* [Present past] returns to the "antagonisms, unsuturability, and contingency" (Barthes, *Camera* 220) of history represented in *Crónica*, then weaves into the narrative a series of erotic characters and experiences akin to those of Paloma and Inmaculada. Based loosely on the lives of Mexican intellectuals during the decades of the 1950s and 1960s in the metropolis, *Pasado presente* lives up to its name by conflating the past and the present into one fluid moment filled with traces of endings and beginnings. As Huyssen concludes of late twentieth-century Berlin, so we posit for Mexico City of the same time frame: "every posttraumatic new beginning bears the traces of traumatic repetition, even though increasing temporal and generational distance from the original experience may alter the discursive structure of the . . . symptom" (151). As high-rises fill the skies, as subways stretch out to new settlements, as the frenetic activity of construction clouds the air with debris, the inhabitants of modernizing Mexico are confronted daily with consumer products and with calls to rehabilitate the patrimony of the nation through its archaeological vestiges and remains. At the heart of the culture industry lies tourism, the nation as product, but also those "contact zones" (Joseph, Rubenstein, and Zolov 16) in which chronological time and its constructs seem to be purely contingent and totally 'unsuturable.'

While the image of the megalopolis began to emit traces of decay in earlier texts by García Ponce, his work from 1993 depicts only faint traces of what the city once was. The official architectural monuments to past glories have become inhabited by ghosts and rats. As artists and architects try to "piece together the scattered jigsaws of antiquity" (Woodward 10), narrators are faced with scenarios of transformation whose excitement lives on only in momentary fits and starts. The city as a whole scene of enjoyment is now a marvelous ruin (marvelous in the sense of fascination that Paz holds for the pre-Columbian Indian). During long moments of contemplation, the narrator Hugo looks out over scenes of devastation which from "his times" (9), whatever that implies for carryovers from past to present, have been changed once and for all. There is no return to the past, and no recovery from decay, yet there is no golden vision of the (modern) future. The past was not a golden one in any case; things have just gone from bad to worse. As the experiential dimension of instability continues, assumptions of "learning from history" and "mediating conflicts" (Huyssen 1, 2) become the debris from which "a fundamental crisis in our imagination of alternative futures" (Huyssen 2) is constructed. Hugo tells us that

> Todo ha ido empeorando, pero ni siquiera podría precisar con qué ritmo. . . . Es natural que todo cambie, tuve que admitir mientras manejaba hacia el Palacio de Bellas Artes. Después de mi recorrido [por el centro], tan plagado de recuerdos que parecían perdidos para siempre si no los conservaba para mí mismo, di vuelta a la izquierda. Pasé frente a nuestra Alameda central.
>
> [Everything has gotten worse, but I can't even say how long it's taken. . . . It's natural that everything changes, I had to admit as I drove toward the Palace of Fine Arts. After my spin around downtown, so full of memories that they seemed lost forever if I didn't preserve them for myself, I turned left. I drove by our Alameda park.] (10–11)

The narrative voice tells us here that chronological time is unstoppable (a fact), and that it is up to him to maintain the fragments of the past alive in his thoughts (the desire to preserve the ruin and one's place within it). No one else will do so since the nation's greatest project is to cancel the past and strive, without looking back, toward the modern future. So it is *his* Alameda park, not an objective geographical place in the city, to which he refers. This zone is a place that evokes specific experiences for him and for the person to whom he addresses his remarks; the Alameda is pure contingency rather than an architectural place or a social space. He goes as far as calling it *nuestra Alameda* or our shared park, one to which he can return time and again in his memories even if those he has shared it with are long deceased and if the times they spent together have ended. As he recreates the city in his imagination, Hugo responds to the fragments of baroque allegory that Benjamin finds so promising for their revelatory potential. As

Hanssen recalls, Adorno interprets these urban landscapes in terms of a still life, a *naturaleza muerta* whose mimesis is that of death and not life (3). Alive in his thoughts alone, modern Mexico is for Hugo a remnant, a ruin, "a falling away from pure 'historical' time into inauthentic 'spatialization' amd a temporality of transience" (Hanssen 3). The pull of memory and the transience of modernity find common ground in the ruinous narratives of García Ponce's Hugo.

Whatever the sacrifices might have been—the lives of those who died during the Olympics, those who are unemployed or chronically sick from the pollution of the modernized industrial parks, those who feel alienated and outside even in their homes and cities of birth—the nation forges ahead. The narrator of *Pasado presente* unites the temporal dimension of the contingent experiences we have already examined in *Crónica, De ánima* and *Inmaculada* with the spatial dimension into one overwhelming feeling of despair:

> ¡Melancolía, melancolía! Esa palabra sagrada no se puede dejar de sentir. Alguien, tal vez yo, en mis muchas mañanas, tardes y noches de ocio, tiene que hacer la crónica de esa época desaparecida no sólo en el tiempo, sino también, en gran medida, en el espacio. Después de todo, durante esa temporada muchos de entre nosotros tratamos de ser escritores.
>
> [Melancholy, melancholy! That sacred word is all I can feel. Someone, maybe even me, in my many mornings, afternoons, and evenings of idleness, has to write the chronicle of that bygone era that has disappeared from both time and space. After all, during those days many of us tried to become writers.] (*Pasado* 11)

Rather than an obstacle to writing, this narrator's melancholic lament leads him to compose the personal and allegorical chronicle entitled *Pasado presente* that represents frustrated desire for a recovery of that lost era while simultaneously recognizing once and for all that this is impossible. Hugo is not deprived of his homeland; he is not physically exiled, but he feels the loss of something he cannot quite name (Kristeva, *Powers* 145). In the midst of that lost paradise, as he tours the streets and neighborhoods that were once 'his,' Hugo compensates for a sentiment of disconnection from this historical reality by creating a fiction in which he recovers himself as an actor, as a subject in a series of roles he must play. The storyteller does not die but lives to narrate this melancholic compulsion. As a coda to his novel, García Ponce ends with a brief paragraph that could be a summation of the image of the Angel of History. Only this time around, the rubble at his feet are pages.

> Esto está acabado. Un hombre viejo contempla un alto montón de cuartillas, como dice Thomas Mann. Terminó la ilusión del comienzo, como dice Musil. Lo demás es larga espera de la muerte, como dice Bataille. O para citar un nombre aún más ilustre *the rest is silence*, como dice Shakespeare. Hago una atroz mezcolanza de escritores favoritos de Geneviève, Lorenzo y míos; termino con un nombre ilustre, favorito de todos los amantes de la literatura.
>
> [It's all over. An old man contemplates a huge pile of pages, as Thomas Mann says. The illusion of the beginning is over, as Musil says. Everything else is the long wait for death, as Bataille says. Or, to quote an even more illustrious name, *the rest is silence*, as Shakespeare says. I make a dreadful mixture of Geneviève's, Lorenzo's, and my own favorite writers; I end with an illustrious name, the favorite of all lovers of literature.] (349)

Thomas Mann writes from a sanatorium that no longer exists, Musil writes from the Austro-Hungarian Empire that has ceased to be, and Shakespeare is as much of a mystery today as he has ever been. Each is the object of speculation and each inhabits a space of invention. Hugo is not the exception.

Hugo is made to stand aside and observe himself, from both past and present, as part of a national spectacle even if he concludes that he is merely fulfilling the expectations of others and that the fluidity of his 'flesh' seems more a one-way street than a two-way passage of experiences. In what Homi Bhabha calls the "problematic boundaries of modernity" (142) within which these characters function, language and culture are constantly being appropriated by discourses of the modern used to promote some evidence of national goals held in common by all. But, as Bhabha points out, these shreds and traces of cultural moments and historical events are patched and sutured together, not in an arbitrary fashion but rather with definite ends in mind. He reminds us that "[t]he language of culture and the community is poised on the fissures of the present becoming the rhetorical figures of a national past" (142). It is in his Benjaminian confrontation with this process—one which is not contingent but a very consciously planned strategy, in spite of carefully orchestrated appearances to the contrary—that Hugo finds both a loss and a recovery of himself at the same time. Like a survivor in the underground tunnels of Mexico City after an earthquake (the natural disaster of 1985 that functions as a leitmotif in the novel), a singular voice heard amid the ruins of culture, Hugo writes his own version of the chronicle of the nation. This new Orpheus finds his stories in the fissures of the present that other discourses attempt to pave over.

APPENDIX

MEXICO AND MODERNITY: CULTURAL AND HISTORICAL CONTEXTS FOR GARCÍA PONCE'S TEXTS

1867 Execution of Emperor Maximilian of Austria in Querétaro. Return to national rule. Benito Juárez, elected in 1858, was restored to the presidency. Édouard Manet painted three versions of *The Execution of Maximilian* in three successive years, 1867–69.

1910–11 Francisco I. Madero won the presidential elections and the Mexican Revolution began.

1910 To celebrate the one hundredth anniversary of Mexican independence from Spain, President Porfirio Díaz began work on the project of a new national theater. By 1932, this became the art deco structure known today as El Palacio de Bellas Artes. For the same centennial celebrations, the statue of El Ángel de la Independencia was erected in central Mexico City, having been commissioned by Porfirio Díaz in 1902. By 1925 was made into a mausoleum for the ashes of heroes of the Mexican Independence, such as Nicolás Bravo, Miguel Hidalgo, José María Morelos, and Guadalupe Victoria. Its structure (the winged victory) and function as a locus for both celebration and protest are similar to the Victory Column in Berlin.

1920s Between 1924 and 1925 Walter Benjamin wrote his work the *Trauerspiel* (*Origins of German Tragic Drama*), which was published in 1928.

1920s Between 1927 and 1929 he also collected the fragmentary notebooks that were published posthumously as *The Arcades Project*.

1929 Founding of the Partido Nacional Revolucionario [National Revolutionary Party], the political party that became the PRI (Partido Revolucionario Institucional) [Institutional Revolutionary Party] and that held the presidency until the elections of 2000.

1932	Juan García Ponce was born in Mérida, Yucatán, September 22, into a family of landed aristocracy (on his maternal side). His recollections of these early days are filled with idyllic moments shared with siblings and numerous relatives. The prose fragments of *Personas, lugares y anexas* revolve around recollected autobiographical episodes from those years, articulated around recovered feelings and nostalgic losses.
1930s–40s	Flourishing of Mexican muralism in the government-sponsored public works projects of artists such as Diego Rivera, José Clemente Orozco, and David Alfaro Siqueiros. Murals, intended as art to be shared among all citizens in a collective venue, were commissioned for government buildings and other public monuments such as the Mexico City water works.
1934–40	Presidency of Lázaro Cárdenas. Expropriation of land and nationalization of oil industry in 1938. Landowning families abandoned the provinces for the capital, having lost their regional hold on haciendas and workers. The García Ponce family was spurred only in part by these political changes to abandon their native territory of Yucatán for the capital city; the other factor was more personal and was connected to marital infidelity on the part of his father, a fact retold in *Personas, lugares y anexas.*
1934	As Secretary of Public Education, Samuel Ramos published *El perfil del hombre y la cultura en México* [Profile of People and Culture in Mexico] as a concomitant to Minister of Education José Vasconcelos's national projects. Ramos concentrated on ontological questions and national identity, and his writings influenced politicians and intellectuals in Mexico and elsewhere.
1940–46	Presidency of Manuel Ávila Camacho. Under his rule a change of paradigm began to occur as young generations began to migrate to Mexico City from the ruined haciendas of the provinces. Ávila Camacho's taste in cinema ran to the *charro* archetype of Jorge Negrete as a national prototype. The paradox is that incipient urbanization did away with this icon, whose place was later taken by the actor-comedian Cantinflas.
1945	García Ponce and his family moved to Mexico City, where Juan began to attend a Marist private school for boys. In *Personas, lugares y anexas,* he reconstructs home life, school days, and his adolescent longings during these years, especially from the perspective of an inhabitant of interiors looking out.
1946–52	Presidency of Miguel Alemán Valdés. With the social and economic tensions of the war years over, Mexico entered a "boom" along with much of the rest of the West. Amid the prosperity of the Alemán years was the golden age of Mexican cinema production. The quantity of films, as well as the profits earned from them, peaked between 1946 and 1952. Genre films—musicals, *comedias rancheras* [Western come-

dies], and melodramas—guaranteed commercial success but left many of the more experimental filmmakers out of the industry. One particular notable figure among these excluded directors is the exiled Spaniard Luis Buñuel whose so-called Mexican phase of filmmaking produced such works as *Los olvidados* (1950) [The Forgotten/sometimes titled The Damned]. United in their rejection of the film, Mexican critics and moviegoers preferred Jorge Negrete and other recognizable faces and stories. García Ponce personalized the meaning of the films of the 1940s and 1950s for him as a young man in the fragment "Mi primera casa en México" [My First House in Mexico City] in the collection *Personas, lugares y anexas*. His preference for imports such as *The Portrait of Dorian Grey* had more to do with the nanny who accompanied him than with the intrinsic quality of the film. For more details on this work see my article "All Streetcars are Named Desire: The Lost Cities of Juan García Ponce's *Personas, lugares y anexas*."

1950 Formation of the generación de medio siglo (aka Generación de la Casa del Lago, aka Generación de la Ruptura [Generation of the House on the Lake, Generation of Rupture]) among artists and writers born between 1930 and 1935. These young intellectuals challenged the aesthetic norms and nationalist goals of the postrevolutionary era. Their models were Alfonso Reyes and Octavio Paz and their goal was to renovate narrative forms and pictorial representation. Juan García Ponce and Fernando, his artist brother, formed part of the core of the generación.

1951 Opening of the new, model campus of the UNAM (Universidad Nacional Autónoma de México) [National Autonomous University of Mexico], an educational project whose architecture combines historical, traditional motifs (on the facades) with innovative structural designs. This was declared to be the mythical home of knowledge for future projects. "Construir la patria" [building the nation] was the slogan used to describe the vast public works of the Alemán era. This ranged from highways to bridges to dams, in particular the Cuernavaca road from that city to the capital and the Mexican part of the Pan American Highway. The modernization of Acapulco for foreign tourists owes its impetus to President Alemán.

1950s Construction and development of the Zona Rosa [Pink Zone] in downtown Mexico City as a magnet for tourists, young intellectuals, and wealthy urbanites interested in exploring cultures other than their own and in feeling part of the birth of a "new" Mexico. Explosion of suburban spaces around the capital, beginning with the planned residential Ciudad Satélite [Satellite City] and its utopian vision of democratic commuter neighborhoods extending throughout the city. Urbanization also took the form of multifamily high-rises for lower-to-middle income groups to accommodate immigration to the capital; these included the complex at Tlatelolco which later becomes the scene of the disasters of 1968.

1956 García Ponce received the Premio Ciudad de México [Mexico City Prize] from President Adolfo Ruiz Cortines.

Construction of the Torre Latinoamericana [Latin American Tower] office building in the center of Mexico City. With this relatively tall skyscraper (by D.F. standards it stood alone), Latin America acquired its first visible symbol of modernity.

1957 In July an earthquake centered in Guerrero provoked serious damage in Mexico City. The Ángel de la Independencia statue fell from its pedestal, suffering some damage, which was repaired over the course of the next year. This event forms part of García Ponce's reminiscences in *Pasado presente*. The statue survived intact during the devastating quake of 1985.

1960s Emergence of the Onda and Escritura movements, whose aesthetic interests diverged into popular modes, on the one hand, and experimental texts on the other. Another space of encounter between opposing answers to the rising questions of national identity.

1961–63 García Ponce was awarded a Rockefeller Grant for travel to the United States.

1964–70 Presidency of Gustavo Díaz Ordaz under whom student and worker repression was intensified and reached a crescendo in the massacre in Tlatelolco in 1968.

1966 Art exhibit entitled Confrontación de 1966 in which José Luis Cuevas, Manuel Felguérez, Vicente Rojo, Fernando García Ponce, and other young artists staged a challenge to the pictorialism of previous generations, especially the hallowed muralist tradition. Akin to the French artists' Salon de Refusés during Manet's time.

October 2 student massacre by government troops sent at the behest of President Díaz Ordaz to the Plaza de las Tres Culturas [Plaza of the Three Cultures], Tlatelolco, enclosed on all sides by the same high-rises built to house urban families. Aside from the overtly political aspect of these acts, generational gaps also were opened by what was seen as an attack of the father figure on an entire generation of his children. The material toll of human deaths was in the hundreds, and the long-term cultural toll was just as great. Two days later, as a representative of the Asamblea de Intelectuales y Artistas [Assemby of Intellectuals and Artists], García Ponce was arrested as he left the offices of the newpaper *Excélsior*, where he presented a manifesto in support of the student protests. The arrest was later rescinded since police may have confused him with a student leader.

1968 October 12, postponed from the traditional summer schedule due to what the federal government called political unrest, the Olympic Games opened in Mexico City. The modern sports venue, including many of the swimming and track spaces of the UNAM, was meant as a public homage to Mexico's definitive entrance into modernity. The economy took a tremendous hit from this enormous federal investment of funds, and the political ramifications were on the front page of the nation's woes for a long time. Both U.S. track and field protesters (with black gloves for the Black Panthers) and Mexican protesters over govenment policies shared the spotlight.

1968 García Ponce published *Desconsideraciones*, a collection of essays on the visual arts, culture, cinema, and social values such as "chauvinismo" [chauvinism] from the 1960s.

1970–76 Presidency of Luis Echevarría Alvarez. The term "Mexican miracle" began to be applied to the modernizing influences. What is now called the Guerra Sucia [Dirty War] against remnants of the political opposition of the 1960s began.

1970 First Mundial de Fútbol [World Soccer] games held in Mexico. This was another touted step toward modernity in the eyes of the media and the government.

1971 June 10, Jueves de Corpus [Corpus Christi Day], the Halconazo, or attacks by the paramilitary groups known as the Halcones [Falcons] against demonstrators in Mexico City. Despite clear and mounting evidence to the contrary, Echevarría remained officially innocent of any involvement as of 2005.

1971–72 García Ponce won a Guggenheim Fellowship.

1972 García Ponce published *La invitación*, a novel whose backdrop is composed of a general cacophony of the events of the Halconazo of 1971.

1975 García Ponce published *Teología y pornografía. Pierre Klossowski en su obra: una descripción* [Theology and Pornography. Pierre Klossowski in His Works: A Description].

1976–82 Presidency of José López Portillo. Devaluation of the peso and boom in the petroleum industry. His inaugural address mentioned the national "crisis."

1980 García Ponce won the Medalla Yucatán, the first of four prizes for contributions to culture presented by his home state. He is the only *yucateco* to be awarded all four of these honors.

1981 García Ponce won the Premio Anagrama de Ensayo [Anagrama Essay Prize] for *Teología y pornografía*. He was also awarded the Cruz de Honor por Ciencias y Artes de Primera Clase [First Class Cross of Honor for Arts and Sciences] by the Republic of Austria.

1982–88 Presidency of Miguel de la Madrid Hurtado. During times of severe economic inflation, he promised not to promise the impossible.

1982 García Ponce published *Crónica de la intervención*, a two-volume historically framed novel which weaves together family chronicles and national narratives to form a tale of tradition faced with modernity.

In the same year he published the collection of essays on the arts and literature entitled *Figuraciones*.

1984 García Ponce published *De ánima*, an epistolary novel filled with erotic episodes.

1985 García Ponce was awarded the Premio de la Crítica [Critics Prize] for *De ánima*.

September 19 earthquake devastated Mexico City. Rebuilding took years, and even decades. In some cases, the rubble was cleared to make way for skyscrapers and modern office complexes rather than reconstruction of the buildings of the past. This natural disaster cleared the way for a new skyline for a metropolis that still sought to prove its modernity. About 10,000 died in the earthquake and aftershocks, and many more were left homeless years later. The rubble revealed the flaws at the heart of the system that could not cope with such disasters and on whom citizens could not count for relief. The disaster spurred an exodus from the city that overpopulated provincial capitals by the end of the century.

1986 Second Mundial de Fútbol held in Mexico despite the devastating effects that lingered from the disaster the year before.

1987 García Ponce published *Apariciones*, a collection of essays on writers such as Jorge Luis Borges, Malcolm Lowry, and Vladimir Nabokov, and on artists Vicente Rojo, José Luis Cuevas, and Paul Klee. He also included two essays on Pierre Klossowski and Georges Bataille.

1988–94 Presidency of Carlos Salinas de Gortari. Fraudulent elections brought to power a technocracy that created tremendous wealth for a few, promoted foreign-educated technocrats, and continued the electorate's growing disenchantment with politics. Never indicted officially for fraud or any other crime, Salinas ended up living in exile in Ireland and working as a finanical consultant.

1989 García Ponce received the Premio Nacional de Literatura [National Prize for Literature].

García Ponce published *Inmaculada*, in which the concepts of innocence and perversity are inverted, and the antinomies of guilt and innocence no longer stand in opposition. The human body becomes the medium through which the experiences of the social world are filtered.

1991 García Ponce won the second of the series of cultural awards from Yucatán, the Premio de Literatura Antonio Mediz Bolio.

1992 García Ponce received the Premio de Narrativa Colima [Colima Prize for Narrative] for *Crónica de la intervención*.

1993 García Ponce was named Creador Emérito [Writer Emeritus] by the Sistema Nacional de Creadores [National Association of Writers].

García Ponce published the novel *Pasado presente*, his last before his death in 2003. A chronicle of a very personal sort, this text reexamines the events of the twentieth century as they cause innumerable changes in the people, places, and society of Mexico. The deterioration of the utopian city is the background for a narrative of promiscuity and indifference, ending with questions about who is to blame.

1994 January 1, the first appearance on television of Subcomandante Marcos and the Zapatistas in the state of Chiapas. President Salinas and many politicians were taken by surprise. The Zapatistas declared war on the federal government. Neither the indigenous "question" nor the question of national identity seem to have been solved by 2006. In March, PRI presidential candidate Luis Donaldo Colosio was murdered in the Lomas Taurinas section of Tijuana while campaigning for his party's nomination. A scandal broadcasted on all of the media across satellite networks, this event provoked more questions than answers even though a suspect was caught and jailed. The eye of the television camera did not seem to be reliable enough to catch the tricks of politics.

Implementation of NAFTA (North American Free Trade Agreement) [The Tratado de Libre Comercio] created an atmosphere of privatization, including in such public institutions as the Aeropuerto Internacional de la Ciudad de México Benito Juárez [Mexico City, Benito Juárez Airport] and in a variety of communications and banking networks. The maquiladora sweatshops on the U.S.-Mexico border began to provide cheap labor for exported goods, inducing a massive immigration out of Mexico.

1994–2000 Presidency of Ernesto Zedillo Ponce de León. The economic crisis continued, as did the policies of Salinas under this handpicked successor.

1995 García Ponce published a collection of short stories entitled *Cinco mujeres* [Five Women] as a homage to Austrian writer Robert Musil.

1996 García Ponce won the third of the series of cultural awards from Yucatán, the Medalla Eligio Ancona.

García Ponce published *Personas, lugares y anexas*, a collection of short prose pieces, which form a constellation of autobiographical remembrances beginning with his childhood in Yucatán and Campeche. Rather than a chronology of events, he returns to people, places, and spaces (as the title reflects) to evoke emotionally-charged connections to them.

2000 Election of Vicente Fox Quesada as president. A member of the PAN party [Partido de Acción Nacional], which created an alliance with other oppositional parties, Fox displaced the PRI for the first time in seventy-one years with promises of "cambio" [change].

2001 García Ponce won the XI Premio de Literatura Latinoamericana y del Caribe Juan Rulfo. Awarded by the Consejo Nacional para la Cultura y las Artes de México, the University of Guadalajara, the government of the state of Jalisco, and the Fondo de Cultura Económica, this prize recognizes life achievement.

2003 García Ponce won the fourth award in the series presented for his contributions to culture, the Medalla de Honor Héctor Victoria Aguilar. December 27, García Ponce died at his home in Mexico City after a long illness.

Sources (also cited in Works Cited) for the above timeline are Sergio Aguayo Quezada, *El Pequeño Almanaque Mexicano*; Enrique Krauze, *Mexico: Biography of Power. A History of Modern Mexico, 1810–1996*; Elena Poniatowska, *La noche de Tlatelolco*; and the website for the Ángel de la Independencia, http://en.wikipedia.org/wiki/El_%C3%8ingel.

Information on the details of García Ponce's biography come from references in all of his texts and from http://www.garciaponce.com, an incredibly complete source about the author compiled by Magda Díaz y Morales with links to many other sites.

NOTES

CHAPTER 1: TRACES OF THEORY, TROPES OF MODERNITY

1. As he writes of the current state of the humanities and the university in crisis, Dominick LaCapra turns, perhaps not unexpectedly, to the trope of ruin and the works of Habermas and Benjamin as referential of the ruin in more positive terms than negative. In a detailed footnote LaCapra mentions that this metaphor does not belong only to those philosphers mentioned but also to Adolph Hitler and Albert Speer, whose turn toward monumental relic contradicts the absence of nostalgia in Benjamin's view of the ruin. The Third Reich gives a "ruin value" to the architectural feats (LaCapra 202) that Benjamin disputes. We might in a future study examine the links between dictatorial figures and the architectural ruin that survives their reigns.

2. In his book on modern Mexico, Rubén Gallo designates five fronts on the battleground of the early postrevolutionary nation of the 1920s and 1930s: the camera, the typewriter, the radio, cement architecture, and the public stadium. Although, as I write, his book has not yet been published, we appear to coincide somewhat in the deployment of these 'tropic' items in that I have chosen to approach García Ponce and the second half of the century from the perspectives of three of these, namely the photograph, the architectural structure, and the sports stadium. Gallo is to be admired for his exploration of cultural practices and modes of representation that indicate a break with the past. I hope to signal the shadowing of "the break and the period" in written and visual texts of this later era.

3. In the sixteenth-century text *Crónica Mexicáyotl*, the *cronista* Fernando Alvarado Tezozómoc emphasizes the eight cultural and linguistic groups that merge in the valley of Mexico to form what will become Tenochtitlán. But his contemporary, the indigenous historian Domingo Francisco de San Antón Chimalpahin Cuauhtlehuanitzin, builds into the alternative version of events contained in his narrative not merely the patronymics of the founding of the city but the first acts of construction. In *La fundación de México* [The Founding of Mexico] he describes the procuring

of food from the lagoons as a communal activity, followed by the physical founding of a place. He writes: "E inmediatamente fueron a vender y a comprar, regresaron luego y tomaron piedra y madera, aquélla pequeñita y ésta delgadita; y al punto cimentaron con ellas, al borde de la cueva; pusieron así la raíz del poblado aquel: la casa y templo de Huitzilopochtli" [And immediately they went out to sell and to buy, then they returned and took up stone and wood, the first very small and the second very thin; and at that moment they built a foundation with them outside the cave; they gave root that way to that settlement: the house and temple of Huitzilopochtli] (18). It is obvious that, for this chronicler at least, the material building of a community is an early sign of an imagined collectivity that shares structures of belief (the temple) and of exchange (buying and selling). Unless otherwise indicated all translations from Spanish are my own.

CHAPTER 2: THE STORYTELLER'S RUINS

1. Writing on politics and aesthetics in the Latin American novel, critic Raymond Williams notes that, in the case of Mexico, Carlos Fuentes, Juan García Ponce, Fernando del Paso, and others of that generation "were the producers of the grand narrative, memorable characters, and [that] their interests were fundamentally epistemological" (41). I tend to disagree with this statement to the extent that García Ponce's texts, while interested in history, are not historicist. If the "grand narratives" survive, they do not look like they did before. Perhaps Williams and I would agree to call this writer a modernist (Williams goes on to say he is not postmodern) for two reasons: one, there are still semblances of plot and character, if fragmented; two, he is the epitome of modern aesthetics in Habermas's terms of unfinished projects. The grand narratives do not spin into nothingness, but they do not correspond to the official projects of celebratory nationhood either.

2. In her useful overview of the Mexican novel between 1968 and 1988, Cynthia Steele dedicates one entire section of her book to a category designated as "The Novel of Tlatelolco" and to the narratives and documents produced as a result of the events of 1968. By extension, Vittoria Borsò refers to the novels subsequent to this heterogeneous group as "la novela postlatelolco" [post-Tlatelolco novel] (66). Steele finds some thirty novels covering a variety of forms, among them the testimonials of *La noche de Tlatelolco* [Massacre in Mexico] by Poniatowska and *Los días y los años* [The Days and the Years] by Luis González de Alba. She also mentions Fernando del Paso's *Palinuro de México* [Palinurus of Mexico] and Jorge Aguilar Mora's *Si muero lejos de ti* [If I Die Far From You], but García Ponce's *Crónica de la intervención* [Chronicle of an Intervention] does not appear among those works listed. It is impossible to second-guess the reason, but given the length of the novel (over 1,000 pages) and the shrouding of external events

in the guise of interior monologues and baroque erotic fantasies, one could conclude that either or both of these factors precludes inclusion in a more overtly political group of works. On the other hand, García Ponce's fictions have been easily placed among "an infamous series of high-class erotic novels" (Castillo 143) and, upon his death last December, obituaries across the board seemed to deem it necessary to include the tag line "No sería exagerado afirmar que la literatura mexicana le debe su erotismo a Juan García Ponce" [It would not be an exaggeration to affirm that Mexican literature owes its eroticism {erotic component} to Juan García Ponce] (Poniatowska, "Jardín" 36). Now to state that all of erotic writing in Mexico has as its source García Ponce would, in opposition to what the line states, indeed be an exaggeration. But hyperbole aside, the emphasis on the lived bodies of men and women does permeate his narratives, and it is one of the crucial aspects of the European texts and pictorial aesthetic that he finds most stimulating to conjure up within the context of a Mexican readership.

3. The new millennium opened with another opening: that of the case against Echevarría and his government over the Guerra Sucia [Dirty War] that had at its lowest point the persecutions of students and protesters in June 1971. In 2004, Mexican newspapers were filled with the legal steps being taken to prosecute the ex-president, as well as with his lawyers' steps to win him amnesty. The 'miracle' was clouded from the beginning with the blood of those who did not agree with the sacrifices to the new gods of the international market.

CHAPTER 3: MONUMENTS AND RELICS, I

1. Regarding the idea of doubling and "replication," see Gliemmo (24); for the role of repetition in the structuring of the novel, see Moreno Durán (42). Both underline the Mariana/María Inés relationship rather than a consideration of the text in its totality of thirty chapters and the interplay among them.

2. It should be noted here that incest, a theme explored frequently by García Ponce's narrators, occurs in every other of his novels among the rich. In *De ánima*, for instance, Paloma and her uncle are involved physically and the language used to describe their encounters is always positive in the sense of proposing a transgressive force against restrictive social norms. (Each one transgresses in a different way, nevertheless.) Another example appears in *Inmaculada* where traces or suggestions of an incestuous relationship are present when Inmaculada and her brother share an apartment. Once again, the act is represented as a discovery of sexuality and a desired erotic experience on the part of both the participants. In the end, however, incest is defended by García Ponce as a necessity for the survival of a way of life and a social class. For him, it is a 'natural' instinct to preserve the innate beauty of

the bourgeoisie when faced with the ugliness of society. In the essay "Infancia en Mérida y Campeche" on the author's early years in Mérida and Campeche, García Ponce writes of his mother's family and their rejection of his father's mercantile background and lack of important family tree. Although he is of Spanish descent, this fact is not enough. Upon hearing of their impending marriage, his maternal grandfather remarks about his future son-in-law: "¿Qué pata puso ese huevo?" [What duck laid that egg?] (16). This is followed by a second set of nuptials between his father's sister and his mother's brother Fernando. The author continues: "¿Familia incestuosa? Para nada: familia de gente guapa cuyos miembros se enamoraban de los hermanos de los otros sin tener ningún parentesco. Mi primo Manuel Barbachano Ponce se casó con mi prima Teresa Herrero García y así podría seguir ad infinitum" [An incestuous family? Nothing of the sort: a family of beautiful people whose members fell in love with brothers and sisters of others without having any family {blood} relationship. My cousin Manuel Barbachano Ponce married my cousin Teresa Herrero García and I could go on like this ad infinitum] (16). Aside from the obvious commentary on provincial society, there is more here. One can catch the allegory of a closed (and "beautiful") nation amid this description of an impenetrable and self-reproducing family image. The paradox lies in the fact that the beauty is carried by social class and not nation, however, with crossovers among those who qualify despite borders and geographical distance.

3. The ruination of modernity's projects now stands at the gates of the heart of the city. The Zona Rosa in 2004 was seen as the "Zona Horro-Rosa," an embodiment of the allegory of construction and destruction taking place very visibly in the Distrito Federal. In an interview with the head of the then business association of the Zona Rosa, Edmundo Cazarez writes that on its streets "la decadencia es total" [decadence is complete and total] (10A). From chic neighborhood for foreign investment and diversion, this monument to the dreams of the 1970s has fallen into urban deterioration and is the victim of projects never carried out to their conclusion, a "rehén" [hostage] of globalization. But these forces came on the scene late, and the Zona is several decades ahead of them.

CHAPTER 4: MONUMENTS AND RELICS, II

1. Bruce-Novoa has discovered crossovers between the *costumbrismo* of the novel *Doña Perfecta* by nineteenth-century Spanish novelist Benito Pérez Galdós and the presentation of provincial society in García Ponce's early plays, finding that the traditional family life in both is centered around enclosures and patios: the spaces of familial relations and activities but also of closeted individual frustrations and sacrificed desires. He concludes: "Lives are wasted; dreams abandoned. . . . Youth is suppressed by

tradition, religion, and fear—a conflict metaphorical for traditional society's suppression of the individual. Any outside presence, especially from Mexico City, threatens stability through the possibility of change" (6). He notes in particular the same type of provincial/urban opposition found later in *Crónica*. Yet it seems that in the later novel, rather than a simple case of opposition, the two sides or panels reflect cycles of fear and repression back onto each other; they cannot be escaped in either setting.

2. Pellicer finds a parallel between the ironic narrator of *Crónica* and the narrator of Robert Musil's *The Man Without Qualities* when each talks about the planning of public rituals of the State. Pellicer writes that there are coincidences between "cuando se refieren, uno al Festival Mundial de la Juventud y el otro a la Campaña Colateral y las celebraciones del que sería el Año Austriaco o tal vez el Siglo Austriaco o mejor aún un Año Austriaco-Universal y al ambiente burgués que rodeó los preparativos de esas grandes celebraciones" [when they speak of, in the first case, the World Youth festival and, in the second, the Collateral Campaign and the celebrations of what would be the Austrian Year or maybe the Austrian Century or even better the Austrian Universal Year and the bourgeois atmosphere that surrounded the preparations for these grandiose celebrations] (169). It is evident in both cases that the building up of monumental and grandiose images of national projects is accompanied by a revelation of the decadence of the bourgoisie that promotes them. Whether national, continental, or "universal," these projects hold hidden secrets of coercion that only surface in the internal conflicts of the characters.

CHAPTER 5: *DE ÁNIMA, DE CORPORE:* THE RUINS OF THE BOURGEOIS WORLD

1. McCarthy notes in his Introduction to Tanizaki's memoirs that there is a striking resemblance between them and the diaries of his characters. With regard to the themes of "woman as mother, as *femme fatale*, and as harlot" (McCarthy vi) this is the case, much as it is for other erotic concerns such as fetishes, passions, and obsessions. The episodic nature of the memoir (McCarthy xi) reflects the structure of *The Key* as well. This structural concern arises from Tanizaki's interest in expanding the Japanese canon of writing to include influences from the West. For him, France was a particular source of aesthetic inspiration. The same holds true for García Ponce, although the Mexican writer's interests span other European cultures and those of Asia as well. Perhaps the traditional values at stake in a modernizing Japan, for instance, spoke to him as much as those of twentieth-century Europe do.

2. For one possible literary source of such rules or conventions of the erotic, see Pauline Réage's *Story of O*, written in 1954, five years before Klossowski's text and almost three decades before *De ánima*.

3. My reference is to the philosophical view that spiritual values are not reducible to material things and processes, whereas Bataille emphasizes the crucial importance of corporeality and materialism.

4. This concept is explored in the selections of Bataille's writings collected in the volume *Visions of Excess*, in particular the essays entitled "The Sorcerer's Apprentice" and "The Practice of Joy Before Death."

5. This character is found in one of Bataille's short stories originally published in 1956. The tale bearing her name deals with the narrator's visit to the brothel of Madame Edwarda in search of 'liberation' through the physicality of the love-passion he finds there in the form of this woman-as-God gone awry.

6. In the section of *Visions of Excess* entitled "The Notion of Expenditure" (and quite aptly subtitled "The Insufficiency of the Principle of Classical Utility"), Bataille discusses the concept of what he terms "the regrettable condition . . . of productive social activity" (117) which considers "violent pleasure . . . as pathological" (116) in contrast to a proposal of human "insubordination" through which "the human race ceases to be isolated in the unconditional splendor of material things" (128). In this statement, the social body of the State and the human body of its citizens are posited in direct opposition to one another.

CHAPTER 6: MODERNITY, CONTINGENCY, COMPENSATION

1. My reference to 'paralysis' has much less to do with any supposition of authorial disease than it does with a text infused with an enervated and devitalized social class facing its own demise.

WORKS CITED

Aguayo Quezada, Sergio, María Yolanda Argüello, and Alejandro Cabello. *El pequeño Almanaque Mexicano*. Mexico City: Hechos Confiables, 2004.

Aguilar Camín, Héctor, and Lorenzo Meyer. *In the Shadow of the Mexican Revolution: Contemporary Mexican History, 1910–1989*. Trans. Luis Alberto Fierro. Austin: U of Texas P, 1993.

Anderson, Benedict. *Imagined Communities: Reflections on the Origin and Spread of Nationalism*. Rev. ed. London: Verso, 1991.

Avelar, Idelber. *The Untimely Present: Postdictatorial Latin American Fiction and the Task of Mourning*. Durham: Duke UP, 1999.

Bammer, Angelika, ed. Editorial. Spec. issue of *New Formations* 17 (1992): vii–xi.

Barthes, Roland. *Camera Lucida: Reflections on Photography*. Trans. Richard Howard. New York: Hill and Wang, 1981.

———. *A Lover's Discourse (Fragments)*. Trans. Richard Howard. New York: Noonday, 1978.

Bataille, Georges. *Erotism, Death, Sensuality*. Trans. Allan Stoekl, Carl R. Lovitt, and Donald M. Leslie, Jr. San Francisco: City Lights Books, 1986.

———. *Visions of Excess: Selected Writings, 1927–1939*. Ed. Allan Stoekl. Minneapolis: U of Minnesota P, 1985.

Benjamin, Walter. *The Arcades Project*. Trans. Howard Eiland and Kevin McLaughlin. Cambridge: Harvard UP, 2002.

———. "A Berlin Chronicle." *Reflections: Essays, Aphorisms, Autobiographical Writings*. Ed. Peter Demetz. Trans. Edmund Jephcott. New York: Harcourt, 1978. 3–60.

———. *Charles Baudelaire: A Lyric Poet in the Era of High Capitalism.* Trans. Harry Zohn. London: Verso, 1985.

———. "Marseilles." *Reflections: Essays, Aphorisms, Autobiographical Writings.* Ed. Peter Demetz. Trans. Edmund Jephcott. New York: Harcourt, 1978. 131–36.

———. "One-Way Street." *Reflections: Essays, Aphorisms, Autobiographical Writings.* Ed. Peter Demetz. Trans. Edmund Jephcott. New York: Harcourt, 1978. 61–94.

———. *The Origin of German Tragic Drama.* Trans. John Osborne. London: New Left Books, 1977.

———. "The Storyteller: Reflections on the Works of Nokolai Leskov." *Illuminations: Essays and Reflections.* Ed. Hannah Arendt. Trans. Harry Zohn. New York: Schocken, 1968. 83–109.

Bhabha, Homi. *The Location of Culture.* London: Routledge, 1994.

Bolz, Norbert, and Willem van Reijen. *Walter Benjamin.* Trans. Laimdota Mazzarins. Atlantic Highlands: Humanities P, 1996.

Borsò, Vittoria. "El nuevo problema del realismo en la novela 'post-latelolco.'" *Literatura mexicana hoy: del 68 al ocaso de la revolución.* Ed. Karl Kohut. Frankfurt: Vervuert Verlag, 1991. 66–82.

Bruce-Novoa, Juan. "Introduction: Juan García Ponce in Context." Introduction. *The House on the Beach.* By Juan García Ponce. Ed. and Trans. Margarita Vargas and Juan Bruce-Novoa. Austin: U of Texas P, 1994.

Buck-Morss, Susan. *The Dialectics of Seeing: Walter Benjamin and the Arcades Project.* Cambridge: MIT P, 1989.

Calefato, Patrizia. "Fashion, the Passage, the Body." *Cultural Studies* 2.2 (1988): 223–28.

Carbone, Mauro. *The Thinking of the Sensible: Merleau-Ponty's A-Philosophy.* Evanston: Northwestern UP, 2004.

Casanova, Pascale. *The World Republic of Letters.* Trans. M.B. DeBevoise. Cambridge: Harvard UP, 2004.

Cascardi, Anthony. *Consequences of Enlightenment.* Cambridge: Cambridge UP, 1999.

Castañeda, Quetzil E. "The Aura of Ruins." *Fragments of a Golden Age; The Politics of Culture in Mexico Since 1940.* Ed. Gilbert Joseph, Anne Rubenstein, and Eric Zolov. Durham: Duke UP, 2001. 452–67.

———. *In the Museum of Maya Culture: Touring Chichén Itzá.* Minneapolis: U of Minnesota P, 1996.

Castillo, Debra A. *Easy Women: Sex and Gender in Modern Mexican Fiction.* Minneapolis: U of Minnesota P, 1998.

Cazarez C., Edmundo. "La Zona HorroRosa." *Excelsior.* 7 July 2004: 10A.

Chimalpahin Cuauhtlehuanitzin, Domingo Francisco de San Antón. "La fundación de México." *Seis siglos de la ciudad de México.* Ed. Salvador Novo. Mexico: Fondo de Cultura Económica, 1995. 16–20.

Coe, Andrew. *Archaeological Mexico: A Traveler's Guide to Ancient Cities and Sacred Sites.* 2nd ed. Emeryville: Avalon Travel, 2001.

Corona, Ignacio. "Entre la Jouissance y el deseo mimético: el voyeurismo del marido eterno." *Cánones literarios masculinos y relecturas transculturales. Lo trans-femenino/masculino/queer.* Ed. Ileana Rodríguez. Barcelona: Anthropos, 2001. 135–56.

Davenport, Guy. *A Balthus Notebook.* New York: Ecco, 1989.

Deleuze, Gilles, and Félix Guattari. *A Thousand Plateaus: Capitalism and Schizophrenia.* Trans. Brian Massumi. Minneapolis: U of Minnesota P, 1987.

Demetz, Peter. Introduction. *Reflections: Essays, Aphorisms,Autobiographical Writings.* By Walter Benjamin. New York: Harcourt, 1978. vii–xliii.

d'Entrèves, Maurizio Passerin. Introduction. *Habermas and the Unfinished Project of Modernity: Critical Essays on the Philosophical Discourse of Modernity.* Ed. Maurizio Passerin d'Entrèves and Seyla Benhabib. Cambridge: MIT P, 1996. 1–37.

Diacon, Todd A. *Stringing Together a Nation: Cândido Mariano da Silva Rondon and the Construction of a Modern Brazil, 1906–1930.* Durham: Duke UP, 2004.

Duncan, J. Ann. *Voices, Visions, and a New Reality. Mexican Fiction since 1970.* Pittsburgh: U of Pittsburgh P, 1986.

Eiland, Howard and Kevin McLaughlin. Translators' Foreword. *The Arcades Project.* By Walter Benjamin. Cambridge: Harvard UP, 2002. ix–xiv.

Ellman, Maud. "Eliot's Abjection." *Abjection, Melancholia, and Love. The Work of Julia Kristeva.* Ed. John Fletcher and Andrew Benjamin. London: Routledge, 1990. 178–200.

Feal, Rosemary Geisdorfer, and Carlos Feal. *Painting on the Page: Interartistic Approaches to Modern Hispanic Texts*. Albany: State U of New York P, 1995.

Ferguson, Harvie. *Modernity and Subjectivity: Body, Soul, Spirit*. Charlottesville: U P of Virginia, 2000.

Fischer, Sibylle. *Modernity Disavowed: Haiti and the Cultures of Slavery in the Age of Revolution*. Durham: Duke UP, 2004.

Forero, Juan. "Explorers Still Seek El Dorado in the Mountains of Peru." *New York Times*. 13 May 2004: A3.

Foucault, Michel. "The Prose of Actaeon." Preface. *The Baphomet*. By Pierre Klossowski. Trans. Sophie Hawkes and Stephen Sartarelli. Hygiene: Eridanos P, 1988. xix–xxxviii.

Fowler, Roger, ed. *A Dictionary of Modern Critical Terms*. New York: Routledge, 1987.

Freud, Sigmund. "The 'Uncanny.'" *Writings on Art and Literature*. Ed. Neil Hertz. Stanford: Stanford UP, 1997. 193–233.

Friedrich, Otto. *Olympia. Paris in the Age of Manet*. New York: Harper, 1992.

Fuentes, Carlos. *The Buried Mirror: Reflections on Spain and the New World*. Boston: Houghton, 1992.

———. "Mexico's New Wave." *Venture: The Traveler's World*. Dec.–Jan. 1967: 125–31.

Gallo, Rubén. *Mexican Modernity: The Avant-Garde and the Technological Revolution*. Cambridge: MIT P, 2005.

Garb, Tamar. *Bodies of Modernity: Figure and Flesh in Fin-de-Siècle France*. London: Thames, 1998.

García Ponce, Juan. *Ante los demonios. A propósito de una novela excepcional: 'Los demonios' de Heimito von Doderer.* Mexico City: El Equilibrista, 1993.

———. "Autobiografía." *Apariciones: Antología de ensayos*. Ed. Daniel Goldin. Mexico City: Fondo de Cultura Económica, 1987. 497–528.

———. "Balthus: el sueño y el crimen." *Las huellas de la voz*. Mexico City: Coma, 1982. 25–33.

———. *Cinco mujeres*. Mexico City: Lectorum, 2000.

———. *Crónica de la intervención*. 2vols. Barcelona: Bruguera, 1982.

———. *Cruce de caminos*. Xalapa: Universidad Veracruzana, 1965.

———. *De ánima*. Mexico City: Montesinos, 1984.

———. "De la ausencia." *Desconsideraciones*. Mexico City: Joaquín Mortiz, 1968. 39–43.

———. "De la ausencia." *Desconsideraciones*. Mexico City: Aldus, 2001. 13–17.

———. "Enigma." *Figuraciones*. Mexico City: Fondo de Cultura Económica, 1982.

———. "El escritor como ausente." *Apariciones: Antología de ensayos*. Ed. Daniel Goldin. Mexico City: Fondo de Cultura Económica, 1987. 329–32.

———. "Infancia en Mérida y Campeche." *Personas, lugares y anexas*. Mexico City: Joaquín Mortiz, 1996. 13–24.

———. *Inmaculada o los placeres de la inocencia*. Mexico City: Fondo de Cultura Económica, 1989.

———. Introduction. *The Baphomet*. By Pierre Klossowski. Trans. Sophie Hawkes and Stephen Sartarelli. Hygiene: Eridanos P, 1988. xi–xviii.

———. *La invitación*. Mexico City: Joaquín Mortiz, 1972.

———. "Los medios del fin." *Desconsideraciones*. Mexico City: Aldus, 2001. 73–78.

———. "Lo viejo y lo nuevo." *Desconsideraciones*. Mexico City: Aldus, 2001. 19–24.

———. "María Luisas." *Personas, lugares y anexas*. Mexico City: Joaquín Mortiz, 1996. 155–65.

———. "Mi primera casa en México." *Personas, lugares y anexas*. Mexico City: Joaquín Mortiz, 1996. 51–56.

———. "Mi última casa en Mérida." *Personas, lugares y anexas*. Mexico City: Joaquín Mortiz, 1996. 43–45.

———. "Otras voces, otros ámbitos." *Personas, lugares y anexas*. Mexico City: Joaquín Mortiz, 1996. 25–38.

———. *Pasado presente*. Mexico City: Fondo de Cultura Económica, 1993.

———. "La pintura y lo otro." *Apariciones: Antología de ensayos*. Ed. Daniel Goldin. Mexico City: Fondo de Cultura Económica, 1987. 393–409.

———. "¿Qué pasa con la novela en México?" *Apariciones: Antología de ensayos*. Ed. Daniel Goldin. Mexico City: Fondo de Cultura Económica, 1987. 146–55.

———. "El tamaño de los libros." *Desconsideraciones*. Mexico City: Joaquín Mortiz, 1968. 15–19.

———. *Teología y pornografía. Pierre Klossowski en su obra: una descripción.* Mexico City: Era, 1975.

———. "Transfiguración y muerte de la imagen." *Desconsideraciones*. Mexico City: Joaquín Mortiz, 1968.

———. *Una lectura pseudognóstica de la pintura de Balthus*. Mexico City: El Equilibrista, 1987.

Giddens, Anthony. *The Consequences of Modernity*. Stanford: Stanford UP, 1990.

Gill, Jerry H. *Merleau-Ponty and Metaphor*. New Jersey: Humanities P, 1991.

Gilloch, Graeme. *Myth and Metropolis: Walter Benjamin and the City.* Malden: Blackwell P, 1997.

———. *Walter Benjamin: Critical Constellations*. Malden: Polity, 2002.

Givner, Joan. *Katherine Anne Porter: a Life*. Rev. ed. Athens: U of Georgia P, 1991.

Glantz, Margo. "Onda y escritura en México: Jóvenes de 20 a 33." *Repeticiones (Ensayos sobre literatura mexicana)*. Xalapa: Universidad Veracruzana, 1979. 89–113.

Gliemmo, Graciela. "*Crónica de la intervención*: El desnudo de una escritura." *Hispamérica: Revista de Literatura* 20 (58). Apr. 1991: 17–27.

Goldin, Daniel. "Prólogo." *Juan García Ponce, Apariciones: Antología de ensayos.* Ed. Daniel Goldin. Mexico City: Fondo de Cultura Económica, 1987. 7–15.

Grosz, Elizabeth. *Volatile Bodies: Toward a Corporeal Feminism*. Bloomington: Indiana UP, 1994.

Gutmann, Matthew C. *The Meanings of Macho: Being a Man in Mexico City.* Berkeley: U of California P, 1996.

———. *The Romance of Democracy: Compliant Defiance in Contemporary Mexico*. Berkeley: U of California P, 2002.

Habermas, Jürgen. "Modernity—An Incomplete Project." Trans. Seyla Ben-Habib. *The Anti-Aesthetic: Essays on Postmodern Culture*. Ed. Hal Foster. Seattle: Bay P, 1983. 3–15.

Hanssen, Beatrice. *Walter Benjamin's Other History: Of Stones, Animals, and Angels*. Berkeley: U of California P, 1998.

Harvey, David. *Paris, Capital of Modernity*. London: Routledge, 2003.

Horkheimer, Max, and Theodor Adorno. *The Dialectic of Enlightenment*. Trans. John Cumming. New York: Seabury, 1972.

Huyssen, Andreas. *Present Pasts: Urban Palimpsests and the Politics of Memory*. Stanford: Stanford UP, 2003.

Jameson, Fredric. *A Singular Modernity: Essay on the Ontology of the Present*. London: Verso, 2002.

Jerez Ferrán, Carlos. *El expresionismo en Valle-Inclán: Una reinterpretación de su visión esperpéntica*. A Coruña: Do Castro, 1989.

Jonas, Hans. "The Nobility of Sight: A Study in the Phenomenology of the Senses." *The Philosophy of the Body. Rejections of Cartesian Dualism*. Ed. Stuart Spicker. Chicago: Quadrangle, 1970. 312–33.

Jonsson, Stefan. "A Citizen of Kakania." Rev. of Karl Corino, *Robert Musil: Eine Biographie. Reinbeck bei Hamburg: Rowohlt, 2003. New Left Review*. May–June 2004: 131–41.

———. *Subject without Nation: Robert Musil and the History of Modern Identity*. Durham: Duke UP, 2000.

Joseph, Gilbert M., Anne Rubenstein, and Eric Zolov. "Assembling the Fragments: Writing a Cultural History of Mexico since 1940." *Fragments of a Golden Age: The Politics of Culture in Mexico since 1940*. Ed. Gilbert M. Joseph, Anne Rubenstein, and Eric Zolov. Durham: Duke UP, 2001. 3–22.

Kaes, Anton. *From 'Hitler' to 'Heimat': The Return of History as Film*. Cambridge: Harvard UP, 1989.

Klossowski, Pierre. *The Baphomet*. Trans. Sophie Hawkes and Stephen Sartarelli. Hygiene: Eridanos P, 1988.

———. *Les Lois de l'Hospitalité (La Révocation de l'Edit de Nantes; Roberte Ce Soir; Le Soffleur)*. Definitive ed. Paris: Gallimard, 1965.

———. *Roberte Ce Soir and The Revocation of the Edict of Nantes*. Trans. Austryn Wainhouse. New York: Grove P, 1969.

Krauze, Enrique. *Mexico: Biography of Power. A History of Modern Mexico, 1810–1996*. Trans. Hank Heifetz. New York: Harper, 1997.

Krell, David Farrell. *Archeticture: Ecstasies of Space, Time, and the Human Body*. Albany: State U of New York P, 1997.

Kristeva, Julia. *Black Sun: Depression and Melancholia*. Trans. Leon S. Roudiez. New York: Columbia UP, 1989.

———. *Powers of Horror: An Essay on Abjection*. Trans. Leon S. Roudiez. New York: Columbia UP, 1982.

LaCapra, Dominick. *History in Transit: Experience, Identity, Critical Theory*. Ithaca: Cornell UP, 2004.

Larsen, Neil. *Modernism and Hegemony: A Materialistic Critique of Aesthetic Agencies*. Minneapolis: U of Minnesota P, 1990. vol. 71 of *Theory and Literature*.

Lingis, Alphonso. "Sex Objects." *SubStance* XXIII.3 (1994): 30–45.

Lomnitz, Claudio. *Deep Mexico, Silent Mexico: An Anthropology of Nationalism*. Minneapolis: U of Minnesota P, 2001.

Lucie-Smith, Edward. *Latin American Art of the Twentieth Century*. London: Thames, 1993.

MacAdam, Alfred J. "Writing and the Visual Arts in Mexico: The Generation of Juan García Ponce." *Review: Latin American Literature and the Arts*. Jan.–June 1988: 5–13.

Marks, Laura U. "Fetishes and Fossils: Notes on Documentary and Materiality." *Feminism and Documentary*. Ed. Diane Waldman and Janet Walker. Minneapolis: U of Minnesota P, 1999. 224–43.

Martré, Gonzalo. *El movimiento popular estudiantil de 1968 en la novela mexicana*. Mexico City: Universidad Nacional Autónoma de México, 1986.

Masiello, Francine. "Gender, Dress, and Market: The Commerce of Citizenship in Latin America." *Sex and Sexuality in Latin America*. Ed. Daniel Balderston and Donna J. Guy. New York: New York UP, 1997.

McCarthy, Paul. Introduction. *Jun'ichiro Tanizaki, Childhood Years: A Memoir*. Tokyo: Kodansha International, 1989. v–xiii.

Merleau-Ponty, Maurice. "Eye and Mind." *The Primacy of Perception and Other Essays on Phenomenological Psychology, the Philosophy of Art, History and Politics*. Ed. James M. Edie. Trans. Carleton Dallery. Evanston: Northwestern UP, 1989. 159–90.

Monsiváis, Carlos. "La cultura de los años recientes." *Historia general de México*. Ed. Daniel Cosío Villegas. 2 vols. Mexico City: Colegio de México, 1981. 1485–505.

———. *Mexican Postcards*. Trans. John Kraniauskas. London: Verso, 1997.

———. "Modernity and Its Enemies." Exhibition Catalogue. *Images of Mexico: The Contribution of Mexico to 20th Century Art*. Trans. Marjory Matingly. Ed. Erika Billeter. Dallas: Dallas Museum of Art, 1987. 72–80.

Moreno-Durán, Rafael Humberto. "La escritura como pasión y liturgia." *Quimera: Revista de Literatura*. 20 (June 1982): 50–53.

Mulvey, Laura. *Fetishism and Curiosity*. Bloomington: Indiana UP, 1996.

———. "Visual Pleasure and Narrative Cinema." *Visual and Other Pleasures*. Bloomington: U of Indiana P, 1989. 14–26.

Nietzsche, Friedrich. *The Will to Power*. Trans. Walter Kaufmann and R.J. Hollingdale. New York: Random, 1968.

Osborne, Peter. "Small-scale Victories, Large-scale Defeats: Walter Benjamin's Politics of Time." *Walter Benjamin's Philosophy: Destruction and Experience*. Ed. Andrew Benjamin and Peter Osborne. London: Routledge, 1994. 59–109.

Ott, Frederick W. *The Great German Films*. Secaucus: Citadel P, 1986.

Paz, Octavio. "América Latina y la democracia." *Tiempo nublado*. Mexico City: Origen-Planeta, 1983. 161–88.

———. Introduction. *Encounters*. Trans. Helen Lane. Hygiene: Eridanos P, 1988. ix–xvii.

———. *Vislumbres de la India: Un diálogo con la condición humana*. Barcelona: Seix Barral, 1995.

———. "Will for Form." Exhibition Catalogue. Introduction. *Mexico: Splendors of Thirty Centuries*. New York: Metropolitan Museum of Art, 1990. 3–38.

Pellicer, Juan. *El placer de la ironía: Leyendo a García Ponce*. Mexico City: UNAM, Dirección de Difusión Cultural, 1999.

Pereira, Armando. "La generación de medio siglo." *Juan García Ponce y la Generación de Medio Siglo*. Ed. Magda Díaz y Morales. Xalapa: Universidad Veracruzana, 1998. 127–32.

———. "Sobre la Generación de Medio Siglo." *sábado*. Suplemento cultural de *unomásuno* 3 Dec. 1994: 6.

Pollack, David. *Reading Against Culture: Ideology and Narrative in the Japanese Novel*. Ithaca: Cornell UP, 1992.

Poniatowska, Elena. "Taking Mexican Popular Culture By Storm." Foreword. *Fragments of a Golden Age: The Politics of Culture in Mexico since 1940*. Ed. Gilbert Joseph, Anne Rubenstein, and Eric Zolov. Durham: Duke UP, 2001. xi–xiv.

———. "El jardín de las delicias de Juan García Ponce." *La Jornada* 28 Dec. 2003: 36, 3a.

———. *La noche de Tlatelolco*. Mexico City: Era, 1983.

Rama, Angel. "El arte intimista de Juan García Ponce." *La nueva novela latinoamericana*. Vol. I. Ed. Jorge Lafforgue. Buenos Aires: Paidós, 1969. 180–93.

Ramos, Samuel. *El perfil del hombre y la cultura en México*. 5th ed. Mexico: Espasa-Calpe Mexicana, 1972.

Reed, Alma. "A Primer of Mexican Archaeology." *Venture: The Traveler's World*. Vol. 3, no. 6 (Dec./Jan. 1967): 156–59.

Rodríguez-Hernández, Raúl. "All Streetcars are named Desire: The Lost Cities of Juan García Ponce's *Personas, lugares y anexas*." *The New Centennial Review* 5:3 (2005): 35–64.

Rosen, Charles. "The Ruins of Walter Benjamin." *On Walter Benjamin: Critical Essays and Recollections*. Ed. Gary Smith. Cambridge: MIT P, 1988. 129–75.

Rountree, Melissa. "Retablos: Devotional Images of Mexico." Exhibition Catalogue. *Retablos: Devotional Images of Mexico*. Feb.–Apr. Chicago: Mitchell Museum, 1990. 1–13.

The Route of the Mayas. Knopf Guides. New York: Knopf, 2003.

Rubenstein, Anne. "Bodies, Cities, Cinema: Pedro Infante's Death as Political Spectacle." *Fragments of a Golden Age: The Politics of Culture in Mexico since 1940*. Ed. Gilbert Joseph, Anne Rubenstein, and Eric Zolov. Durham: Duke UP, 2001. 199–233.

Ruffinelli, Jorge. Interview. "La perversa candidez de Juan García Ponce." *Plural* Dec. 1974: 23–30.

Schmidt, Arthur. "Making it Real Compared to What? Reconceptualizing Mexican History since 1940." *Fragments of a Golden Age: The Politics of Culture in Mexico since 1940*. Ed. Gilbert Joseph, Anne Rubenstein, and Eric Zolov. Durham: Duke UP, 2001. 23–68.

Scott, David. *Conscripts of Modernity: The Tragedy of Colonial Enlightenment*. Durham: Duke UP, 2004.

Sefchovich, Sara. *México: país de ideas, país de novelas. Una sociología de la literatura mexicana*. Mexico City: Grijalbo, 1987.

Smith, Paul Julian. *The Moderns: Time, Space, and Subjectivity in Contemporary Spanish Culture*. Oxford: Oxford UP, 2000.

Smith, Verity. *Ramón del Valle-Inclán*. New York: Twayne, 1973.

Sobré, Judith Berg. *The Development of the Painted Retable in Spain, 1350–1500*. Columbia: U of Missouri P, 1989.

Sontag, Susan. "The Pornographic Imagination." *A Susan Sontag Reader*. Ed. Elizabeth Hardwick. New York: Vintage, 1983. 205–33.

———. "Under the Sign of Saturn." *A Susan Sontag Reader*. Ed. Elizabeth Hardwick. New York: Vintage, 1983. 385–401.

Steele, Cynthia. *Politics, Gender, and the Mexican Novel, 1968–1988*. Austin: U of Texas P, 1992.

Stephens, John Lloyd. *Incidents of Travel in Yucatán. With Engravings By Frederick Catherwood.* Ed. Victor Wolfgang von Hagen. 2 vols. Norman: U of Oklahoma P, 1962.

Stern, J. P. Introduction. *Friedrich Nietzsche, Untimely Meditations*. Trans. R. J. Hollingdale. Cambridge: Cambridge UP, 1983. vii–xxxii

Stoekl, Allan. Introduction. *Visions of Excess: Selected Writings, 1927–1939*. Ed. and trans. Allan Stoekl. Minneapolis: U of Minnesota P, 1985. ix–xxv.

Tanizaki, Jun'ichiro. *The Key*. Trans. Howard Hibbett. New York: Vintage International; Random, 1988.

Traba, Marta. *Art of Latin America: 1900–1980*. Washington: Inter-American Development Bank, 1994.

Ulanov, Ann, and Barry Ulanov. *Transforming Sexuality: The Archetypal World of Anima and Animus*. Boston: Shambala, 1994.

Valle-Inclán, Ramón María del. *The Tyrant (Tirano Banderas): A Novel of Warm Lands*. Trans. Margarita Pavitt. New York: Holt, 1929.

van Delden, Maarten. *Carlos Fuentes, Mexico, and Modernity*. Nashville: Vanderbilt UP, 1998.

von Doderer, Heimito. *The Demons*. Trans. Richard and Clara Winston. Los Angeles: Sun and Moon P, 1993.

Waldman, Amy. "A Glorious Survivor: The Taj Mahal, in Teeming Agra, Where it Has Endured Centuries of Strife, Transcends its Time and Place." *New York Times* 16 May 2004: 9, 14.

Walsh, Thomas F. *Katherine Anne Porter and Mexico: The Illusion of Eden*. Austin: U of Texas P, 1992.

Weiss, Allen S. *The Aesthetics of Excess*. Albany: State U of New York P, 1989.

———. *Perverse Desire and the Ambiguous Icon*. Albany: State U of New York P, 1994.

Williams, Raymond L. *The Postmodern Novel in Latin America: Politics, Culture, and the Crisis of Truth*. New York: St. Martin's, 1995.

Wilson-Bareau, Juliet. *Manet: The Execution of Maximilian. Painting, Politics, and Censorship*. London: National Gallery Publications; Ewing: Princeton UP, 1992.

Woodward, Christopher. *In Ruins: A Journey Through History, Art, and Literature*. New York: Vintage, 2003.

Zea, Leopoldo. "The Actual Function of Philosophy in Latin America." *Latin American Philosophy for the 21st Century: The Human Condition, Values, and the Search for Identity*. Ed. Jorge J. E. Gracia and Elizabeth Millán-Zaibert. Amherst: Prometheus, 2004. 357–68.

Zolov, Eric. "Discovering a Land 'Mysterious and Obvious': The Renarrativizing of Postrevolutionary Mexico." *Fragments of a Golden Age: The Politics of Culture in Mexico since 1940*. Ed. Gilbert M. Joseph, Anne Rubenstein, and Eric Zolov. Durham: Duke UP, 2001. 234–72.

INDEX